AFTER THE
CIVIL WAR

AFTER THE CIVIL WAR

THE HEROES, VILLAINS, SOLDIERS, AND CIVILIANS WHO CHANGED AMERICA

JAMES ROBERTSON

NATIONAL GEOGRAPHIC

Washington, D.C.

Published by the National Geographic Society
1145 17th Street N.W., Washington, DC 20036

Library of Congress Cataloging-in-Publication Data

Robertson, James I.
After the Civil War : the heroes, villains, soldiers, and civilians who changed America / James Robertson.
    pages cm
Includes bibliographical references and index.
ISBN 978-1-4262-1562-9 (hardcover : alk. paper)
1. United States--History--1865-1898--Biography. 2. United States--History--Civil War, 1861-1865--Influ-ence. 3. United States--Biography. I. Title.
E663.R67 2015
973.8--dc23
                      2015006104

The National Geographic Society is one of the world's largest nonprofit scientific and educational organi-zations. Its mission is to inspire people to care about the planet. Founded in 1888, the Society is member supported and offers a community for members to get closer to explorers, connect with other members, and help make a difference. The Society reaches more than 450 million people worldwide each month through *National Geographic* and other magazines; National Geographic Channel; television documentaries; music; radio; films; books; DVDs; maps; exhibitions; live events; school publishing programs; interactive media; and merchandise. National Geographic has funded more than 10,000 scientific research, conservation, and exploration projects and supports an education program promoting geographic literacy. For more informa-tion, visit www.nationalgeographic.com.

National Geographic Society
1145 17th Street NW
Washington, DC 20036-4688 USA

For information about special discounts for bulk purchases, please contact National Geographic Books Special Sales: ngspecsales@ngs.org

For rights or permissions inquiries, please contact National Geographic Books Subsidiary Rights: ngbookrights@ngs.org

Interior design: Melissa Farris and Katie Olsen

Printed in China

15/RRDS/1

To my wife, Betty—who is always there

CONTENTS

INTRODUCTION

TODAY, 150 YEARS AFTER THE FINAL SHOTS echoed over the land, the Civil War remains the most riveting period in our nation's history. The four years of the country's struggle against itself—North versus South, brother versus brother—still has the power to stir our interest and imagination. What receives less attention is the tremendous impact that the war had on America's future.

Appomattox was not an end; it was the beginning of an unprecedented period of growth. The same industrial forces that propelled the Union armies to victory continued to expand until they vaulted the United States to world power. Thomas Jefferson's vision of a nation of farmers evaporated in the headlong rush following 1865.

Many engaged in the war had a personal role in influencing the future. Their impacts showed in ways both expected—such as radicals seeking reprisal on the impoverished South—and unexpected, such as teenager James Hanger's loss of a leg leading to modern prosthetics. This book traces the stories of those war heroes, villains, soldiers, and civilians and draws out their enduring legacies. War's effects on these private lives also changed the collective life of the nation.

Abraham Lincoln had hoped for a peace with malice toward none and charity for all. That would not come to pass for the conquered South. Those who succeeded the martyred president insisted that slavery be abolished and the Confederacy punished for its sins. Radical Republicans led by Thaddeus Stevens and Charles Sumner quickly took control from Secretary of State William Seward and his moderate associates.

Beyond Washington politics, the harsh new laws enforced by military occupation implanted discontent in the South for decades to come. Robert E. Lee's pleas to Southerners to bind the nation's wounds fell on deaf ears. Strident voices such as Jubal Early's created a cult of "The Lost Cause." Any Southerner who dared take advantage of Federal control—even wartime heroes such as James Longstreet and John Mosby—were traitorous scalawags. Only when Reconstruction ended in 1877 did reconciliation begin.

The Civil War's long shadow reached future warfare. The advent of the rifle, especially Christopher Spencer's repeating carbine, provided an accurate, murderous fire that changed military tactics forever. William Sherman, "the father of total war," initiated a pattern of wholesale destruction that wreaked havoc on the states—and in time, the world. Bedford Forrest's cavalry strategy of quick-strike advances foreshadowed tactics the German Blitzkrieg employed in World War II.

The war also brought major advances in medicine, thanks in large part to Dr. Jonathan Letterman's determination to treat men immediately on the field. Quartermaster General Montgomery Meigs pioneered the logistics of equipping and moving hundreds of thousands of soldiers, setting a new precedent for staff officers.

What happened in 1861–65 was likewise the grandest media event in American history. Mathew Brady's photographs brought the impact of battle into parlors in astonishing detail. Battleground sketches and newspaper drawings by such powerful postwar artists as Winslow Homer and Thomas Nast turned inanimate scenes into human pathos. Among the ranks of military nurses were famous authors Louisa May Alcott and Walt Whitman.

As reunification painfully began, national attention turned toward the unspoiled West. The Great Plains and beyond had as residents only Native Americans and buffalo. While some army commanders sallied forth heedlessly (George Custer was a classic example), a more steely-eyed leader like Philip Sheridan ruthlessly slaughtered everything in his path. Towns sprouted wherever roads crossed. A handful of adventurers, as personified by Montana territorial governor Thomas Francis Meagher and murderous lawman William Hickok, would spawn popular legends in the Wild West.

Many veterans used wartime fame as a springboard into politics. A prime example is George McClellan, a general who ran for president while the war was still raging. Ambrose Burnside, an equally incompetent but far more amiable general, found repeated success in the political arena. Name recognition also enabled rascals like Daniel Sickles and Judson Kilpatrick to embarrass the nation in a way that their less-than-exemplary military careers could have foretold.

Seven American presidents are associated with the Civil War. Abraham Lincoln towers above them all. Late 19th-century presidents—starting with James Buchanan and Andrew Johnson—are remembered as mediocrities who let the country flounder through unrest. In a span of 40 years, three of the presidents were murdered. A look at the assassins provides striking insight to the fitful times.

If these presidents were ineffectual, hardly the same could be said of the private sector. Industrial titans such as Andrew Carnegie, Philip Armour, and John D. Rockefeller seized on wartime opportunities, while financial legends Jay Gould and J. P. Morgan netted high profits from Union needs. These controversial magnates would go on to build legendary empires, entrenching the roots of capitalism that catapulted America onto the world scene.

Others buoyed the nation in a different way. Clara Barton created the American Red Cross, which revolutionized humanitarian efforts across the nation. Civil rights pioneer Frederick Douglass continued his crusade, lighting the way for successors George Washington Carver and W.E.B. DuBois.

This book is filled with a delightful cast of characters—some fighters, some thinkers, some rogues, some leaders—who made their mark on a changing nation. The legacy we share comes from people who devoted their lives to this unbreakable union. In looking at their successes and errors, we can face the future with better assurance. After all, history is the best teacher. ✧

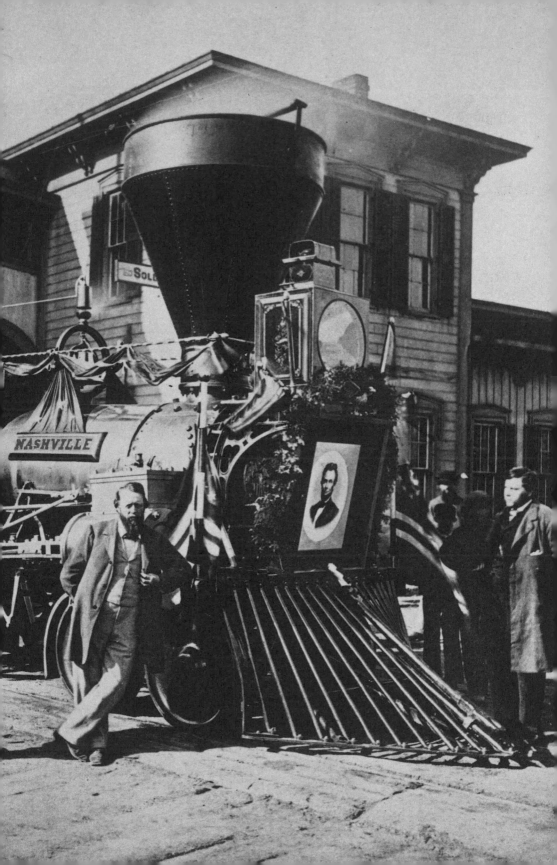

CHAPTER 1

IN THE

SHADOW

OF LINCOLN

ONLY FIVE DAYS AFTER Robert E. Lee surrendered the Confederate Army, a 26-year-old actor named John Wilkes Booth pulled the trigger of a derringer. The one-ounce pellet was the heaviest bullet ever fired in American history. It killed President Abraham Lincoln, who, after four years of indescribably bloody war, had hoped for a peace with malice toward none and charity for all. Not only did the conquered South lose the best friend it had for the unknown future, but also the victorious North, with Lincoln's steady hand no longer at the helm, fragmented into political and social chaos that lasted far beyond the years of combat on the battlefields.

For the first half of the 19th century, Democrats had controlled Congress and the presidency. After the election of 1860, the exodus of 11 solidly Democratic Southern states left the newborn Republican Party firmly holding the reins of government. Yet the party had dangerous factions.

Moderates such as Abraham Lincoln wanted to proceed carefully both during the war and in the peace that followed. A radical Republican element wanted slavery abolished immediately and the South severely punished. The Radicals never attained a majority among Republicans,

OPPOSITE: *Lincoln's funeral train journeyed 1,650 miles to Springfield, Illinois.*

but they were the most determined and most aggressive members of the party. Many chaired important congressional committees.

Knowing clearly what they wanted, and talented enough to achieve their aims in the midst of war, Radical Republicans became more influential as the conflict continued. By 1865, Lincoln was advocating reconciliation. Radical Republicans wanted retribution.

With Lincoln's assassination, anger surged through the North. Many of the Northerners felt that the murder of the president was a final atrocity committed by the dying Confederacy. One of the Radicals shouted, "Lincoln had been too much the milk of human kindness to deal with these damned rebels! Now they will be dealt with according to their deserts!"

Vice President Andrew Johnson, a Southern Democrat placed on the Republican ticket in 1864 for wider appeal, had been viewed with disgust from the beginning. Secretary of State William Seward, the third link in the presidential chain, had been critically wounded by one of Booth's co-conspirators. The nation, at a critical moment, was leaderless.

What followed was the ugliest power struggle in all American politics. For a decade, revenge and civil rights, egotism and impeachment, stretched the reaches of the government and marred the progress of a new nation trying to gain its footing.

The tide of revenge began with a Cabinet member who first assumed and then abused federal power to an extent not seen since the days of Andrew Jackson. Secretary of War Edwin Stanton assumed the reins of leadership in the power vacuum before the government returned from the long years of war to the normal balance exercised by its three branches. His primary scapegoat was Captain Henry Wirz, the commander of Georgia's infamous Andersonville Prison even though his responsibility for the mass starvations was unclear at best. With President Johnson rendered largely ineffective by the Radical Republicans, Representative Thaddeus Stevens and Senator Charles Sumner promulgated the rights of the newly emancipated slaves as well as established

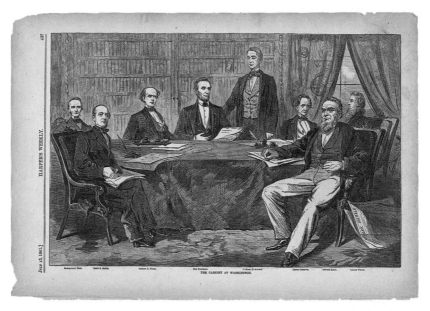

Lincoln meets with his Cabinet, unaware of the scale of the tumult ahead.

the military occupation of the South that would enforce these new laws. The edicts they rammed through dominated the ruined Confederate states for more than a decade, until 1877. Left on the sidelines were two of the most capable members of Lincoln's Cabinet, Secretary of State William Seward and Secretary of the Treasury Salmon Chase. Yet both these men left legacies that helped to shape America's future in important ways.

The immense tides stirred by the long war continued to pit North against South long after the last shot was fired. In similar fashion, the men who did so much to direct the war continued to cast long shadows over the nation's future. As harrowing as it had been, the Civil War proved to be only the foundation for the profound changes to come. ℘

EDWIN McMASTERS STANTON

SEIZING CONTROL AMID
THE CHAOS

As Lincoln lay dying, Secretary of War Edwin McMasters Stanton, on his own initiative, became de facto commander in chief of the American government. He summoned General Ulysses S. Grant to return immediately to Washington to assume command of the city's defenses. Stanton ordered the 72 miles of forts and earthworks surrounding the capital to be heavily reinforced. All roads leading from the District of Columbia were closed and patrolled. Rail service came to a halt. Special vigilance was ordered at all jails in the area. Dozens of telegrams went out to put the North on alert, for fears existed in those chaotic hours that Booth's act might be only the first of a series of attacks by still belligerent Southern bands.

Meanwhile, as a cold rain fell on the day of Lincoln's death, Stanton launched the first major manhunt by the U.S. government. Federal troops tracked down and killed Booth. Four of his accomplices were captured. "For better security against conversation," Stanton ordered the quartet placed in separate cells. Each of their heads was shrouded by a canvas bag, cotton pads were placed over their eyes and ears, their hands were cuffed to the ends of a 14-inch iron bar, and their feet were chained to 75-pound cannonballs.

*The War Department offers a sizable reward for the apprehension
of Booth and conspirators.*

That was merely Stanton's first act of retaliation. On the heels of the executions of the four conspirators, the secretary kept Northern anger at fever pitch with a rigged trial and execution of Captain Henry Wirz, commandant of Andersonville, the South's largest prisoner-of-war compound.

The humorless Cabinet member could exert supreme power at the moment because the country had been on a war footing for so long. Stanton had always endorsed Lincoln's actions about overriding law for wartime expediency—for example, in the numerous suspensions of the writ of habeas corpus. Lincoln had admired the unbendable strength of his war secretary and had spent a good deal of time asking his advice and following his suggestions. Stanton's loyalty to Lincoln, and his willingness to act quickly and decisively, impressed the chief of state. So it was easy for Stanton to jump to the forefront—and often exceed his authority. It was his unyielding strength that would ultimately prove his fatal undoing.

Born in Steubenville, Ohio, Stanton became a successful lawyer and eventually moved to Washington, D.C. However, in the short space of a decade, he lost two wives, a daughter, and a brother, who publicly committed suicide by slashing his throat. The personal tragedies turned Stanton into an unsmiling, often rude attorney. In the courtroom he became a crafty, aggressive lawyer who treated witnesses and opposing attorneys alike with contempt.

Bespectacled, pudgy, with hot little eyes and a graying beard that extended to his chest, Stanton seemed to enjoy alienating people. He viciously pursued some of his secretarial duties, and he invited enmity with his demands. One official noted that the secretary "fears that the administration will go to pieces without victories, and he is so impatient for them that he doesn't stop to consider how they are won." Overlooked by historians is a physical explanation for Stanton's dourness: He suffered progressively through the war years and thereafter from attacks of asthma.

The war secretary and Lincoln had maintained a warm relationship. The two were both Midwesterners, raised in poverty, and dedicated to the Union. They disagreed sharply in only two areas. First, Lincoln favored a lenient peace and a quick reconciliation between North and South, while Stanton thought that the conquered Confederacy should pay heavily for its sins of secession. Second, lacking any sense of humor, Stanton detested the witty stories that the president told to sustain himself throughout the terrible years of war.

By 1865, Stanton and his ally, Pennsylvania congressman Thaddeus Stevens, had gained control of the Radical Republicans and became key figures in "the age of hate" that ensued.

Following the arrest of the Lincoln conspirators, Stanton convinced himself that Lincoln's murder was a last-ditch effort led—or at least approved—by President Jefferson Davis. Federal soldiers captured the Southern leader a month after Lee's surrender, and Davis spent two years of harsh solitary confinement at Fort Monroe, Virginia. During that period, the anger from war receded. Northern public opinion shifted from siding with Stanton to having sympathy for Davis. The secretary was forced to back off and release the former Confederate president.

In the meantime, fiery Andrew Johnson had assumed his rightful place as president. He and Stanton worked well together for the first year after the war. Stanton demobilized the army and ran his department efficiently. The secretary then broke with the president over the latter's lenient policies toward the South. When Stanton joined the Radical Republicans at the outset of Reconstruction, an outraged Johnson demanded his resignation. That was not so easily done, however, because Congress had passed—over Johnson's veto—the Tenure of Office Act. It stipulated that just as an appointed Cabinet member had to be confirmed by the Senate, the firing of one also required senatorial permission.

Stanton refused to leave his post, whereupon Johnson in August 1867 suspended him and named Grant as his replacement. Congress refused to act on the request, and Grant stepped down to avoid the political infighting. Johnson instead appointed Adjutant General Lorenzo Thomas to head the War Department.

Stanton did not go quietly. On February 21, 1868, his last day as secretary, he barricaded himself in his office, placed soldiers around the

Grant looks on as the grizzled Stanton directs a canon at President Johnson in an 1868 newspaper cartoon.

War Department building, and slept on a sofa. When General Thomas, a tall, gaunt desk general of limited ability, arrived that morning to assume his duties, Stanton had him taken into custody. A judge quickly released Thomas, who thereupon angrily stormed into Stanton's office. The two men engaged in a shouting match for several minutes. Then Stanton faced reality, accepted defeat, and offered Thomas a drink. As Thomas was leaving, he said to Stanton, "The next time you have me arrested, please do not do it before I get something to eat."

Later that day, Congress passed impeachment charges against the president. Stanton remained at his post throughout the congressional trial of the president. When impeachment failed, Stanton in May 1868 resigned as head of the War Department.

Stanton returned to his home in Steubenville. He was physically tired, mentally beaten, financially strapped, and beset with increasing asthma.

He did not seem to realize that he was dependent on the charity of his few friends and relatives. By late 1869, he was found sitting by the hearth, his flabby limbs and heavy body wrapped in blankets to fend off the autumn chill.

That fall a vacancy occurred on the Supreme Court. Stanton wanted it badly, and he persuaded 118 congressmen to petition President Grant on his behalf. Grant made the appointment, and confirmation followed without even a committee hearing. But it was too late. On December 23, Stanton died of heart failure following a prolonged coughing spell.

Grant called Stanton "a martyr to the Union." While it is true that the irritable, unpleasantly intense war secretary gave Lincoln a loyalty that deserves remembrance, his legacy following the war showed the negative aspects of his domineering personality. He thrust himself into the forefront of those who wanted to impose their will on the fallen South. As a result, his positive achievements as war secretary are unfortunately marred by his postwar vindictiveness. ☙

HENRY WIRZ

SCAPEGOAT FOR WAR'S TOLL

HAD LINCOLN LIVED, he would have insisted on overseeing a new union favoring orderly reconciliation rather than insensitive recrimination. But that spirit of charity was replaced by Edwin Stanton's series of harsh reprisals to punish Southerners in rebellion against their nation. Stanton's vindictiveness to the defeated South showed most blatantly in his targeting of Captain Henry Wirz, the former commandant of Andersonville Prison. In the show trial to come, fairness and the rights of the accused were thrown aside in the rush to execute a symbol of the hated Confederacy.

The accused was an unusual figure. Although records about Wirz are few and contradictory, it is confirmed that he was born in Zurich, Switzerland, to middle-class parents. Early in life he declined to take over the family's mercantile business, and he rejected their Calvinistic faith in favor of Catholicism. Wirz married and had two children, but legal troubles led to a brief imprisonment followed by a divorce.

In 1849 he migrated to America. He lived first in Kentucky, married a second time, and then settled in New Orleans. On two occasions Wirz became an apprentice to a physician, and even though he practiced medicine on occasion thereafter, no evidence exists that he ever received a medical license. With the outbreak of the Civil War, he enlisted in the Fourth Louisiana Battalion. Wirz had attained the rank of sergeant when, in the May 31, 1862, Battle of Seven Pines, he received an extensive wound above his right wrist. The injury never fully healed and left Wirz partially incapacitated and often in pain.

Reassigned to guard prisoners of war in Richmond, Virginia, he came to the favorable attention of Provost Marshal John H. Winder, the Confederacy's police chief, who promoted him to adjutant with the rank of captain. For a short period, Wirz commanded a small prison camp in Tuscaloosa, Alabama. In 1863 he delivered dispatches of an unknown nature to Europe, and upon his return in February 1864, the 40-year-old officer was assigned command of the uncompleted prison camp at Andersonville, Georgia.

No amount of training could have prepared Wirz—or anyone else—for the supervision of the largest and most notorious Civil War compound. Some 33,000 prisoners of war were herded together on bare ground without shelter. A small stream coursing through the camp was used as both water supply and latrine. Filth, starvation, exposure, disease, lack of medical care—all combined to produce mass suffering and death. In Andersonville's first year of existence, at least 13,000 Federal prisoners died. Survivors were mere skeletons who never forgot the living hell through which they had passed.

How responsible Wirz personally was for the horrors is conjectural. In that waning year of the war, the Confederacy was suffering heavily from hunger and want. Wirz was unable to get medical supplies, food, even the manpower required to bury the dead properly. An extenuating factor was the cessation of a prisoner-of-war exchange by Federal authorities. Certainly, Wirz's strict disciplinary practices played a role. His most constant nightmare, he stated, was that a prison breakout would unleash thousands of desperate Federals through the countryside of the Deep South.

No inmate likes his jailer, and there was much about Wirz to hate. He was a foreigner with a thick accent, a Catholic, filled with nervous energy, and quick to anger and profane language. To the prisoners he became "the Andersonville savage," "inhuman wretch," and "the infamous captain." Yet in his favor, Wirz did not join other prison officials who fled at war's end.

*Federal prisoners await meager rations at Georgia's alarmingly
overcrowded Andersonville Prison.*

He remained at Andersonville, and he was still attempting to remedy the
horrible situation when Federal soldiers arrested him.

Lynch mobs waited at train stations as the captain was transported to
Washington and placed in Old Capitol Prison. Then Secretary Stanton
went after Wirz with the intensity of an assassin. Stanton orchestrated
every detail of the military commission: establishing the charges (12
counts of murder and inhuman cruelty to all inmates), handpicking the
military judges, and hiring many of the 160 ex-prisoners who testified
for the prosecution.

On August 25, the proceedings began. Witnesses seemed to vie to paint
Wirz in the worst way. The bulk of the testimony was hearsay, double
hearsay, exaggeration, or complete fabrication. Every witness presented

an unsubstantiated story. Prosecutors could not even produce the names of the 12 men Wirz supposedly killed. Whenever the defense sought to cross-examine a witness, the prosecution took umbrage at such attempts to impugn brave Union soldiers, and the judges concurred.

The legal travesty lasted 63 days before the court abruptly announced that it had heard enough. Wirz was adjudged guilty on all counts and sentenced to death. On the chilly morning of November 10, 1865, he was taken from his cell to a scaffold built in the prison courtyard. In a scene reminiscent of the French Revolution, soldiers chanted, "Andersonville! Andersonville!" A mob of civilians screamed for blood and vengeance.

When the trapdoor sprang, a last act of revenge occurred. One of the executioners had improperly positioned the noose. The fall should have broken Wirz's neck and ended life instantly, but instead, his body oscillated back and forth as he was strangled to death.

The published record of the Wirz proceedings exceeded 5,000 pages and became a basic reference tool for ex-Union prisoners who penned their own "memoirs" of suffering in Confederate compounds. One soldier's printed account dramatized the terrible treatment he had received at Andersonville—a year before the prison came into existence. He added that Captain Wirz personally shot him three times.

The huge population and death toll at Andersonville probably precluded other commandants—on either side—from being indicted for similar mistreatment. Indeed, in later years, former Confederates as well as a number of ex-prisoners came to Wirz's defense. A highly controversial act occurred in 1909, when the United Daughters of the Confederacy dedicated at Andersonville a stone monument to the only Confederate executed after the Civil War.

A victim was found, tried not before a jury of his peers but before a military tribunal in an atmosphere ruled by the mob. It was one of the most blatant contraventions of the laws on which our country was founded. How ironic it is, in a nation so proud of its justice system, that on the site where Wirz was legally lynched now stands the U.S. Supreme Court Building. ⨍

THADDEUS STEVENS

THE FATHER OF RECONSTRUCTION

BIOGRAPHERS DISAGREE ON WHY Thaddeus Stevens had such an intense passion against slavery. To some writers, he saw the abolitionist cause early on as a good avenue for his political ambitions. Others feel that he identified with the oppressed, based on his own physical deformity. In either event, Stevens worked to achieve an interracial democracy and reacted savagely to those who differed with him.

When the Southern states started a war in great part to preserve human bondage, Stevens's rage was uncontrollable. He could not fight in the field, but he did succeed in gaining control of the House of Representatives and becoming the father of postwar reconstruction.

The most extreme of a Radical Republican, Thaddeus Stevens certainly looked the part. He was a fascinating mixture of idealism and hatred. Born in 1792 to poor parents and then abandoned by his father, he was clubfooted, tall but bent, and crowned by an ill-fitting wig after he lost his hair prematurely. He had burning eyes, a perpetual scowl, and a splenetic personality. His harshness of temper created enemies wherever he went, and that lack of comity frustrated many of his plans.

He never attended church. "I am one of the devil's children," he would say and point at his deformed foot. If one stared too long at it, Stevens would stick out his leg and snarl, "There! Look at it! It won't bite!" He never took a wife, although for 20 years he maintained a relationship with a widowed mulatto housekeeper, Lydia Smith. Marriage he considered "licensed copulation."

Vehemently antislavery, the passionate Stevens rallied Radical Republicans around retribution on secessionist states.

*The gravely ill Stevens is carried into Congress in 1868 to argue
for Johnson's impeachment in his final weeks.*

A successful lawyer, railroad operator, and iron furnace owner in Lancaster, Pennsylvania (James Buchanan was a neighbor), Stevens served in the state legislature prior to his election to Congress in 1848. After two terms, his strong antislavery views brought him defeat at the polls. Yet his signing on early with the Republican Party led to congressional reelection in 1858. Stevens took his seat three days after the hanging of abolitionist John Brown.

His efforts were always driven by dogged pursuit of the abolition of slavery and inspired by "the grand idea of liberty, equality, and the rights of man." One historian asserted that Stevens's "single-minded devotion to the principles of the Declaration of Independence were so all-consuming that to Northerners he seemed the incarnation of radicalism and to Southerners he was the embodiment of aggression and vindictiveness."

President-elect Abraham Lincoln considered Stevens for a Cabinet post until a Pennsylvania official warned, "If you want to add fuel to the flames already kindled," the appointment of Stevens "would be the likely course to dictate." Instead, Stevens spent the Civil War years as chairman of the House Ways and Means Committee, which set the agenda for the lower chamber. He often criticized Lincoln's actions, particularly with regard to slowness over the question of slavery.

His enmity of the South became deep and relentless. "Free every slave—slay every traitor—burn every Rebel mansion, if these things be necessary to preserve the temple of freedom," Stevens thundered. The North must "treat this [war] as a radical revolution, and remodel our institutions."

By 1865 Stevens's power in the House of Representatives had earned him the title "Dictator of Congress." This brought him into head-on confrontation with conciliatory "president by accident" Andrew Johnson. Stevens came to hate the Tennessean passionately. Johnson's generous terms for Reconstruction, his openly racial views with regard to civil rights, and his outspoken intransigence were unacceptable policies for the president, Stevens insisted. The only hope of the nation moving forward was for Congress to take the initiative. "The foundations of Southern institutions must be broken up and relaid, or all our blood and treasure have been spent in vain."

When the Radical Republicans gained outright control of the legislature in the 1866 elections, Stevens stood in the spotlight. He chaired the Committee of Fifteen, which guided the passage of the 14th Amendment, granting federal and state citizenship to blacks and guaranteed several basic rights—but not suffrage.

His treatment of the South seemed paranoid to many. Stevens fathered the 1867 Military Reconstruction Act, which divided the former Confederacy into five military districts. The commanding general of each was to preserve order (real or imagined) by any means. All citizens except former Confederates would enact new constitutions that would qualify a state for readmission to the Union. Congress, not the president, would determine the legality of each statehood request.

Throughout this period the crippled and humorless Stevens was the dominant figure as Congress regularly overrode presidential vetoes. Then he turned his full attention on Johnson. He charged that the president was more like King Charles I of England, who lost his head under circumstances similar to those of Johnson's vetoes and other usurpations. In the movement to impeach him, Stevens was the most relentless advocate. By then the congressman was in his seventies and wracked by stomach ailments, rheumatism, and dropsy. Two young boys bore him by chair from place to place. A New York newspaperman described Stevens as "a recluse remonstrance from the tomb . . . the very embodiment of fanaticism, with not a solitary leaven of justice or mercy."

When it was Stevens's turn to speak at the impeachment trial, he fortified himself with a mixture of raw eggs and brandy. Yet he was unable to deliver more than a few sentences before halting for breath. Finally he asked his colleague, Benjamin F. Butler, to finish the long address.

The motion to impeach failed by a solitary vote. Stevens was "black with rage and disappointment." For several weeks thereafter, he submitted new sets of impeachment charges, but to no avail. In August 1868, he died—bitter to the end. His remains were but the third (after those of Henry Clay and Lincoln) to lie in state in the Capitol's rotunda. Black soldiers served as honorary guards.

Stevens was buried, according to his wishes, in an integrated cemetery in Lancaster. A New Orleans newspaper exclaimed, "May his new iron works wean him and the fires of his new furnace never go out!" More positive is a recent appraisal: "His policies often sounded harsh, whether vindictive or not, but his legacy made possible racial progress in the twentieth century, finally showing that his life had not been a failure."

Indeed, Stevens was far ahead of his time. While his methods were as harsh as the institution of slavery he fought against, the amendments he marshaled through Congress became the foundation of the civil rights movement a hundred years in the future. ∾

CHARLES SUMNER

SELF-RIGHTEOUSNESS
IN THE SENATE

SONOROUS AND FORCEFUL, Charles Sumner once ridiculed a Southern senator as having "chosen a mistress who, though ugly to others, is always lovely to him; though polluted in the sight of the world, is chaste in his sight—I mean the harlot, Slavery."

The Massachusetts-born Sumner was a thoroughly dislikable man who spent 23 critical years in the U.S. Senate. He and Thaddeus Stevens were principal Radical Republican agitators in their respective chambers of Congress. Colleague Stephen Douglas once observed, "Sumner is a damned fool who will get himself killed by some other damned fool." That almost came to pass.

A Boston blue blood who followed his father's path as a Harvard-trained lawyer, Sumner was unsuccessful in his first legal efforts. So, he turned briefly to academia before going abroad for three years and hobnobbing in European high society. He returned home full of reform ideals. The ensuing crusade brought out the worst in him.

In his case, personal appearance and personality lay at opposite poles. One of the most handsome men of his time, he had a mane of dark hair flowing down a massive neck to powerful shoulders that gave the impression of great strength. His dress was immaculate: plaid jackets over trousers tapered down to white spats. A senator once wondered aloud how Sumner might look in his nightshirt.

Throwing decorum to the wind, a congressman knocks Sumner unconscious after his two-day rant against the South.

On the other hand, he was an arrogant moralist and Congress's most vigorous champion of black emancipation. Sumner was also vain and condescending. His breadth of knowledge led him to talk too much about everything. A friend observed that listening to Sumner was like standing under Niagara Falls.

Sumner had never held public office before he was appointed to the Senate in 1851. Just as Henry Clay, the master of the century's famous compromises, made his exit, militant abolitionist Sumner appeared on the national stage. He instantly became known for his scathing speeches against slavery. They were always performances to be watched: memorized totally and rehearsed privately in front of a mirror. A Sumner oration had no humor, as he himself acknowledged. "You might as well look for a joke in the Book of Revelation," he confessed.

In May 1856, following Sumner's two-day tirade against the South and its dependence on human bondage, Congressman Preston Brooks of South Carolina assaulted Sumner in the Senate chamber. How seriously the senator was injured remains a bone of contention. That Sumner was knocked unconscious and bled heavily from head wounds and that three years passed before he returned to his duties are indisputable. Southerners insisted that the senator provoked the attack and feigned injuries for the sake of martyrdom. Northerners howled at the blatant affront of one lawmaker by another. Some felt that the vacant chair in the Senate chamber meant more than Sumner's presence ever could. In any event, when Sumner returned to the Senate, not one Democrat greeted him.

Until 1871, he chaired the Senate Foreign Relations Committee, with a constant eye on English and Mexican affairs. Yet he gave his greatest efforts to the eradication of slavery. The Civil War, as Sumner viewed it, was from the beginning a struggle to abolish the peculiar institution. Perpetuation of the Union was secondary. He also insisted that freedom for black people would be useless without their having the right to vote. "A righteous government cannot be founded on any exclusion of race," he argued repeatedly.

Sumner's wartime relations with Abraham Lincoln were mixed. The president moved far too slowly on the slavery question to please Sumner. Generally, however, he supported presidential policies and became socially intimate with the Lincolns. Much like Stanton, Sumner had no appreciation of the president's humorous sidebars. On one occasion, Lincoln asked Sumner to stand and see which of the two was the taller. Sumner grumpily replied that it was time for uniting their fronts, not their backs.

As might be expected, the vain, arrogant elitist from Massachusetts never found common ground with the low-class ex-tailor Andrew Johnson. Radical Republicans, in Johnson's view, were "an irresponsible central directory." He considered Stevens and Sumner to be "traitors to the fundamental principles of government." For their part, the two congressmen were in the forefront of the attempt to impeach the president. Sumner delivered the longest and most virulent of the prosecution speeches.

On the personal side, no woman could hold Sumner's interest for any length of time, and he lived unmarried for most of his adult life. Finally, in 1866, at the age of 55, he wed a young widow. Over time, rumors began circulating of his wife's attraction to a Prussian attaché. Sumner filed for divorce after six years of marriage.

He remained a fervid crusader to the end. Because Sumner openly regarded President U. S. Grant as a corrupt despot, he supported Horace Greeley in the 1872 presidential election. That lost cause cost Sumner much of his influence in the upper chamber. He continued to champion civil rights for freedmen, and he began soliciting support for an academy of arts and letters.

On March 10, 1874, the 63-year-old Sumner had just returned home from the Capitol when he died of a heart attack. His best biographer summarized Sumner by stating that he "combined a passionate conviction in his own moral purity . . . Stumbling into politics largely by accident, elevated to the United States Senate largely by chance, willing to indulge in Jacksonian demagoguery for the sake of political expediency, Sumner became a bitter and potent agitator of sectional conflict." ∾

WILLIAM HENRY SEWARD

THE ENIGMATIC DIPLOMAT

AMERICANS LIKE THEIR HEROES to be unambiguous, but William Henry Seward steadfastly refused to fill that mold. He was an enigma by his own confession: a devoted husband who was rarely home, a reformer closely allied with one of the leading political bosses of the time, and someone who longed for the 1860 presidential nomination but spent half the preceding year on a European vacation. As the new secretary of state, he attempted to gain the power of a prime minister, accepted rebuff for his efforts, and became one of Lincoln's most loyal associates during the Civil War. Afterward, he stood to one side during the Radical surge, but he took the lead in one of America's largest territorial expansions: Alaska.

Born in Orange County, New York, in 1801, Seward was only 29 when he entered politics as a state senator. He forged a 40-year friendship with William "Boss" Tweed, the editor of an Albany newspaper and a major political fixer in New York. In 1838 Seward became governor and won laurels for several proposed reforms. He advocated for the creation of a state board of education and major improvements in public school curricula. Expansion of railroads, a widening of the Erie Canal, and an overhaul of the prison system all brought national attention.

In 1849 Seward won election to the U.S. Senate, where he quickly established himself as a leading antislavery spokesman. He opposed the

*The treaty for the 1867 purchase of Alaska straight
from the Russian minister's desk*

Compromise of 1850 because he believed there was "a higher law than the Constitution, the law of God." Seward was the first to describe slavery as "a crime against humanity." By the mid-1850s he was warning of an "irrepressible conflict" looming on the horizon.

Contrary to Hollywood depictions, Seward was physically unimpressive. Disorderly in dress and slouchy in posture, he had a gravelly voice and "a head like a wise macaw." Seward drank heavily but seemed to suffer only from long-windedness as a result. While a man of warmth and charm, he also could be shrewd, devious, and indiscreet. He wore a politician's mask for so long that nobody could discern when his demeanor was real or contrived. A friend noted that it was not fair to call Seward insecure. "We generally knew what hole he would go in, but we never felt quite sure as to where he would come out."

Rising steadily through the Republican ranks, he became the heir apparent for the 1860 presidential nomination. Yet Seward had made too many enemies in the preceding decade, and his strong abolitionist views had alienated a large sector of the party. On the third ballot, he lost the nomination to dark horse Abraham Lincoln.

The new president, keenly aware of Seward's political clout and abilities, named the New Yorker to the senior Cabinet post, secretary of state. Seward attempted from the start to exert power beyond his office. This immediately brought him into collision with the equally ambitious secretary of the treasury, Salmon Chase. The two men had a mutual dislike of each other because they were so unalike. Chase was a figure of moral righteousness, while Seward was a pragmatist. Seward was as witty as Chase was humorless. At one point, Seward offered his resignation from the State Department to escape Chase's machinations.

Lincoln gently kept Seward in place because he knew Seward was the better administrator. In the ensuing months, a warm congeniality developed between the two. Lincoln turned often to Seward for advice. For example, Lincoln planned to issue his Emancipation Proclamation in the summer of 1862, but Seward persuaded him to wait. Lack of Northern success in the war, the secretary argued, would make the document sound like a panic-inspired move. In addition, the proclamation could not be enforced at the time, and it might offend such border slave states as Kentucky because, Seward stressed, it would enable former slaves to become Union soldiers. Lincoln withheld announcement of the proclamation until Robert E. Lee's Northern invasion in September had been repulsed.

His pivotal role as secretary of state is too often overlooked. His anti-British feelings were unconcealed. Just before his Cabinet appointment, Seward told the Duke of Newcastle that "it will become my duty to insult England, and I mean to do so." In spite of his feelings, Seward displayed amazing diplomatic skills in maintaining support for the Union and opposition to Confederate efforts. Seward blocked the one movement—foreign intervention—that might have brought victory to the Confederate cause.

Seward was also instrumental in the 1864 creation of the National Union Party for the presidential election. To outflank George B. McClellan, Lincoln broke tradition by selecting a Southerner from the other party as his running mate. Likewise, Seward played a key role with wavering congressmen in the January 1865 debates over the 13th Amendment, which, by abolishing slavery, incorporated the principles of the Emancipation Proclamation into the Constitution.

On April 5, Seward was in a carriage accident that resulted in fractures in his jaw, a dislocated shoulder, a broken arm, and a concussion. An iron frame was placed inside his mouth to hold his face together. Nine days later, while he was fighting off the pain from the injuries, Booth conspirator Lewis Payne broke into his bedroom and stabbed Seward several times about the face and neck. Physicians sutured the facial wounds, which Seward endured without anesthesia. As soon as he was able to stand, he resumed his secretarial duties in the 1865–68 Johnson Administration. Seward had little role in Reconstruction policies, yet his support of the president during the impeachment attempt made him an outcast in his party.

Instead of becoming involved in the postwar punishment of the South, Seward exhibited his own nationalistic spirit by engineering the purchase

*Seward and President Johnson welcome caricatures of the
new territory's senators to Washington, D.C.*

of Alaska from Russia in May 1867. Seward displayed extraordinary far-sightedness in this deal. For the paltry price of $7.2 million (about $120 million by modern-day standards), he obtained a region twice the size of Texas. Ironically, Seward signed the purchase agreement on March 30, 1867, four weeks to the day after Congress overrode a presidential veto and enacted the Military Reconstruction Act, dividing the South into five military districts.

Critics dubbed Alaska "Seward's Folly" and "Mr. Seward's Ice Box," but time has shown the importance of the acquisition. Besides his being Lincoln's chief adviser, historians consider this his greatest contribution as a statesman. The new territory opened the door for American commercial expansion in the Pacific Great Circle route. The strategic importance of the so-called wilderness became evident in World War II, when the Japanese spent the better part of two years trying in vain to get a toehold on the Aleutian Islands off the coast of Alaska. Yet even that consideration pales beside the fact that the largest field of oil in North America was found in its far north, in Prudhoe Bay.

With Grant's election in 1868, Seward relinquished his State Department duties. The following year he suffered a progressive paralysis of the hands and feet. The condition steadily worsened. Seward was dictating a travel book he wanted to publish when he died on October 10, 1872. Physicians put pneumonia as the cause of death. However, modern-day diagnoses strongly suggest that the fatal malady was amyotrophic lateral sclerosis (Lou Gehrig's disease).

Friendly and outgoing as he was, something within Seward blocked his giving to others the affection they gave to him. He lacked the moralistic fervor that could move the minds and hearts of men. Yet with his canny political maneuvering and crystalline foresight, he emerged as one of the ablest secretaries of state in American history. ᴄ⌀

SALMON PORTLAND CHASE

JUSTICE TRUMPS AMBITION

S ALMON PORTLAND CHASE wanted two things in his life: the abolition of slavery and the presidency of the United States—in reverse order of priority. Unfortunately, this last of the Radical Republican leaders found that his convictions thwarted his considerable ability. He was one of those rare individuals who achieved sterling accomplishments in two fields, finance and justice. Yet he fell victim to personal ambition so raging that it could be termed self-destruction.

Born in Cornish, New Hampshire, Chase grew up in Ohio with an uncle, an Episcopal bishop, who freely meted out corporal punishment and verbal abuse. Chase studied law under Attorney General William Wirt and in 1830 opened a law practice in Cincinnati. He was an early enlistee in the abolition movement. When defending captured bondsmen, Chase argued repeatedly that since they had tasted freedom, by right they were entitled to have it. That earned him the title Attorney General of Runaway Slaves.

The Free Soil element in Ohio engineered his 1849 election to the U.S. Senate. He proved as stalwart an abolitionist as Charles Sumner. Two terms as Ohio governor set him on a course for the presidency. Chase helped organize and lead the Republican Party. Yet his self-righteous attitude and his blind ambition tended to repel first-time greeters as well as strain established friendships.

*Chase officiates the oath of office to Andrew Johnson in
a private ceremony in the Kirkwood House parlor.*

He was unlucky in love as well. He married three times, and all three
wives died prematurely. Hence, his equally ambitious daughter Catherine
(Kate) became her father's confidante and chief adviser.

Chase fully expected to push aside William Seward and gain the 1860
Republican nomination for president. He was certain that his intelligence
and majestic appearance outweighed what any other candidate offered.
Yet Chase's antislavery radicalism, along with his aloof manner, earned
him too many enemies. Still, after he failed to win the Republican nod,
he campaigned hard for his fellow Midwesterner Abraham Lincoln. Chase
hoped to be named secretary of state. He received instead the Treasury
Department; more disappointingly, he learned the news from a newspaper
rather than from a member of the new administration.

This helped fuel a long-standing contentiousness with Secretary of State
Seward. Chase had all the dignity and ostentation that Seward lacked. Yet the

State Department operated on the greased rails of tact and diplomacy. Chase also found it difficult to serve under a president of lesser abilities. Even though a member of Lincoln's inner circle, Chase often criticized Lincoln's "blunders."

Amid all his political maneuvering, Chase succeeded as Treasury Department head almost despite himself. He had innate ability but little financial training. This showed in his failure to propose tax measures early in the war, when public enthusiasm was high, and that lack of funding proved a lasting problem. To make up for this lack of financial experience, he was smart enough to call on individuals with expertise in the field. Financier Jay Cooke and Congressman Elbridge Spaulding were major influences behind the hallmark National Banking Act of 1863. It created the first network of federally chartered banks from the 1,600 privately owned, state-chartered banks that had often issued their own currency. In lieu of gold and silver coin, the government issued paper currency ("greenbacks") that were redeemable anywhere for anything.

Buoyed by public acceptance and carefully managed to avoid inflation, paper currency—in the words of *Harper's Weekly*—"circulated like the fertilizing dew." In time, Chase's banking changes would be the forerunner of the Federal Reserve System.

On the negative side, Chase manipulated for the 1864 Republican nomination throughout his secretarial tenure. Twice he submitted letters of resignation, in addition to continual verbal threats of stepping down from the Cabinet—a move designed to cause Lincoln difficulties with the Radical wing of his party. The president, quite aware of the ploys, refused to let Chase go until he was certain of his own renomination. Then, to the shock of all, Lincoln accepted Chase's third official resignation. "You and I," he told Chase, "have reached a point of mutual embarrassment that cannot be overcome and is no longer in the interest of the public service."

Before Chase could recover from the blow, Lincoln named him to succeed Roger Taney as Chief Justice of the United States. Chase could not decline the offer, even though the high judicial seat removed him from the political arena. As an example of his new impotence, Chase followed administering the presidential oath to Andrew Johnson by sending him five long personal letters on how the nation should be put back together again. He received no response.

As Chief Justice, Chase was a surprising moderate on the Court. For starters, he blocked the movement to have Jefferson Davis tried for treason. One man should not be singled out as responsible for the Civil War, Chase stated. He coined the phrase "Universal Amnesty and Universal Suffrage." He opposed military occupation of the South and the Tenure of Office Act, but he was helpless in blocking either.

In the impeachment charge against Johnson, Chase thought that Radicals were acting more stubbornly and irresponsibly than President Johnson was. Since this was the first indictment of a president, Chase set the ground rules that are still in effect. The House would issue the indictment; the Senate would act as a jury with a judge presiding, and the judge would cast the deciding vote in the event of a tie.

It was a trying time for Chase. Old friends were ranged against him politically; he had to maintain order in an almost circuslike atmosphere. In the turmoil, some newspapers accused Chase of exercising undue influence for acquittal by cajoling wavering senators. The charge was untrue but could not be addressed by Chief Justice Chase.

All the while, his hunger for the presidency persisted. Chase angled for the Democratic nomination in 1868, but neither party would have anything to do with him.

During his service on the highest court in the land, Chase displayed his tremendous ability once again. He rendered two highly important court decisions. In *Ex parte Milligan,* the Court decreed that a military trial of a civilian was unconstitutional. The problem stemmed from Lincoln's use of military expediency to have individuals arrested and held without charge. (The Baltimore city council spent the entire war in a Boston prison for "suspect loyalties.") For the decision before the Chase court, General Benjamin Butler was chief defense attorney, but his loquacious orations fell on deaf ears. The court's ruling that it was unconstitutional for military courts to try civilians in regions where civilian courts functioned sharply limited federal powers in judicial matters.

*The $10,000 bill, discontinued in 1934, honors Chase
for issuing the first greenback bills in 1862.*

The other signal case, *Texas* v. *White,* dealt directly with the issue of secession. Texas would always be a state, the Court proclaimed, even though its government and its citizens might have "formed an alien group."

In 1870, having worked too hard and eaten too much, Chase had the first of two heart attacks. On March 4, 1873, a skeletal figure with slurred speech and diminished abilities administered the oath of office to U. S. Grant. The ceremony, conducted in frigid weather, sapped much of Chase's remaining strength. On May 7, he died of a stroke. His passing also signaled the era of a Radical Republicanism that, beneath the shadow of Lincoln, had left a great deal of political damage for successors to mend.

Today, Chase National Bank is named for the wartime treasury secretary. Perhaps fitting his ambition, his portrait appears on the $10,000 bill, the largest denomination of currency ever printed. (Only 300 such bills are in circulation.) A deeply pious man, Chase attended church three times on Sunday and often quoted psalms while in the bathtub. It was Secretary of the Treasury Chase who ensured that the national motto, "In God We Trust," appeared on all American currency.

Nevertheless, the ambition and the pomposity could not be hidden. Ohio senator Benjamin Wade once observed, "Chase is a good man, but his theology is unsound. He thinks there is a fourth person in the Holy Trinity." ↝

CHAPTER 2

WHEN THE REBELS CAME MARCHING HOME

Y THE SPRING OF 1865, the great Old South lay ravaged. Southerners were a proud people who had staked all and lost all. Cities, homes, and barns were burned, once prosperous fields were in ruins, railroads had no tracks, roads lacked bridges. Law and order no longer existed to stop guerrillas and deserters who plundered defenseless civilians.

A quarter of a million of the South's young men were dead. Close to the same number were crippled by wounds or broken in health. Almost half the South's livestock and farm machinery had been destroyed. Equally damaging was having to adjust to political and social changes brought about by defeat, as well as by the emancipation of 3.5 million slaves.

The compassionate hand of Abraham Lincoln was gone. General George Pickett's reaction was typical of thousands of former Confederates: "The South has lost her best friend and protection in this her direst hour of need."

Northern victory brought immediate problems, all tainted by vindictiveness. Radical Republicans controlling Congress regarded secession as

OPPOSITE: *Soldiers survey the ruins of Richmond, Virginia, in 1865.*

rebellion. The South had committed "state suicide." What had been the Confederacy was now inhabited by non-American residents, to be treated as the criminals they were.

Almost naturally, Southerners looked to their great military leader, Robert E. Lee, for guidance. The 58-year-old general became in his last five years the leading spokesman for reconciliation between the two sides. As Lee told an angry mother whose sons wanted to move to the North, "Madam, abandon all those local animosities and make your sons Americans." Unfortunately, Lee's efforts often seemed to be a solitary crusade.

Defeat and its accompanying humiliation were more than many Southerners could tolerate. Federal law required each former Confederate to obtain a parole. That often was the hardest task to perform. Requesting a pardon meant admitting a wrong. Diehards like General Jubal Early felt no consciousness of having done anything illegal, and they resisted or disobeyed pledging allegiance to conquerors. Instead, and somewhat ironically, they took the brief, stormy existence of a nation and spent the remainder of their lives in reshaping it in their hearts as a sacred ideal. Vestiges of the "Lost Cause" cult remain in evidence today.

Confusion in peace follows organization in war. This is especially the case with the losing side. Confederate officers like Early and Harvey Hill never relinquished their hatred of the North—and never missed an opportunity to say so. Former spy Belle Boyd felt the same way, yet her postwar stage performances (with a little fact mixed in a flurry of fiction) made her Southern prejudices entertaining if not acceptable.

As for Jefferson Davis, former president of the Confederacy, his innate dislike for people would plague him both during the war and after. His underlying fault may have been that he was too much the commander-in-chief and too little the political steward of his people. Only late in life would his people forgive him for the role he played in the Confederacy's defeat.

Two new classes appeared in postwar Southern society. Both generated lasting ridicule. "Carpetbaggers" were Northern whites who came to the South (many as Union soldiers) and remained there seeking profits.

A portrait of a man whose freedom was hard-won

"Scalawags" were native white Southerners who joined the Republican ranks because they thought it was in the South's best interest—as well as their own—to cooperate with the North. In the second category were military heroes James Longstreet and John Mosby, as well as extraordinary espionage agent Elizabeth Van Lew. Also scorned, but for a different reason, was George Pickett, made famous for his futile charge at Gettysburg. Beneath the flamboyant appearance was an ordinary man, both during and after the war.

Other major figures in the South realized that the past is prologue. Helping the war-torn South back on its feet and functioning again in the national mainstream slowly gained prominence. In South Carolina, Wade Hampton overcame war wounds and assumed a leadership role, while Louisiana's Francis Nicholls used his two missing limbs as springboards in replacing military rule and political corruption with honest state government.

Not until Reconstruction ended in 1877 did the former Confederate states fully rejoin the Union. By that time, the camps of both hatred and healing had made lasting marks that influenced the New South for years to come. Changing laws proved easier than changing hearts. ෴

ROBERT EDWARD LEE

THE MODEL GENERAL

ROBERT EDWARD LEE is to millions an American icon. Next to George Washington and Abraham Lincoln, he may be our most admired historical figure. That is indeed a strange phenomenon. Washington founded a nation; Lincoln preserved one. Yet Lee commanded an army in a revolution whose purpose was the dissolution of that nation. For a leader of a failed revolt to be held subsequently in such universal esteem is unprecedented.

One historian has explained the dichotomy this way: "In the confused councils of war and peace that Lee was forced to share, he bore the contention of swaggers and braggarts with dignity because it was his duty as a soldier to be patient and his obligation as a Christian to be humble."

Born into a Virginia aristocratic family that had fallen on hard times, Lee spent his teenage years caring for a mother dying of tuberculosis. He chose West Point because his family could not afford to send him to college. In an early sign of his sterling character, Lee graduated second in his class and was among a handful of cadets who acquired no demerits while enrolled at the academy.

Thirty-two years of devoted service to the Army followed without a single blemish on his record. Lee was a hero in the Mexican War,

Painter Jean Leon Gerome Ferris's "Let Us Have Peace"
commemorates the war's end.

superintendent of West Point, second-in-command of the prestigious Second U.S. Cavalry, and protégé of General in Chief Winfield Scott.

The turning point in Lee's life came on April 17, 1861, when Virginia voted to secede from the Union. Three days later, Lee resigned from the Army. While the United States was 70 years old, the Lee family had lived in Virginia for 225 years. Lee opposed both slavery and secession, but nevertheless, he stated, "I cannot draw my sword against my birthright."

He spent the next four years defending the Old Dominion. Desk duties and acting as President Davis's troubleshooter occupied the first 13 months of the war. Then, on June 1, 1862, he received command of the Confederacy's premier force, which he named the Army of Northern Virginia. By this point, dispirited Southerners had been pushed back to the gates of Richmond. Under his brilliant leadership, however, Lee would lead the army into legend.

Lee was the physical embodiment of a soldier. Tall, well built, and with a calm voice and a dignity that commanded respect, he stood out in any crowd. He had the brown eyes of the Lees. The war changed his hair—and the beard he cultivated—to silver gray. An officer who often saw him remarked: "He assumed a common interest in a common venture with the person addressed . . . He was less of an actor than any man I ever saw."

Possessed of "a fierce and violent temper," Lee had the willpower to keep it under almost perfect control. (Two of the four known instances when he gave way to anger came when he saw horses being abused.) The love he had for his soldiers was reciprocated by the thousands who called him "Marse Robert" and referred to themselves as "Lee's Miserables." A sense of invincibility permeated the Southern ranks throughout the middle half of the war.

In battle after battle, Lee used audacity against an always superior enemy. He took risks, did the unpredictable, gambled against the odds. Sometimes it failed (Malvern Hill and Gettysburg); sometimes it succeeded (Second Manassas, Chancellorsville, the Wilderness). Always it kept Union forces off-balance, uncertain, fearful of making a mistake that Lee would exploit.

Not until 1864 did General U. S. Grant, utilizing fully the North's more powerful resources, begin the continual hammering that mercifully ended on April 9, 1865, at Appomattox. British military writer J.F.C. Fuller, though one of Lee's early critics, later acknowledged that "few generals have been able to animate an army as [Lee's] self-sacrificing idealism animated [his force] . . . What this bootless, ragged, half-starved army accomplished is one of the miracles of history."

"The Great American Tragedy," as the Civil War is often termed, left the South in destruction and despair. Lee knew that the eyes of the public were upon him and that he needed be a model of how the South accepted defeat. If he felt resentment, he concealed it well. Humiliation as a general changed to humility as a civilian. The federal government refused to grant him a pardon, but Lee did not complain. He never returned to his beloved Arlington estate overlooking Washington. Nor did he forget Grant's magnanimity at the surrender. Ex-Confederates would not merely be paroled. Thereafter at home, they were not to be molested by Union authorities as long as they obeyed the law. Reconciliation would prevail in place of retribution. Ever after, Lee reacted strongly to any criticism he heard of his Union counterpart.

Only once in those stormy years did Lee express indignation. The passage in 1867 of the Military Reconstruction Act, whereby the Southern states were placed under Union Army occupation, seemed to Lee a gross betrayal of the contract of conciliation that he and Grant had signed at Appomattox.

In spite of his brilliance as a field commander, Robert E. Lee also made lasting achievements in the five years after the Civil War. Penniless and in ill health, he agreed in 1865 to accept the presidency of impoverished Washington College. He had no reason to become involved in the postwar education problems of the South save one: his lifelong sense of duty. "I have led the young men of the South into battle," he declared. "I have seen many of them dead on the field. I shall devote my remaining energies to training young men to do their duty in life."

An honor code was among the first of many innovations Lee made in transforming the threadbare Lexington school into one of the most desirable educational centers in the postwar years. Lee set himself apart from those who wanted to perpetuate the unhappy memories of North versus South. He refused to write his memoirs, attend reunions, or speak at dedications. When Lee was out walking and a contingent of Virginia Military Institute cadets marched past him, Lee made a point of staying out of step.

To an angry Confederate widow who complained of the future, Lee said, "Madam, dismiss from your mind all sectional feeling, and bring up your children to be Americans." Famed abolitionist Henry Ward Beecher and newspaper giant Horace Greeley endorsed Lee in 1868 for president of the United States—even though, lacking citizenship, he was ineligible to serve.

Healing the wounds of a terrible war was Lee's final duty, and he did it so well that his death from a stroke on October 12, 1870, brought an outpouring of grief nationwide. Eulogies gushed forth in the hundreds.

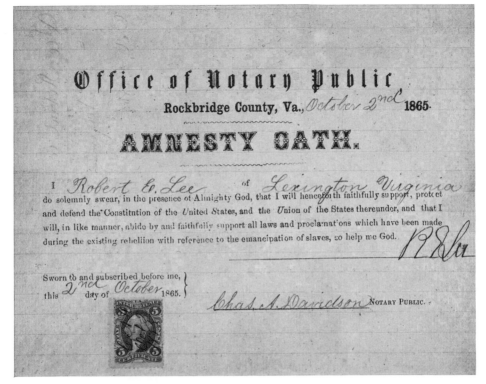

Robert E. Lee's Amnesty Oath, signed October 2, 1865,
reaffirms his loyalty to the U.S. Constitution.

New Englander Julia Ward Howe—whose stirring lines in "The Battle Hymn of the Republic" were the most inspiring song for Billy Yanks (the common name for Union soldiers)—wrote of Lee: "A gallant foeman in the fight / A brother when the fight was done / And so, thy soldier grave beside / We honor thee, Virginia's son." Lee is buried beneath the chapel on the campus of what today is Washington and Lee University.

In October 1865, Lee signed an oath of allegiance to the Union. Mysteriously, it became lost and wasn't discovered until 105 years later. A bill was rushed through Congress, and on August 5, 1975, President Gerald Ford officially restored citizenship to a man who had been the model of defeat for the land he loved. ☙

JUBAL ANDERSON EARLY

THE FIREBRAND CONFEDERATE

J UBAL ANDERSON EARLY was the South's answer to Thaddeus
Stevens. General Robert E. Lee referred to Early, when he was
one of his corps commanders, as his "Bad Old Man." In a war
filled with characters, "Old Jube" stood in the forefront. His snappish
nature was hardly curbed by defeat. Unreconstructed, irreconcilable,
outspoken, and argumentative, he rallied behind him an influential flock
of followers who preferred to live in the past rather than in the present.
After the war, he became one of the leading voices against the changes
imposed under Reconstruction.

Raised in rural Virginia, the third of ten children, Early entered West
Point in 1833 and exhibited good academics and poor behavior. He saw
duty against the Seminole and Cherokee tribes. In the Mexican War, a
severe rheumatic condition rendered his gangly figure stooped and aged
beyond his years. He left the army to become a lawyer. Through most of
the 1850s he was commonwealth attorney for Franklin County in the
Virginia Piedmont.

In 1861 the staunchly Whig conservative was elected to the Virginia
secession convention. Early first voted against secession because of his
home area's close tobacco ties with Northern markets. What changed his
mind was the majority's belief that the federal government did not have

the right to send soldiers across Old Dominion soil without the state's permission. To him that amounted to "coercion." The Constitution, he declared, "does not prevent our State authorities repelling invasion."

Early led the 24th Virginia Regiment into the war. By firm and sometimes outstanding leadership, he rose steadily through the military chain of command to become one of Lee's most reliable soldiers. Bluntness was but one of his peculiarities. At the 1862 Battle of Williamsburg, where he received a severe shoulder wound, Early sent his troops forward into action with the words "The safest place after getting under fire will be at the [Union] guns themselves, and so I advise you to get there as quickly as you can!"

By the end of that year, Old Jube was known by sight and reputation throughout the Army of Northern Virginia. He was respected by all but liked by hardly anybody. With his dark eyes and beard, and wearing a dirty white hat adorned with a black plume, Early had a hunched-over manner that made him look, wrote one soldier, "solemn as a country coroner going to his first inquest." Constant pain made him irritable and irascible. He spat tobacco and—in his high, piping voice—oaths with reckless abandon. A staff officer remarked that if Early "had a tender feeling, he endeavored to conceal it and acted as though he would be ashamed to be detected in doing a kindness."

He was the only man who dared curse in Lee's presence. The commander tolerated it because his subordinate was so dependable. In May 1864 Early was promoted to lieutenant general and assigned to defend the Shenandoah Valley. His first engagement came when he brought seasoned reinforcements to dislodge Federals from Lynchburg. They were used to the likes of John Mosby's cavalry rangers, and as Early arrived on the outskirts of the city, he hollered toward the Union lines: "No butternut rangers after you now, you God-damned Blue-Butts!"

Early cleared the valley of enemy troops and, with 14,000 soldiers, swept across the Potomac River, won a victory at Monocacy, Maryland, and marched to the outskirts of Washington. The capital was too well defended for Early's small force to attack, but as he withdrew, he exclaimed, "Major, we haven't taken Washington, but we scared Abe Lincoln like hell!" While retiring to the west, Early sent a detachment to burn Chambersburg, Pennsylvania, as retaliation for Federal depredations in the Shenandoah Valley.

That autumn, in the Second Valley Campaign, overwhelming numbers of Federals under General Philip Sheridan badly defeated Early in three major engagements. The South lost the region known as the "Breadbasket of the Confederacy." Early received heavy criticism even though a Confederate general praised the "fearlessness with which he fought against all odds and discouragements." However, public outcry forced Lee to relieve Early from command a month before the war ended.

Old Jube sternly refused a pardon from his hated enemy. Over the next few years he fled successively to Texas, Mexico, and Canada. He eked out a living from checks sent by family members and friends. While in Canada, Early published his version of the Second Valley Campaign, *A Memoir of the Last Year of the War for Independence, in the Confederate States of America.* The 125-page apologia was the first printed narrative by a Southern general—and the first among many printed recollections and accusations he would write.

Early's initial intention was to move permanently to New Zealand to get as far from the federal government's occupation as possible. He had made no effort to gain a pardon or regain citizenship, but on Christmas Day 1868, President Johnson announced an unconditional amnesty to all former Confederate leaders. This enabled Early to return to Virginia. In 1869, he moved to Lynchburg and began a leisurely law practice. When he received word of newspaper speculation that he was running for governor, the old soldier quashed the report at once by writing to the editor, "If I were made governor, I would have the whole state in another war in less than a week."

To the contrary, he toiled endlessly to keep the Confederacy alive. Always clad in gray suits, Early served as president successively of the Lee Monument Association, Southern Historical Society, and Association of the Army of Northern Virginia. Former general P. G. T. Beauregard chose Early to co-manage the Louisiana Lottery. The job entailed little work, so Early spent much of his time engaged in vicious public debates with anyone who criticized the South.

Southern pride personified, Jubal Early poses for a portrait.

The cult of the "Lost Cause" was largely his creation. To Early, the Civil War was simply defined: a contest of might over right. He used the monthly magazine *Southern Historical Society Papers* as a platform. His vehemence of irreconcilability made him the chief spokesman for the defeat-with-honor movement. As one historian wrote, Early "fashioned himself into a passionate architect and defender of 'The Lost Cause,' and he went to great lengths to control the contents of early histories of the war." For the rest of Early's life, a veteran noted, "no man ever took up his pen to write a line about the great conflict without the fear of Jubal Early before his eyes."

Early's conception of the Lost Cause had three major prongs: Johnny Rebs, as the Confederate soldiers were called, were better fighters; Robert E. Lee was the consummate commander; and James Longstreet betrayed Lee and the Confederacy by his near-treasonable performance at Gettysburg. Longstreet's joining the Republican Party after the war added fuel to Early's fire. He went so far as to call Longstreet a "renegade" and "viper." The two men engaged in a war of words that echoed far beyond their deaths.

Early never married, although evidence is strong that he fathered at least one child. In mid-February 1894 he was preoccupied with a bundle of mail when he fell down the post office's marble steps. A physician found no broken bones, but Early's speech thereafter was incoherent, and he had severe back pain. On March 2, two weeks after the accident, he died quietly at home. He was buried in Lynchburg's Spring Hill Cemetery.

One eulogist stated after the funeral, "Virginia holds the dust of many a faithful son, but not of one who loved her more, who fought for her better, or would have died for her more willingly." This most thoroughly beaten of Confederate generals spent the last 30 years of his life as the most adamantly unreconstructed of the Rebels. Fortunately for history, Early's followers dwindled in number as the years healed the sores. Well into modern times, one historian asserted, Early's followers believed that "northern advantages of men and resources, the righteousness of the Confederates' own activities, and Lee's greatness resonated powerfully among a people who had sacrificed so much in a failed war." ❧

DANIEL HARVEY HILL

IRASCIBLE PATRIOT

J UBAL EARLY'S STRIDENT DEFENSE of the old South was matched by Daniel Harvey Hill's utter hatred of the North. His men called him "Old Rawhide" because he turned biting sarcasm into a fine art. Though Hill was an excellent educator, his virulence toward Yankees emblematizes the bitterness of so many defeated Rebels. Military occupation, the thievery of carpetbaggers, and the corruption of political appointees only reinforced beliefs in "Yankee heathens."

The basis for his acerbic nature stemmed from his austere childhood. He was the youngest of 11 children born to South Carolina parents who were fervent Presbyterians. A boyhood illness left him bent in stature and always in some degree of pain. Nevertheless, he graduated from West Point in 1842 and won praise for gallantry at Contreras and Chapultepec in the Mexican War.

Hill married the daughter of the president of Davidson College in North Carolina, and in 1848 he left the Army to pursue a teaching career. Hill was a professor for six years at Washington College (the same school that Robert E. Lee resurrected after the Civil War). One of his closest friends was Major Thomas J. Jackson of the nearby Virginia Military Institute. The two men enjoyed a militant faith that emphasized the Jehovah of the Old Testament. They became brothers-in-law after Hill departed to teach at Davidson College.

Hill's level gaze hides a quick temper easily triggered by
perceived Northern offenses.

Why Harvey Hill came to detest Northerners so violently is unknown, but it became flagrant during the Davidson years. For instance, he wrote a mathematics textbook for use in his classes, and one question began, "A Yankee mixes a certain quantity of wooden nutmegs, which cost him one-fourth cent, with a quantity of real nutmegs, worth four cents . . ."

In 1859, Hill left Davidson to become superintendent of the newly created North Carolina Military Institute in Charlotte. That made him a natural choice for appointment at war's outset as colonel of the First North Carolina Infantry Regiment. Hill displayed commendable leadership in June at Big Bethel, Virginia, the first major skirmish of the Civil War. In terms that would have made John Calvin proud, Hill wrote to his wife after the engagement, "Oh, God, give me gratitude to thee, and may we never dishonor thee by weak faith."

Big Bethel brought Hill promotion to brigadier general in a young nation badly in need of high-ranking officers. He devoted the next months to strengthening the defense of his adopted state. His love of God was as fierce as his hatred of the enemy. "If conquered by the Yankees," he asserted, "there is no insult and no indignity which those infernal wretches will not inflict upon us."

Promotion to major general preceded solid service in the 1862 Peninsula Campaign. Hill was an instructive rather than inspiring leader. Small, thin, and dark-complexioned, he rarely smiled. An occasional cigar was his only vice. He was stiff and sharp when on duty, negative and critical when not. His fighting skills and disregard for personal safety were widely known. Yet the spinal ailment and chronic dyspepsia constantly sharpened his tongue.

Hill once stated that he had never seen a dead Confederate wearing spurs—a sweeping indictment of cavalry. On another occasion Hill observed, "Our Regimental Chaplains as a general thing are as trifling as the Regimental Surgeons, which is the strongest denunciation I can use." Lacking in patience, Old Rawhide regarded any straggler as "generally a thief and always a coward, lost to all sense of shame." When a member of one of the army bands once asked for a furlough, Hill returned the application with a four-word reply: "Disapproved—shooters before tooters." Even his generosity toward his men was sometimes negative. "If our brave soldiers are not permitted to visit their homes, the next generation in the South will be composed of the descendants of skulkers and cowards." The Carolinian's battle reports occasionally found fault with superiors, and his "croaking" complaints made him unwelcome around his fellow officers.

In the 1862 Maryland Campaign, Hill was unfairly blamed for losing a copy of Lee's marching orders that a Union soldier found and delivered to General George McClellan. Yet Hill's all-day resistance at the Battle of South Mountain gave Lee a day to consolidate his army at Antietam, and Hill's staunch defense of the Bloody Lane, where his force of 2,600 men held off Federal forces double that number, was masterful. Yet his leadership received only passing attention in the press and public.

Hill "had such a queer temperament," Lee told an associate, "I can never tell what to expect of him." The commander soon wearied of Hill's carping and dispatched him to repulse Federals congregating along the North Carolina coast. Hill's poor performance there convinced Lee that while his lieutenant was "an excellent executive," operating alone made him "embarrassed and backward to act." Nor did Hill endear himself to local Carolina inhabitants. He described one home guard unit as consisting of "three field officers, four staff officers, ten captains, thirty lieutenants, and one private with a misery in his bowels."

Transfer to the western theater brought no improvement to his fortunes. Hill and army commander Braxton Bragg quickly came to loggerheads. Following the empty Southern victory at Chickamauga, Georgia, President Davis sided with Bragg rather than his mutinous subordinates. Davis refused to send Hill's promotion to lieutenant general to the Senate for confirmation. Hill spent the remainder of the war in minor assignments, trying to clear his name.

"My great sin," he wrote late in life, "was hatred of the Yankees." It never wavered. In 1866 he began editing *The Land We Love,* a monthly magazine supposedly devoted to the agricultural and industrial development of the postwar South. Yet during its three-year run, the periodical increasingly became a military journal containing official battle reports, officers' memoirs, and Hill's editorial denunciation of Northerners and Reconstruction. His short-lived Charlotte weekly, *The Southern Home,* was equally vindictive. Hill's strong anti-Reconstruction views brought occasional threats of assassination, he told Early in 1869. On an occasion in Charlotte, someone in a boisterous mob shot and wounded Hill's youngest son as the lad walked down a city street. The shooter forgot the incident. The father never did.

Hill was not a defender of everything Confederate. At one point he urged the North Carolina governor to authorize a book on that state's participation in the Civil War. "North Carolina led the fighting and Virginians have written the history," he complained, "and from the history it is difficult to discover that our State took any part in the Confederate struggle." His cadre of friends dwindled when Hill stated publicly, "My impression of Genl. Lee is not so enthusiastic as that of most men who served under him." Hill even criticized more than once his own brother-in-law, General Stonewall Jackson. Hill's reputation also slipped with a number of articles he wrote of war experiences. One that generated wide anger was Hill's summation of Lee's leadership at the 1862 Battle of Malvern Hill: "It was not war—it was murder."

In 1877, Hill attained the presidency of the all-male University of Arkansas. Able as always, he increased funding, enrollment, and the size of the campus. His seven-year tenure, however, ended in his angry resignation when the school's governing board refused to adopt Hill's strict code of student conduct.

In 1885, Hill accepted the superintendent's position at Middle Georgia Military and Agricultural College. Return to a military atmosphere brought him momentary peace of mind and seeming improvement from spinal pain and stomach cramps. Early in 1889 he was diagnosed with inoperable stomach cancer, the result of years of dyspepsia. He resigned from the military school and returned to Charlotte. For the remaining time, he lived on a morphine diet. Hill died on September 24, 1889, as a rainstorm raged outside his home. Burial services were held at the Davidson College cemetery.

Hill's devotion to the South was unimpeachable. His dedication to postwar education in the shattered South deserves praise. What crippled him in both endeavors was his tendency toward harsh and reckless criticism. Free with his opinions, whether on "the mercenary vandals of the North" or Southerners too concerned with sentimentality, Harvey Hill was an ever present thorn in his time. ❧

MARIA ISABELLA BOYD

SHOWBOAT SPY

MARIA ISABELLA BOYD HATED YANKEES. However, she exploited her prejudices in the postwar years through stage performances and other self-promotions that were as comical as they were successful. Around her astounding career as a Confederate activist, spy, fugitive, prisoner of war, international actress, and touring performer swirls so thick a combination of fact and fiction that historians have never agreed on the perimeters of the truth. A respected writer termed her "one of the most active and reliable of the many woman agents of the Confederacy." Her defenders hailed her as the "Siren of the Shenandoah," the "Famous Amazon in Secessia," and the "Southern Cleopatra." A New York reporter dismissed her as "an accomplished prostitute," while another author concluded that she was a myth and never existed.

That last claim is definitely not true. The daughter of a successful merchant in the northern end of Virginia's Shenandoah Valley, "Belle" Boyd received an above-average education at a Baltimore female academy. With South Carolina's secession in December 1860, she became an ardent Southern sympathizer. Her first "military" action came on July 4, 1861, when a group of drunken Union soldiers attempted to raise the American flag atop the Boyd home in Martinsburg. One of the soldiers

Never shying from the spotlight, the spry Boyd pauses for a photo.

insulted Mrs. Boyd, whereupon her 17-year-old daughter pulled out a pistol and killed him.

Authorities brought no charges against the teenager. She hardly looked like a threat to the Union. Tall, supple, with blue eyes and lighter hair than her photographs show, she had other features too irregular to make her

*Boyd braves the Union army stockade at Manassas Junction
to gather intel for the Confederacy.*

attractive: a long, narrow face, a prominent nose, and protruding teeth.
A Winchester, Virginia, diarist thought her "too horsy."

As a spy she bore dispatches for a year between the major Confederate
Army east of the Blue Ridge Mountains and another force in the Shenandoah
Valley. Unsophisticated in the ways of espionage, she sent messages in her
own handwriting, and this led to a brief imprisonment in Baltimore. Upon
her release, Boyd went to Front Royal to live inside Confederate lines with an
uncle and aunt. They owned the town hotel, a center for reports and rumors.

On May 23, 1862, Boyd performed her greatest exploit. Stonewall
Jackson was pursuing the Federal army northward when Boyd obtained
information on Union movements. She dashed across open fields outside
Front Royal as a fusillade of bullets sprayed around her. (Later stories had
Boyd riding a great horse in clear view of Federal riflemen.) In any event,
Jackson used her information to maximum advantage and continued his
Valley Campaign.

Two months later, Boyd was captured and placed in Washington's Old Capitol Prison. She enjoyed her celebrity status. A fellow inmate observed, "Her prejudices were very strong and she hated the North with a bitterness I never saw equaled before in a woman." A local reporter found her "smart, plucky, and absurd as ever."

Boyd gained her freedom once again in a December 1863 prisoner exchange. She agreed to carry a packet of official Confederacy papers to England, but a Union warship intercepted the vessel, and she was again taken captive. This time, however, U.S. Navy Lieutenant Samuel Hardinge fell in love with his prisoner. The two married shortly after their arrival in England.

Union authorities subsequently ordered the arrest of Hardinge, and when the Civil War ended, Boyd and an infant daughter were left penniless in London. Boyd quickly compiled her wartime "memoirs." *Belle Boyd in Camp and Prison*, published in both London and New York, had all of the drama, excitement, flamboyance, and manufactured conversations that one could expect. Her characters are real, some of the escapades are factual, and the work as a whole is captivating. Two editions appeared in rapid order. This marked the debut of Boyd's second career.

In 1866, out of financial desperation, she turned to the English stage. Her debut in a well-known comedy, *The Lady of Lyons,* was a smashing success. The enthusiasm of the "celebrated Confederate heroine," a London critic purred, "resembled the enthusiasm of Joan of Arc."

Boyd returned to the United States and rave notices of her acting. In 1860, she married John Hammond, an English traveling salesman in the tea and coffee business who was 15 years her senior. Their marriage was stormy and tragic, however. The couple moved to California, and Boyd became pregnant and increasingly erratic. She was committed to an insane asylum, where a son was born and died.

Following a six-month confinement, Boyd resumed traveling with her husband, and eventually gave birth to three more children. But love evaporated with time, and divorce came in 1884. She again was alone—but not for long.

Six weeks later, she wed again. Nathaniel High was 17 years her junior, playing juvenile roles in an acting company. The newlyweds faced financial strains, though, which forced Boyd to return to the stage. With High as her manager, she toured the country with solo recitals of her Civil War "experiences." Usually the show went by the title *The Perils of a Rebel Spy.*

She insisted on being introduced as "captain and honorary aide-de-camp of General Stonewall Jackson." Generally she appeared on stage in a decorative Confederate officer's uniform and wearing a hat that, she maintained solemnly, cavalry chief James Ewell Brown "Jeb" Stuart had been wearing at the time of his 1864 death. She also elicited tears with the quivering announcement that her first two husbands had died gallantly defending their beloved South.

For 14 years Belle Boyd Hardinge Hammond High presented her shows. Although she did much to rekindle goodwill between North and South, her bookings decreased with the passing years. Soon she was reduced to performing before small groups in second-rate theaters.

She was in Kilbourn, Wisconsin, to give a recitation when, on June 12, 1909, she died of a heart attack. Although she was 56 years old, she looked no more than 40. Ironically, the women's auxiliary for the Grand Army of the Republic raised money for her funeral. Four Union veterans bore her casket to a grave in Spring Grove Cemetery. There, deep in the Union, her journey ended.

Boyd's career and personality made her controversial. In an age when women were supposed to be homebodies, the overly bold, outspoken, garrulously dressed, and thrice-married Boyd was an espionage agent and a stage performer. Everything from her chastity to her age became a source of dispute.

Belle Boyd would have liked that. ✎

JEFFERSON DAVIS

ICON OF THE "LOST CAUSE"

U NLIKE HIS FAMOUS MILITARY LEADER, Confederate president Jefferson Davis would provide no direction to his former nation after the war. His political and military experiences were many, but so were his personality defects. He led a confederation of 11 loosely linked sovereignties trying to break away from the most powerful nation in the Western Hemisphere. Davis had the misfortune of being the Southern counterpart of Abraham Lincoln, in comparison with whom any statesman would pale. Nevertheless, the Confederacy never had a more devoted torchbearer.

A Kentuckian by birth (he was the tenth child of log-cabin parents), Davis became a Mississippian by adoption. He attended Transylvania University and graduated from West Point. In 1835 he wed the daughter of General Zachary Taylor. The couple fell ill with malaria three months later, and after Sarah Davis died, her grief-stricken husband spent seven years in seclusion on his brother's plantation. Davis read vociferously and learned everything he could about politics and history. He emerged from his self-imposed exile, entered Mississippi politics, and married a Natchez belle 17 years his junior.

With no loss of momentum, Davis moved up both military and political ladders. He succeeded John C. Calhoun as chief spokesman for the South. When the "fire-eaters" accomplished their goal of secession, they sought a conservative who would keep a calm hand on the steering wheel. That led to Davis's election as president of the Confederate States of America.

*Following the Confederate attack on Fort Sumter, a cartoon lampoons Davis
as a circus acrobat in a delicate balancing act.*

"All we ask is to be left alone," he repeatedly said as he assumed the double burdens of chief of state and commander in chief of military forces.

Davis possessed more assets for a president than any other figure in American history. A tall, dignified man with chiseled face, he was well educated and impressive in appearance as well as in manner. Everyone admired his unquestionable courage and integrity. Davis was so honest that he would never compromise what he knew to be right. And the crises pressing on the Confederacy permitted Davis no margin for error.

His political career included a term in the House of Representatives and multiple elections to the Senate, and Davis possessed even better military credentials. A graduate of West Point, he was a colonel in the Mexican War (a rank that neither Lee nor Grant could match), and he limped home a hero.

In 1853 Davis became secretary of war in the Franklin Pierce Administration. He increased the size of the Army by 50 percent, adopted an advance system of infantry tactics, studied revolutionary breech-loading rifles, and sent officers abroad to monitor European military techniques. At one point he even experimented with using camels instead of horses in the desert country of the Southwest. In the late 1850s he chaired the Senate Committee on Military Affairs, a position that made him familiar with both military thinking and the army personnel then on duty.

Davis's liabilities, unfortunately, negated his strong points. He was notoriously inept at getting along with people. A Richmond, Virginia, newspaper thought Davis "ready for any quarrel, with any and everybody, at any time and at all times." This weakness cost him popular appeal. Northerners praised their leader as "Uncle Abe" and "Father Abraham." To embattled Southerners, their chief executive was "the president" or simply "Davis."

He wasn't just a poor administrator; he also neglected critical political matters in favor of military affairs where his presence wasn't needed. Similarly, Davis was so ardent a patriot that he expected others to give blind support to his programs. The president and the Confederate Congress all too quickly began staring at each other across a widening chasm of disagreements. Davis increasingly came to see that a nation armed with state rights ideals would fail. They needed a centralized government to fight a war in which the South was inferior in every way except courage. Yet Davis's piecemeal approach to nationhood was a dream that never neared reality.

Perhaps worst of all, Davis lacked the capacity of growth vital to successful presidents. While Lincoln gained increasing stature during the war, Davis fretted about his problems, fought back at his opponents, shriveled in spirit, and declined in public esteem. He was an ingrained conservative attempting to lead a revolution. The paradox was impossible to overcome.

Then there were the host of physical maladies that plagued him: neuralgia, nervous indigestion, insomnia, migraine headaches, boils, and the loss of one eye—possibly from glaucoma—a decade before the war.

Davis was captured in May 1865 by Federal soldiers as he fled to the West. He spent two years in a dungeon at Fort Monroe, Virginia, while authorities considered putting him on trial for treason. His wife, Varina, worked ceaselessly for his release, and citizens across the country pleaded in his defense. The government abandoned plans for a trial and in May 1868 set Davis free.

He returned home to a hero's welcome. Davis now received what he so ardently had sought during the war: the respect, if not admiration, of his own people. Financially strapped, he pursued jobs that friends found for him. In none was he successful for any length of time. Then he found a real benefactor: the widow Sarah Dorsey, who owned a 600-acre plantation called Beauvoir near Biloxi, Mississippi. She invited the Davis family to live in a cottage on the estate, and Davis agreed, believing it was an ideal place to work on his wartime memoirs. However, Varina Davis refused for a period to visit her husband as he enjoyed a widow's hospitality.

In 1879, Sarah Dorsey died of cancer. To the surprise of all, she left her entire estate to the man, as she stated in her will, "who is in my eyes the highest and noblest in existence." With a substantial advance in hand, and several collaborators to assist him, Davis labored hard on his two-volume memoirs, *The Rise and Fall of the Confederate Government* (1881). It was a publishing failure, however. A boring rehash of Davis's old arguments, the thick volumes were also a polemic against such adversaries as Joseph Johnston and P.G.T. Beauregard. Most Southerners

The spurs that saw Davis along his final push toward the western theater until being captured in Irwinville, Georgia

couldn't afford the two volumes, and the North was too busy rebuilding the nation to care about them.

At least his last years proved rewarding. Although all four of his sons preceded him in death, the Southern people treated Davis as a living martyr of the "Lost Cause." He argued to the end over the constitutional right of secession and the legitimacy of the Confederate nation. In 1887, he visited Macon, Georgia, where 50,000 people came to cheer him. Confederate veterans broke from the ranks and swarmed around their former commander. When a faded battle flag was drooped over the frail statesman's shoulders, Davis buried his face in the folds and sobbed.

On December 5, 1889, he died in New Orleans of pneumonia, at the age of 82. The U.S. War Department had flown the flag at half-mast following the death of every secretary of war, but officials refused to accord Davis that honor. Nonetheless, thousands came to cheer and weep at his two funerals (in New Orleans in 1889 and Richmond in 1893).

Historian Frank Vandiver's tribute to Davis was concise and profound: "He had a zealot's intolerance and a patriot's haste, and worst of all, he knew he was right." ∞

JAMES LONGSTREET

The Controversy Continues

THE MAJORITY OF SOUTHERNERS accepted defeat and went to work rebuilding careers shattered by war. Some, accepting the "arbitrament of the sword," concluded that joining the victors was the best avenue to recovery. The most famous—or infamous—of these scalawags was Lee's senior corps commander in the Army of Northern Virginia, James Longstreet.

He was born in South Carolina, yet he spent his youth in Gainesville, Georgia, and then his teenage years with an uncle, the noted minister and writer Augustus Baldwin Longstreet. After James graduated near the bottom of his West Point class in 1843, he served the usual frontier duty, received a wound in the Mexican War, and by 1861 was a major and paymaster in New Mexico Territory.

He received one of the Confederacy's first brigade assignments and was prominent in the opening phase of the 1861 Manassas campaign. The action convinced Longstreet that the tactical advantage in war lay with the defense. More specifically, repulsing attacks was the key to Southern victory.

Longstreet's stately appearance was a great asset. A strong man with powerful arms and shoulders, he stood six feet two inches tall and weighed 200 pounds. He wore a full brown beard beneath "eyes of glint steel blue, deep and piercing." He usually attended to his duties with an unlit cigar in his mouth.

His personality was a principal liability. Stubborn, blunt-spoken, sometimes arrogant and sarcastic, Longstreet was cautious by habit. That was tragically augmented in January 1862, when he lost three of his four children in a Richmond, Virginia, scarlet fever epidemic. Any sense of humor he might have had disappeared.

The 1862 Peninsula Campaign was his first real test of battle. He fought well at Williamsburg, but at Seven Pines he took undue caution with orders and displayed anger at a fellow general. Yet, when Lee reorganized the Army of Northern Virginia early in the summer, he assigned Longstreet to command the First Corps. It contained five of the eight divisions in the army.

At the Battle of Second Manassas, while Stonewall Jackson's men sustained heavy losses, Longstreet waited a day before launching a hammerlike attack that shattered the Union line. Three weeks later, at Antietam, an officer described Longstreet withstanding Union charges as "like a rock in steadiness when sometimes in battle the world is flying to pieces." Lee hailed him afterward as "my old war horse."

The lopsided Southern victory at Fredericksburg was further proof to Longstreet that the Confederacy should always seek to fight defensively. That strategy backfired on him, however, after Lee answered Longstreet's desire for an independent command. Early in 1863 he was assigned to secure the southeastern Virginia region, but his lack of aggressiveness made the venture a disappointment.

"Old Pete," as his men called him, rejoined Lee for the 1863 invasion of the North. As far as posterity is concerned, Longstreet's Civil War career climaxed at the three-day Battle of Gettysburg. Opposed from the start to the Confederate foray into Pennsylvania, Longstreet may or may not have purposefully been tardy in his attack on the second day's fighting. He then argued against Lee's decision to send Pickett's division on an illfated charge the next day.

Transferred with two divisions to assist Braxton Bragg's army, Longstreet led a breakthrough at the Battle of Chickamauga that routed half the Federal Army. However, afterward Longstreet became embroiled in an attempt by several generals to have Bragg relieved from command. Bragg removed Longstreet from the scene by sending him to seize Knoxville, Tennessee. Not only did Longstreet fail again at independent command, but also the Union victor at Knoxville was Ambrose Burnside, the victim of the slaughter at Fredericksburg.

Longstreet was back with Lee when U. S. Grant began his massive 1864 offensive in Virginia. The first fighting occurred in the Wilderness. There, as befell Stonewall Jackson a year earlier, Longstreet was a victim of "friendly fire." He was leading his men in the second day's action when a bullet entered his throat and ripped into his right shoulder. The severe bleeding was brought under control, but Longstreet permanently lost the use of his arm and had to learn to write left-handed. The wound also left the general with a husky voice that worsened with time. He returned to the army in the autumn and served with Lee at Appomattox.

The reputation of "Lee's Old War Horse" plummeted after the war, largely because of his own doing. Unlike his impoverished compatriots, Longstreet accepted defeat without bitterness and made an easy transition from military to business life. He settled in New Orleans and steadily became prosperous through an insurance business, stocks, and railroad investments. A rekindled friendship with former schoolmate Grant and acquaintances with a few Radical Republicans stoked angry murmuring in the South.

These sparks were inflamed when Longstreet attended Grant's presidential inauguration and in turn was appointed surveyor of customs in New Orleans. He then committed a major mistake by expressing in a New Orleans newspaper his support for and willingness to cooperate with Reconstruction policies. He was unprepared for the blast of negative reaction to his letter. Overnight in the South he became the most controversial of ex-Confederates. His chief antagonists were such diehards as Jubal Early, William Pendleton, and John B. Gordon. Especially through the pages of a monthly publication, *Southern Historical Society Papers,* Longstreet was blasted as a turncoat, unfaithful to the Confederate cause, and the major factor in Lee's defeat at Gettysburg, "the climactic struggle for independence."

Longstreet orders Gen. George Pickett to initiate what would be a disastrous charge at the Battle of Gettysburg.

Cast as a scapegoat, Longstreet spent the remainder of his life defending his war record. He lashed out indiscriminately by writing five articles for a popular collection of memoirs, *Battles and Leaders of the Civil War.* His criticisms of Robert Lee further blackened his already tarnished reputation. Yet Longstreet continued to be dogged and unbreakable in his views.

In the late 1880s, the physically crippled general began preparing his memoirs, despite his poor memory. "I do not expect to handle facts with gloves in my account," he stated, "but let chips fall where they may." However, he had difficulty locating official reports because few former comrades were willing to share material with him. An 1889 home fire destroyed much of the research he had collected.

Staff members helped as much as they could. A copy editor, Pascal J. Moran of the *Atlanta Constitution,* used a more liberal hand than prudence would advise, but Longstreet approved the publication of the manuscript. *From Manassas to Appomattox* appeared in 1896. One had to go north of the Potomac River to locate a favorable review.

A year later, Longstreet married Helen Dortch, 32 years his junior. She would outlive—and avidly defend—her husband until her death in 1962. After publication of his memoirs, Longstreet's health slowly deteriorated. His right arm hung limply at his side, rheumatism often left him wracked in pain, and in 1903 he contracted cancer in his right eye. The once bull-like general shriveled to 135 pounds and could talk only in a whisper.

Longstreet died of pneumonia on January 4, 1904, at his daughter's home in Gainesville, six days before his 83rd birthday. He was buried in Gainesville's Alta Vista Cemetery.

A sympathetic biographer concluded that "if Longstreet had been his own worst enemy, alienating people through his embittered writings, he had also been a living presence too great to be ignored." To his postwar attackers, on the other hand, Longstreet assumed the aspect of one who would sooner "reign in Hell than serve in Heaven." Recent scholarship has resurrected Longstreet's positive image to a degree. While sympathetic biographers have called more attention to his contributions, love-hate judgments still prevail. The man simply turned the page to his future too soon. ❧

JOHN SINGLETON MOSBY

THE GRAY GHOST

BEHIND JAMES LONGSTREET, the second most noted scalawag had once been hailed as "the Gray Ghost of the Confederacy" for his ability to elude Union troops. John Singleton Mosby, an attorney before the war with no military experience, succeeded because he was a maverick. However, that inclination to follow the road less traveled did not serve him well after the war. His support for U. S. Grant for president caused him to be blackballed by his enraged Virginians. For the rest of his life, he was exiled from the rolling countryside he had defended so well.

Mosby was decisive even in his youth. He once saw a schoolmaster drunk in public, and the spectacle turned Mosby into a lifetime teetotaler. He enrolled in the University of Virginia and was an above-average student until the day he got into a dispute with a campus bully. The confrontation ended when Mosby shot the student in the neck. He served seven months in jail, and then ironically ended up studying law under the prosecutor in the "malicious wounding" trial. In 1858 Mosby married and settled into the tranquil life of a lawyer in the rail town of Bristol on the Virginia-Tennessee border.

His love for his home state induced him in 1861 to sign up for military service. "Virginia is my mother. God bless her!" he exclaimed.

Small and thin, and lacking any knowledge of soldier life, Mosby hardly seemed a promising recruit. Yet with General Jeb Stuart's cavalry, he rose

*"Mosby's Rangers" carried a Confederate flag fashioned by
Virginia's Ladies of Fauquier to the end of war.*

rapidly from private to regimental adjutant. To Stuart, the young lawyer
from the mountains of southwestern Virginia displayed "a shining record
of daring and usefulness."

Mosby had long idolized Francis Marion, the famous "Swamp Fox" of
the American Revolution. The exploits of General Stonewall Jackson's
cavalry chief, Turner Ashby, likewise fascinated him. Six weeks after
Ashby's death in June 1862, Mosby gained permission to recruit a band
of horsemen to wage irregular warfare behind enemy lines in northern
Virginia. The little band grew in number with its successes until it officially became the 43rd Virginia Cavalry Battalion. To friend and foe, it
was "Mosby's Rangers."

They were farmers by day and fighters by night. Most of them lived in
nearby Fauquier and Loudoun Counties, through which ran the main
Union supply and communication lines. From that vantage point, the
band could strike eastward toward Washington, westward into the Shenandoah Valley, and northward to the Potomac River. For almost two years,
they operated in wooded mountains and hills interspersed with fertile
farmlands. Obscure trails provided a network of furtive access and egress.
Homes and small towns offered places for refuge and food.

As Mosby later wrote, "I rarely rested more than a day at a time." He raided troop detachments, rail lines, wagon trains, storage depots, and command outposts. A common tactic of his was an overnight raid with but a few dozen horsemen. Contrary to legend, the troopers carried neither sabers nor carbines. Each man was armed with two revolvers. Assaults were fast and furious, but never haphazard. In lawyerly fashion, Mosby concentrated long over every detail.

In one of his first raids, he and 29 men galloped through the darkness to the Federal command post at the Fairfax Court House. Confederates captured a sleeping general, 32 soldiers, and 38 horses without firing a shot or losing a man. A disdainful Lincoln commented that he did not mind losing a general officer, "for I can make a much better brigadier in five minutes, but the horses cost $125 apiece."

Fauquier and Loudoun Counties became "Mosby's Confederacy." The colonel fired the Southern imagination and became the most successful guerrilla leader in the Civil War. Union authorities dispatched no fewer than 70 missions in a vain effort to capture him. Atop a magnificent gray horse, issuing orders in his high-pitched but powerful voice, Mosby was invincible in his small theater of operations.

Although Mosby commanded fewer than 400 men at any given time, he captured at least 2,900 Federals—more than four times his own losses. He siphoned off 462 Union cavalrymen, four times his own strength, during the Gettysburg Campaign alone. The following year, at the Battle of New Market, the same ratio occurred. Mosby's men consistently stung General Philip Sheridan's efforts "like a wasp down his collar." Mosby's seizure of over 3,500 horses and mules was a significant replenishment of one of the South's most severe shortcomings.

More than half of Mosby's life remained when the Civil War ended. In the postwar chaos he was twice arrested but never brought to trial. In the summer of 1865, General Grant personally signed a parole for Mosby. He resumed his law practice in the northern Piedmont town of Warrenton, hoping to forget the war. Soon he discovered that the fear he had instilled in Northerners had turned to widespread admiration. Mosby enjoyed prosperity while being outspoken in his scorn of Radical Republicans, scalawags, and Southern diehards. On more than one occasion Mosby's abrasiveness led to fistfights.

His initial fortune changed as his friendship with U. S. Grant developed. Mosby switched to the Republican Party, endorsed Grant for president in 1872, and urged ex-Confederates to do the same while joining in a new Union. Reaction in the South was as if Mosby had deserted during the war to the Union Army. One Virginia newspaper labeled Mosby and Grant an "overrated pair of antipodal military hacks." Virginians branded Mosby a "political outcast" and completely ostracized him.

The law practice collapsed. His wife died in 1876, and Mosby never remarried. President Rutherford Hayes appointed him as minister to Hong Kong, a post he held for seven years. His duty was to supervise American commerce in that region of the Far East. Mosby uncovered "utter rottenness" in a commercial trade where seamen stole and government officials embezzled openly. American consular personnel were in the middle of the mess. When the State Department attempted a cover-up, Mosby wrote directly to President Hayes—and submitted copies of the letters to the *Washington Post*.

Democrat Grover Cleveland's 1884 election signaled the end of Mosby's Hong Kong assignment. He could not return to hostile Virginia, so this man without a country appealed again to Grant for help. On the day before he died, Grant asked Leland Stanford of the Southern Pacific Railroad to find a position for the Virginian.

Stanford hired him as an attorney for the rail line, and Mosby settled in San Francisco. His position offered ample time for personal activities. The cavalryman subsequently lectured to large audiences across the nation. He defended Jeb Stuart's conduct at Gettysburg both publicly and in a book published in 1908. Mosby feuded bluntly, and often rudely, with unreconstructed Southerners, notably General Jubal Early.

In 1897 Mosby was accidentally kicked in the head by a horse. The blow fractured his skull and shattered his left eye. Surgeons were able to prevent sepsis, but Mosby thereafter was blind in the eye.

A different type of blow followed in 1900, when the reorganization of the Southern Pacific executive leadership left Mosby without a job. His

*Virginia cavalrymen recuperate between stealth operations
in the area known as Mosby's Confederacy.*

final service was an appointment from President Theodore Roosevelt as
an assistant attorney general in the Department of Justice in Washington.
His term was short-lived because Mosby was so irascible. He once said,
"If all the men claiming to have served under me had been at hand *at
the time,* we would have driven Grant out of Virginia without an effort."

On May 28, 1916, the 82-year-old Mosby, at his own insistence,
underwent surgery for long-standing prostatitis. He died on the operating table, coincidentally, on Memorial Day. His remains were taken to
Warrenton for burial. A brother-in-law completed his memoirs, which
were published the following year. Like Mosby's life, they are fragmented,
abrasive, and exciting.

With a dynamic personality forged in childhood and a predilection for
direct action achieved in manhood, Mosby thrived on controversy. He
defended the South and the North in turn with a single-handed purpose.
This brought him equal shares of praise and damnation. ℮

ELIZABETH VAN LEW

PRINCESS OF ESPIONAGE

ESPIONAGE WAS IN ITS INFANCY during the Civil War. Many volunteer spies on both sides gathered information—and misinformation. The art of analysis was lacking; hence, so was authenticity. However, amid such clandestine confusion emerged Elizabeth Van Lew, whom historians have praised for running "the most productive espionage operation" of the war.

Van Lew was the daughter of a prosperous Richmond merchant. The family lived in a three-and-a-half-story mansion on Church Hill, the highest of the city's seven hills. Diagonally across the street was the church where Patrick Henry had made his "Give Me Liberty or Give Me Death" speech.

"Lizzie" was well educated and intelligent, and after her father's death, she and her mother carried on the family business. In her mid-40s when the Civil War opened, she was only 4 feet 10 inches tall. Darting blue eyes, an oversize nose, and hair in ringlets were her most conspicuous features. In sentiment, she was an outspoken abolitionist and an uncompromising Unionist.

Fighting had not begun in earnest when Van Lew organized a few citizens who shared her views into a spy ring. She justified her actions with the statement "I do not know how they can call me a spy for serving my own country within its recognized boundaries." Her goals were to gather military and political information for Federal use and to help captured soldiers escape from Libby Prison, immediately downhill from the Van Lew home.

*A photo of Libby Prison discloses the grounds
where Van Lew mined information for the Union cause.*

Among her agents were two former slave women, one of whom, Mary Bowser, gained employment in the Jefferson Davis residence. Almost daily Van Lew received valuable news from the Confederate White House. Meanwhile, she converted her mansion into a veritable fortress by triple-locking the heavy doors and building secret passageways to hidden rooms.

The Van Lew wealth and social reputation at first put the family above suspicion. Yet Lizzie's shrewd and resourceful mind developed a unique cover to conceal her activities: She assumed the airs of a lunatic. She would walk the streets of Richmond in outlandish clothing, her ringlets in disarray, singing nonsensical songs to herself. A vacant expression might suddenly turn into wild gestures as her eyes rolled back and forth.

The ruse worked. No one wanted anything to do with "Crazy Betsy," as she was widely known.

Through a combination of charm, innocence, and praise, Van Lew obtained permission from Confederate Provost Marshal John Winder to

Ever resourceful, Van Lew developed her own cipher
for transmitting covert messages.

carry food, books, and medical supplies to captured Union officers held in Libby Prison. She confided to one of her associates, "I can flatter almost anything out of old Winder, his personal vanity is so great." On her frequent visits she obtained tidbits that prisoners had overheard as well as careless remarks made by sentries. Recently captured Federals were very useful because they provided up-to-date information on Southern strength and positions.

In addition, the Van Lew home became a first stop for Federals who escaped from the prison. They would remain, well hidden and fed, until an opportune time to resume their northward flight.

Some Confederate officials suspected Crazy Betsy of espionage activities. She underwent surveillance on numerous occasions, and suspicions of her activities increased through the war years, but she was never caught in any wrongdoing.

On April 2, 1865, as the Union Army was advancing into Richmond, an angry crowd gathered in front of the Van Lew home. The tiny spinster came out to stare them down. "I know you, and you, and you," she shouted, pointing at individuals and calling them by name. "General Grant will be in this city within the hour. If this house is harmed, your houses shall be burned down by noon!" The crowd dispersed.

For Van Lew, the Union occupation of Richmond was redemption as well as vindication. U. S. Grant sent her a letter stating, "You have sent me the most valuable information received from Richmond during the war." Townspeople were first astounded and then irate to learn the extent of her operations in the capital. Ostracism and poverty were her lot until she secured a brief position in the Richmond office of the Freedmen's Bureau.

In 1869, President Grant added insult to injury for local citizenry when he appointed Van Lew postmaster of Richmond. The position was one of the highest federal offices a woman could hold in the 19th century. Not only was the salary substantial, but also the postmaster dispensed patronage by hiring postal employees and controlled the dissemination of political information. Further, the position was often a stepping-stone to better federal ones.

During her seven-year service, Van Lew diligently ran an honest enterprise. She introduced home delivery of mail inside the city limits while championing racial equality. Nevertheless, she could not escape her wartime deeds. She was a living reminder of Reconstruction. Citizens, emboldened by the Lost Cause creed headquartered in Richmond, humiliated her at every opportunity. She received "constant and repeated gross personal insults." When her mother died in 1875, Van Lew stated that "we had not friends enough to be pall-bearers."

Her appointment as postmaster expired with the Grant presidency. Conciliatory Rutherford Hayes named a less controversial figure to oversee Richmond's postal affairs. Financially strapped, Van Lew moved to Washington in search of another postal position. She obtained only a low-grade clerical position, and when an unfriendly superior demoted her to the dead-letter office, Van Lew left the government and returned to Richmond.

She became a frail and bedraggled figure in a dilapidated building that once was an ornate mansion. A group of Massachusetts citizens, remembering the kindnesses she had shown their soldier sons, sustained her financially with an annual payment. Her last years formed a vicious cycle. She became a recluse; when she went out publicly, she was suspicious of the intentions of everybody and fled home.

On September 25, 1900, Van Lew died of edema (dropsy). Few people attended her burial in the family plot of Shockoe Hill Cemetery. Since the family grave site lacked sufficient room, the coffin was buried vertically rather than horizontally—fitting for someone who had thrived in a world where nothing was as it seemed.

GEORGE EDWARD PICKETT

REMEMBERED FOR ONE ATTACK

"**P**ICKETT'S CHARGE" is the most famous failed assault in American military history. This is perhaps not surprising, since the man for whom it is named possessed more than his share of personal problems. He overdressed and on occasion overimbibed. Beneath the ostentation Pickett was a mediocrity, and his postwar fortunes would not alter that view.

Born in 1825 on a large plantation downriver from Richmond, Virginia, Pickett had a highly unusual record at West Point. A brilliant but lackadaisical student, he graduated last in the Class of 1846 and was only five demerits shy of expulsion. Pickett did serve well in the Mexican War, but his 1851 marriage to Sally Minge ended a year later when she died in childbirth. Pickett was so devastated that he took a four-month leave of absence from the Army and seemingly lost his flair for combat.

In 1857, while on frontier duty in the Washington Territory, he may have married a Haida Indian princess named Morning Mist. (Local residents strongly support the tradition.) Although the couple had a son, the mother died from the effects of childbirth. How Pickett felt about the loss is unknown, for he abandoned both his home and the boy.

The coming of the Civil War sparked Pickett's return to Virginia. He received a colonel's commission and was placed in charge of defenses on the lower Rappahannock River. In February 1862, his promotion stemmed more from the need for brigadier generals than from any accomplishment by Pickett. He was a colorful figure among his fellow officers: outgoing, with a romantic mustache and perfumed curly hair.

He showed promise in the opening phase of the Peninsula Campaign against Richmond. On June 27, at Gaines' Mill, while exhibiting less than inspiring leadership, Pickett suffered a shoulder wound that left him impaired for several months. During his convalescence in Richmond, he met LaSalle Corbell, the highly educated daughter of a Virginia planter, who was 23 years his junior. Pickett would leave camp in the middle of the night to see the girl he had every intention of wedding when she came of age. They maintained a steady flow of love letters even after their September 1863 wedding.

Pickett had no chance after the Seven Days' Campaign to distinguish himself. Quite the contrary, he twice was rebuked for inept supervision of his troops. The same carelessness and inattention at West Point had carried over into his war career. Nevertheless, thanks to his close friendship with General James Longstreet, Pickett was elevated to major general and division command late in 1862.

He had seen no action for a year when his turn in the limelight came on the afternoon of July 3, 1863, at Gettysburg. Lee ordered Pickett's men to spearhead an attack on the center of the Union lines. Pickett allegedly responded first by writing his fiancée: "My brave Virginians are to attack in front. Oh, God in mercy help me as He never helped before." Then 14,000 Confederates surged across an open wheat field three-quarters of a mile wide. Vicious fighting occurred for 40 minutes. On the slaughter ground, Pickett lost half his command, including every general and field officer save one.

The stunning defeat permanently sapped much of Pickett's limited ability. Worse, when Lee rejected Pickett's official report as being far from factual, a coolness developed between the two leaders.

Assigned thereafter to command the lawless department of North Carolina, Pickett met another defeat at New Bern and compounded the loss by brashly hanging 22 deserters as their families and friends watched in horror. Nervous exhaustion removed him from field duty for the remainder of 1864.

Pickett's dignified carriage belies his battle record.

Pickett rejoined the army early in 1865 and assumed command of Lee's right flank. His instructions were to hold his position "at all hazards." On April 1, with no action occurring between opposing lines, Pickett rode to the rear to enjoy a meal of baked shad. That afternoon thousands of Federals under General Philip Sheridan assailed Pickett's leaderless position. Half the Confederates surrendered; the remainder fled to the rear in rout. Lee promptly removed Pickett from command. A week later, the war ended at Appomattox.

Without a home and penniless, with the army the only job he had ever known, Pickett had no idea what to do next. He, his wife, and son were forced to flee to Canada when a congressional committee seemed on the verge of indicting Pickett for war crimes because of the North Carolina hangings. Pickett's old army friend, U. S. Grant, interceded to obtain a pardon and a release from court trial.

The ex-Confederate tried a number of occupations and failed in each. He finally found some stability by selling insurance for a New York firm with an office in Norfolk. Pickett remained quiet in the postwar years while other military leaders were writing articles, producing memoirs, or traveling on the lecture circuit. Still, he couldn't forget the nightmare of Gettysburg.

In 1870 he agreed to accompany Colonel John S. Mosby on a courtesy call to Lee. After they left the meeting, Pickett spoke bitterly of "that old man" who "had my division massacred at Gettysburg."

Mosby, ever supportive of Lee, replied, "Well, it made you famous."

On July 30, 1875, Pickett died in Norfolk from what the death certificate stated was "abscess of the liver." He was buried with the thousands of other Confederates in Richmond's Hollywood Cemetery. From that point, LaSalle Corbell Pickett was determined to bring order and fame from life's disappointments. She spent the remaining 50 years of her life transforming her husband's reputation as a mediocre officer into one of the Confederacy's greatest heroes. Stage performances and veterans meetings set a base for voluminous writings that contained fabrications, romanticized tales, and widespread plagiarism. The results were the ruined reputations of both writer and subject.

George Pickett, however, did have one postwar moment of truth. Former Confederate officers were gathered at a Richmond meeting when an argument began over who was responsible for the defeat at Gettysburg. Was it Lee's error of judgment? Longstreet's slowness? Stuart's absence? One man looked over at Pickett, standing nearby, and asked his opinion.

Pickett quietly replied, "Well, the Union Army had a hell of a lot to do with it." ❧

WADE HAMPTON

SOUTH CAROLINA REDEEMER

WADE HAMPTON WAS REPUTED to be the largest landowner in the antebellum South. He certainly held that distinction in his native South Carolina. His father and grandfather fought in America's first two wars. They accumulated cotton plantations in South Carolina and Mississippi as well as a sugar estate in Louisiana.

After graduating from South Carolina College, Hampton studied law before devoting his full attention to the family's holdings. He considered public office an obligation rather than an opportunity. In 1852 he began seven years of service in the two houses of the state legislature. His was a lone voice of moderation amid a rising chorus condemning abolitionists and "Northern usurpation of the law." Hampton stated in 1859, "Unless every patriot in our land strikes once more for the Constitution, I see not how the Union can be or should be perpetuated."

He followed the state's exodus from the Union and enlisted in the army as a private. Governor Francis Pickens made him a colonel and asked Hampton to raise his own command. Hampton reacted like a patrician warrior. At his own expense, he marshaled his neighbors, family, and even some of his slaves (as body servants) into a combination of infantry, cavalry, and artillery known as Hampton's Legion.

Blessed with intuitive leadership qualities and a fighting spirit, Hampton commanded with a calm, confident manner. He was tall and well propor- tioned, with a mustache and muttonchop whiskers. His dark eyes had a peculiar snapping motion. His voice, one soldier recalled, "was tenor and ringing." Rarely did Hampton display excitement. The hotter the fight, the cooler he seemed to become. Steadily, he evolved into one of the great cavalry officers of the Civil War.

Hampton was conspicuous in every battle of which he was a part. By 1863 he was one of two brigade commanders in General Jeb Stuart's mounted arm of Lee's army. Hampton suffered his first family tragedy at the June 9 Battle of Brandy Station, when his younger brother was killed in the action.

The relationship between Stuart and Hampton was not close. The two men had contrasting personalities, with Stuart tending toward the flamboyant and Hampton more introverted. State rivalry also played a role. After one engagement, Hampton declared, "I suppose Stuart will as usual give all the credit to the Virginia brigades. He praises them on all occasions, but does not often give us credit."

At Gettysburg, Hampton's fellow brigadier, Fitzhugh Lee, ordered a cavalry charge in Hampton's absence. The Carolinian rushed onto the field to rally his men. He received two saber strokes to the head as a result, and a surgeon had to shave half of Hampton's skull. The general took it good-naturedly. "Striking, if not beautiful," he wrote of his injuries, although "the flies play the mischief as they wander over the bald side."

It took Hampton four months to recuperate. He gathered fresh troops from South Carolina, returned to duty, and spent the rest of the war confronting threats and staging raids. His victory over General Philip Sheridan at Trevilian Station was a badly needed success during Grant's 1864 Overland Campaign. When Stuart was killed at Yellow Tavern in May, Hampton moved up to command of all of Lee's cavalry.

The September "Beef Raid" was his most publicized feat. Confederates rode 100 miles in 12 hours and captured 11 wagons plus 2,468 cattle that had been grazing only six miles from Grant's headquarters. The meat fed Lee's army for a month, and the hides filled a critical need for foot covering.

In another engagement a month later at Hatcher's Run, Hampton's son Preston fell mortally wounded while his father was directing the action.

PUCK.

A DREADFUL ATTACK OF "PRESIDENTIAL FEVER" IN THE U. S. SENATE.

"Presidential fever" plagues the Senate, Hampton included,
in an artistic expression of disillusionment.

Hampton rushed to the youngster, held him in his arms, and murmured: "My son, my son." The general kissed the boy and returned to the battle.

Hampton was recruiting at home when, in January 1865, he was promoted to lieutenant general. He became one of but three Southern generals without formal military training to attain that rank. The war ended before Hampton could return to Lee's army.

The once wealthy planter faced widespread destruction from Sherman's forces as well as personal poverty. "He looks crushed," a neighbor stated. "How can it be otherwise?"

The ex-general accepted Confederate defeat, but he never conceded that the Southern cause was wrong. Like Robert E. Lee, Hampton went to work to rebuild his home country. "The very fact that our State is passing through so terrible an ordeal as the present," he stated, "should cause her sons to cling the more closely to her."

Radical Republicans levied heavy reconstruction on the South. Hampton toiled constantly to redeem and reunite the Union. He declined offers to run for governor because he sought to strengthen the Democratic Party into an acceptable alternative for Carolinians. It was in their interests to remake the South, Hampton believed, for as the country prospered, so would its people.

At every mass meeting, Hampton urged freedmen to join Democrats for the common good of the state. One observer mistakenly thought such an action was a waste of time. "General Hampton and his friends," he declared, "had just as well try to control a herd of wild buffaloes . . . as the Negro vote."

In 1876, Hampton won election as governor, with a margin of victory of only 1,134 votes. In spite of his detractors, freedmen made the difference. The new executive became known for racial moderation and honest fiscal policies. Shortly after his reelection, Hampton was thrown from a mule while hunting, and his right leg had to be amputated. He was bedridden when he learned of his election to the U.S. Senate.

He served in Washington for 11 years, but his first speech was the most remembered. When a Northern senator made a slur against the South, Hampton was quick to respond: "In the heat of conflict we struck hard blows, and doubtless we spoke harsh words. But does remembering or repeating them now bring us any nearer to the peace and harmony for which the whole country so ardently longs?" Hampton then expressed the wish that more veterans were in Congress. "We learned in a common school how to respect our enemies."

President Grover Cleveland appointed Hampton as commissioner of railroads. It was largely a ceremonial position, but Hampton took the post seriously, traveled by train from coast to coast, and made several recommendations for improvement. With his health beginning to fail, he declined William McKinley's offer of reappointment.

The Carolinian died April 11, 1892, of vascular heart disease. He is buried in Trinity Episcopal Church Cemetery in the capital of the state that he loved so deeply. The most radical of the secession states received an uplift by Wade Hampton in the critical postwar years, but South Carolina returned to the Union on wheels of conciliation and white supremacy. ❧

FRANCIS REDDING TILLOU NICHOLLS

LOUISIANA'S HONEST POLITICIAN

FRANCIS REDDING TILLOU NICHOLLS rode a bandwagon of reform and popularity to postwar success in Louisiana. He did so in part from having donated two appendages to his country. He is an excellent example of how losses in war can prove to be gains in peace.

Born in Donaldsonville, Louisiana, he graduated from West Point in 1855 and had the distinction of being the only Pelican State native in his class. Nicholls spent a year in service before resigning because of gastrointestinal problems. He obtained a law degree from the University of Louisiana (now Tulane) and enjoyed a successful practice until the outbreak of the Civil War. His marriage to socialite Carolina Guidon produced seven children and financial security.

Nicholls's West Point training led to his appointment as lieutenant colonel of the Eight Louisiana. His first battle action came on May 25, 1862, at Winchester, Virginia. A bullet shattered his left elbow and led to his capture. The wound stopped bleeding on its own, which saved his life, but four days of inadequate treatment followed before a Union surgeon amputated the limb. Nicholls was given only whiskey as anesthesia.

Recuperating at home, Nicholls received a promotion to brigadier general and joined Robert E. Lee's army just in time for his second

Brigadier general, governor, and chief justice of Louisiana's supreme court,
Nicholls cut his path as a Southern "Redeemer."

engagement: the 1863 Battle of Chancellorsville. He was trying to bring
order to his confused command in deep woods when a cannon shell
ripped through his horse's stomach and struck Nicholls's left foot. The
general reached down in the darkness and was shocked to find his foot
gone. The leg was amputated a few hours later. Nicholls had engaged in

two battles and had lost two limbs. A wooden leg and one arm holding a crutch hampered him for the remainder of his life.

Carried to Lynchburg, Virginia, to recover from his wound, Nicholls refused to be treated as a cripple. He sought and received appointment as post commander of the rail town, with its prisoner-of-war compound and five military hospitals. Knowing that Lynchburg might well be a target in the 1864 Union offensive, he began military preparations. He first impressed local slaves to construct fortifications along the main roads leading into the city. Next he recruited locals "too old or too young for regular service" and drilled them regularly as militia. When a Union force did advance on the city in June, Nicholls turned to the hospital population. He selected 1,300 convalescing soldiers who could stand and shoot. This group of "walking wounded" became his major defense line. One reason Nicholls was successful in motivating men to the earthworks was because, according to one surgeon, he was "a West Pointer, and a splendid officer and gentleman."

Confederate reinforcements arrived in time to repel the Federal threat. Even so, the crippled general's preparations for a battle were instrumental in saving Lynchburg from probable destruction.

Nicholls enjoyed a quiet postwar law practice until 1876, when he was drawn into state politics. Reconstruction was ending because Radical control in Washington was fading. On the national scene, Rutherford Hayes and Samuel Tilden waged a heated race for president. In Louisiana, Democrats at last saw a chance to regain political control. They proudly nominated "all that is left of General Nicholls" for governor.

The 1876 gubernatorial contest exceeded even Louisiana's penchant for wild politics. One historian concluded, "In such a mass of assertions and denials, bribery and counter-bribery, and of false testimony contradicted and retracted, the truth is well-nigh hopelessly buried." Nicholls was able to keep most of his followers calm. He courted the black vote with assurances that the 14th and 15th Amendments would be implemented. Public funds from the powerful Louisiana Lottery helped finance his campaign to "redeem" the state from crooks and outsiders.

Both sides claimed victory on Election Day, and for a while the state had two governors. Republican Stephen Packard refused to relinquish the office. In January 1877, Republican legislators barricaded themselves in a New Orleans hotel, dubbed "Fort Packard," and admitted only Reconstruction-sanctioned representatives.

Only weeks before the presidential inauguration in Washington, Louisiana politicians reached a compromise. Republicans duly elected would be allowed their seats in the legislature, the two constitutional amendments would go into full effect, and Francis Nicholls would be recognized as governor. His inauguration brought the largest turnout in New Orleans since the announcement of the 1803 Louisiana Purchase.

Nicholls was one of several Southern "Redeemers" elected governor that year, seeking to end the reign of the Radical Republicans. Their victories, coupled with the ascent to the White House of the conciliatory Hayes, enabled several states to return peacefully to the Union. Inside Louisiana, however, Nicholls battled corruption left over from the Reconstruction era.

The general ousted a large number of proven crooks; he chaired the constitutional convention that brought Louisiana into national alignment. The state capital was returned from New Orleans to Baton Rouge. Nicholls continually promoted racial peace and honest government. He expanded state railroads and resurrected state militia. Rich and poor, black and white, were comfortable with state leadership under "Governor Nick." At a large Confederate veterans convention in New Orleans, speaker William Preston Johnston recognized Nicholls, "whose maimed form and empty sleeve are on the platform." What followed was "deafening applause."

Nicholls declined a second term as governor. He also refused election to the U.S. Senate. His return to private life was brief, for public demand sent him to a second term as governor. In 1892 he was offered the position of chief justice of the state's supreme court. Critics who asserted that Nichols was "too one sided to be a judge" were ignored. Spectators always grew silent as two aides helped him mount and dismount from the bench.

The sword and scabbard that led Nicholls in battle

President Grover Cleveland recognized Nicholls's merits by selecting him for a term on the West Point Board of Visitors.

Nicholls resigned from the court in 1911 because of declining health. Shortly thereafter, on January 4, 1912, he died from heart failure. His remains lie in St. John's Episcopal Church Cemetery in Thibodaux, Louisiana.

One eulogist described him as a "brave soldier whose life was one long battle." Yet that life had its rewards. He was the most impressive figure in Louisiana during the last quarter of the 19th century. Nicholls State University bears his name. At the capitol in Baton Rouge stands an impressive statue. It has its left foot, but the arm is only a flap. ∽

CHAPTER 3

THE

FIRST
MODERN WAR

"**T**HE PARAMOUNT FACT about Civil War battles," historian Allan Millett concluded, "was that weaponry had outpaced tactics and communications."

In 1861 regiments went into battle just as soldiers had done for centuries. Massed firepower and the threat of bayonets wielded in great frontal attacks decided the course of combat. A charging line had to be compact so that infantrymen could see or hear commanding officers giving battlefield orders. The charging file had to be small for the sake of coordination. During the Civil War, however, such assaults came to mean, as a Union officer wrote, "a slaughter pen, a charnel-house, and an army of weeping mothers and sisters at home."

The huge armies of the Civil War demonstrated early that the traditional method of open charges was outdated, but no one could suggest an alternate method of attack. Further, the advent in the 1850s of the rifle, with a range five times that of the musket, provided a weapon that began to shift the advantage in battle to the defensive side. When Christopher Spencer introduced a rapid-firing carbine to the Federal arsenal, this new technology elevated the killing process to a slaughterous level.

OPPOSITE: *Wounded survivors of the 1864 Wildnerness Campaign*

Coinciding with more lethal shoulder weapons were sharp advances in how armed forces fought. William T. Sherman is often called "the father of total war," even though fellow officers such as U. S. Grant, Philip Sheridan, and Judson Kilpatrick pursued identical practices. Sherman spelled out in writing his strategy on the eve of the "March to the Sea" campaign that extended from Atlanta to Savannah. If need be, Sherman stated, his army would "take every life, every acre of land, every particle of property, everything that to us seems proper; that we will not cease until the end is attained. That all who do not aid are enemies, and we will not account to them for our acts." No longer a limited war between armies, the Civil War became a fight to the death between peoples.

Another innovation came about because of militarily untutored Bedford Forrest, whom one writer considers "the great natural soldier of the nineteenth century." He was the premier cavalry commander in the Civil War, not just as a fighter but also as a strategist. Unencumbered by old-school concepts taught at military academies, Forrest's strategy was the forerunner of the World War II German Blitzkrieg: infantry moving quickly by vehicle, attacking a surprised foe, and then racing away to the next target.

While Forrest was often accused of using guerrilla tactics, the term would better be applied to those tactics of Confederate naval commander Raphael Semmes. The hopelessly outnumbered Southern navy had to resort to privateering, in which single vessels roamed the sea in search of defenseless merchant ships. The wily Semmes, with his waxed mustache ever gleaming, was by far the most successful captain of the warships preying on supply boats.

On the positive side, the Civil War mercifully brought major advances in the field of medicine. For every man killed in action, two died behind the lines from wounds and disease. Disorganization awaited injured soldiers brought to aid stations. Into the chaos in 1862 strode Dr. Jonathan Letterman. He single-handedly brought order, organization, and vastly improved medical treatment. His major contribution may have been the introduction of a battlefield ambulance corps. This may seem insignificant, but many wounded men lay unattended for days on a battleground.

Letterman's ambulances gathered up the injured as soon as possible and rushed them to treatment centers. It is impossible to say how many thousands of lives were saved by "the father of the emergency medical services."

In a related improvement, little-known James Hanger supplied an important support to soldiers who lost a leg in battle. In one of the first skirmishes of the war, Hanger received a wound that led to the amputation of a leg. He scorned the usual peg leg given to amputees and carved a wooden limb that resembled a leg and was hinged at the knee. Hanger's innovation opened the door to a prosthesis industry that today supplies hundreds of thousands of maimed individuals who can live far more comfortably, thanks to the ingenuity of a teenage Virginia farm boy.

The Civil War even brought an advance in the treatment of dead bodies. Thomas Holmes is regarded as the father of modern embalming and thus of the American mortuary industry. Every human endeavor opens the possibility of advancement, and an undertaker's business is the dead. Operating in Washington during the war, Holmes embalmed more than 4,000 bodies upon the request of the bereaved.

The Civil War triggered the rise of the largest armies ever seen in the Western Hemisphere. In the case of the North, some two million men stepped forward to defend the Union. Of necessity, the four-year struggle brought significant advances in army logistics. Equipping, feeding, and moving armed forces are fundamental tasks that require much attention and effort. The North was blessed with the greatest quartermaster general in our military history. Humorless but meticulous Montgomery Meigs was indefatigable during the war years. Orchestrating the acquisition and assignment of everything from cannon to nails, he spent more money than anyone else in the Civil War—and he could account for every penny of it. When a Federal army moved, one could say, General Meigs was moving with it.

A major reason that supply lines became so fruitful was the railroads that carried them. Herman Haupt became a model for future engineers in his ability to rapidly build rail lines, especially his trestle bridges. As a result, the railroad's capacity for carrying large numbers of people would become a standard element in mass troop movements all over the world.

As the Civil War grew more intense, so did the killing power of weapons. Richard Gatling in 1862 invented the first "machine gun": a six-barrel, hand-cranked implement that could "fire faster than a man can count." The Gatling gun was too problematic in design to be used extensively in the Civil War. However, it took a terrible toll among Native American tribes during the wars in the West. Continued improvements over the years have now made the Gatling gun one of the most feared weapons of all.

The Civil War was a 19th-century watershed in the development of modern warfare. The days when ladies could come with their parasols to watch the brave boys fight, as occurred in the first Battle of Manassas, by degrees gave way to the soul-draining combat of trench warfare at Petersburg, the Confederacy's last stand. The bloodiest war ever fought on American soil changed forever the ways that armies all over the world marched into battle. ☙

CHRISTOPHER MINER SPENCER

WHAT A DIFFERENCE
A CARBINE MAKES

MORE THAN ONE WRITER has felt that Christopher Miner Spencer was the model for Mark Twain's *A Connecticut Yankee in King Arthur's Court*. The Connecticut-born farm boy relied more on incentive and intuition than on formal education. He lived in search of new ideas and solutions. At 13, using a handmade hacksaw, Spencer cut down his grandfather's Revolutionary War musket to carbine size. At 15, he built a working model of a steam engine. In his late 60s, he drove to work in a steam automobile. At the age of 87, he turned to aviation as a field for study and improvement.

In all, Spencer would obtain 42 patents. The most memorable, if not valuable, was a breech-loading, repeating rifle that changed the face of combat.

Spencer spent his formative years as a journeyman machinist in a range of different plants. While employed in a Hartford textile company (which sparked his invention of a silk-winding machine), Spencer had a long conversation with Samuel Colt, in which the gunmaker commented on the army's need for a new shoulder weapon. Spencer toyed with the idea throughout the late 1850s. His basic concept was a repeating rifle that would far outperform the single-shot, muzzle-loading musket used for centuries by infantry.

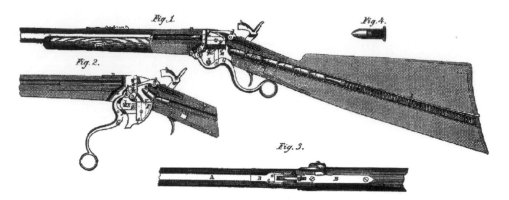

Spencer's repeating rifle was magazine-fed and lever-operated.

The Cheney brothers, at whose mill Spencer worked, were so impressed by Spencer's design that they bought the patent for $5,000 and a royalty of a dollar for each gun sold.

Spencer toiled night and day to perfect the rifle. John Hay, Abraham Lincoln's secretary, later termed the slightly built, bearded Spencer as "a quiet little Yankee who sold himself in relentless slavery to his idea for six weary years until it was perfect."

The weapon Spencer produced was a carbine with a barrel length of only 39 inches (compared with a musket's 48 inches). Instead of storing ammunition in a tube underneath the barrel, Spencer fitted a loading tube into the stock. It contained seven .52-caliber rim-fire metallic cartridges inserted end to end. The gun chamber was loaded simply by working a lever below the trigger. Spencer's carbine could fire a sustained rate of 14 rounds per minute—as compared with the 3 or 4 shots of a muzzle-loading musket.

It was a revolutionary weapon; hence, it immediately encountered a major obstacle. The chief of the Ordnance Department was General James Ripley, an aged officer as rigid in obeying the military manual as he was opposed to innovations that altered standard procedure. Ripley saw little advantage in Spencer's invention, but fortunately, Abraham Lincoln did. The president was mechanically minded, as he showed early in adulthood, when he obtained a patent for a device that allowed river vessels to pass more easily over shoals.

Lincoln acquired a Spencer carbine and ran his own test. Affixing a wooden sight, and tacking some congressman's letter to a tree, the president hit his target 75 feet away with around 12 of 14 shots. The Ordnance Department subjected the weapon to a variety of tests as well, and all were positive. The first order, with Lincoln's endorsement, was for 7,500 guns. Late in 1861, a second order went out for 10,000 more carbines. The Spencer Repeating Rifle Company in Boston was soon thriving.

In August 1863, Spencer traveled to the White House to show the president an improved version of his gun. The two men walked down to a clearing by the Potomac River and took turns shooting at a target from a distance of 40 yards. Lincoln proved the better shot, whether Spencer intended it or not. Orders subsequently increased for the gun.

Colonel John T. Wilder, a foundry owner before the war who commanded an infantry brigade, was so impressed by the Spencer that he took out a personal loan to equip all his men with the carbine. Each soldier agreed to pay for his weapon through payroll deductions. One of Wilder's veterans wrote, "Our men adore them as the heathen do their idols." An embarrassed War Department heard of the situation and bought the Spencers for the brigade.

Confederates understandably feared the rapid-firing gun. They called Spencers "Week Guns" because they were, said one Johnny Reb, "the damn Yankee rifles you load on Sunday and fire all week."

The carbines became the standard arm of Union cavalry. Their short barrels, plus their ability to deliver volleys in quick fashion, made them ideal for mounted soldiers. On New Year's Day 1865, General William Sherman's chief of cavalry wrote to a fellow commander: "There is no doubt that the Spencer carbine is the best firearm yet put in the hands of the soldier . . . Our best officers estimate one man armed with it equivalent to three with any other arm. I have never seen anything else like the confidence inspired by it in the regiments and brigades which have it."

Not until General Ripley's resignation in 1863 did production of the Spencer begin on a large scale. In all, Union soldiers used 1,304,000 shoulder arms in the Civil War. Only 106,600 were Spencer carbines, but their presence in battle had a noticeable and deadly impact.

In the postwar years, Spencer could not keep pace against newer and better rifles such as the 1866 Winchester. Three years later, the near-bankrupt Spencer sold his company to Oliver Winchester and his stock of carbines to the French government. Yet his inventive mind never rested.

Forming a partnership with Charles Billing, Spencer made major improvements in drop-forging—producing complex shapes from metal. He added to his new fortune with inventions in sewing machine shuttles and pistol frames. His 1873 invention of a screw-making machine guaranteed his lifetime wealth.

The success he had known with the Spencer carbine led to the 1882 establishment in Windsor, Connecticut, of the Spencer Arms Company. What Spencer sought to do this time around was to create a revolving-magazine shotgun. It would be the first slide-action (or pump-action) shotgun and would be available in both 10-gauge and 12-gauge caliber. The weapon, however, proved too expensive to manufacture.

In 1901, Spencer designed a steam-powered automobile. He was dabbling with airplane development when he died January 14, 1922, at his Connecticut home. Spencer's inventions, stretching through the last half of the 19th century, made him a leader in the industrial revolution, not only in the United States but also worldwide. Yet, in military circles, he will always be remembered as the man who invented "the gun that ended the Civil War." ↔

WILLIAM TECUMSEH SHERMAN

LEADING THE CHARGE
TOWARD TOTAL WAR

H E WAS "CUMP" TO HIS FRIENDS and "Uncle Billy" to his
soldiers, who idolized William Tecumseh Sherman because
he had a common approach and was a hard fighter. A lean
six-footer, he had little eyes that rarely brightened and nervous hands that
twitched at a scraggly beard. One Billy Yank found him "boiling over with
ideas while discussing every subject and pronouncing on all."

To most historians, he was the Confederacy's worst fear: a ruthless general who waged all-out war as he burned his way through Georgia and
South Carolina in the last year of the Civil War. But the portrait of the
man is far more complex.

Sherman's early years gave few clues to the reputation he would some-
day gain. Though he graduated from West Point in 1840 with high
expectations, results were slow in coming. He spent 13 years at Southern
coastal outposts and in California, cultivating a host of friends wherever
he went. By 1853, having risen only to the rank of captain, Sherman
resigned from the army.

He worked for a San Francisco bank until it closed. Louisiana acquaintances secured for Sherman the superintendent post of the state military
academy. He did well at the Southern school, but as storm clouds of

secession boiled overhead, he left the academy to become head of the St. Louis streetcar system. He wept at the news of Fort Sumter but dutifully asked for reinstatement in the army. A colonelcy promptly followed.

Sherman's solid conduct at the Battle of First Manassas two month later brought him promotion to brigadier general. However, the prospect of the long and bloody struggle ahead, the arduous task of converting uneducated volunteers into seasoned soldiers, and the assignment to backwater duties in Kentucky were more than Sherman could bear. He suffered a nervous breakdown. Newspaper reporters, whom he openly classified as snoopers and liars, gleefully announced that the general had become insane.

Early in 1862, Sherman returned to duty and joined U. S. Grant's forces in the western theater. He served in all the major engagements on the west side of the Appalachian Mountains and became Grant's most trusted lieutenant. Of the close relationship between them, Sherman snapped at a correspondent late in the war, "He stood by me when I was crazy, and I stood by him when he was drunk. Now we stand by each other always."

When Grant took over supreme command of the Union armies in the spring of 1864, he placed Sherman in charge of the western theater. The always unkempt Sherman conducted a less than brilliant campaign to seize Atlanta. But his attitude toward the war had undergone a sharp change. Sherman became convinced that military engagements alone would not bring down the proud South and that war had to be taken to the civilian population via destruction of personal property. Break the Southern will to resist and the Confederacy would die. "If the North can march an army right through the South," Sherman told Grant, "it is proof positive that the North can prevail." Once the South surrendered, he stated, he hoped to regain many lost friendships.

What followed was the introduction of total warfare. Sherman left Atlanta in flames; his 60,000 veterans formed a 40-mile-wide prairie fire of destruction as they swept eastward toward the sea. The Union target, Savannah, fell without a fight. Sherman then proved a man of his word in regard to regaining "friendships." His lenient treatment of Savannah

*The audacious Sherman scans the landscape from the
Union line near Atlanta.*

residents went far in making defeat palatable. Federals then burned their way through South Carolina—"the seedbed of the Confederacy"—but exercised restraint during final operations in North Carolina.

Sherman's "scorched earth" tactics certainly shortened the Civil War. On the other hand, his surrender terms to his opponents were so lenient that the Johnson administration rejected them while the press branded Sherman a traitor. He in turn refused to shake Secretary of War Edwin Stanton's hand at the May 1865 Grand Review in Washington.

With victory secure, Sherman wanted all punishment of the South to cease. It was time to rebuild, he felt. This "soft policy" ran counter to the aims of the Radical Republicans who ran Congress. Sherman was dispatched 1,500 miles away to command the Department of the Trans-Mississippi. However, in 1869, Grant, now president, named him general in chief. Sherman held that post for the next 14 years.

Unfortunately, his racial prejudices shone shamefully for a second time. On the "March to the Sea," the general had ignored thousands of runaway slaves trailing in the army's wake. His biases became more pronounced against Native Americans. Sherman declared, "Both races cannot use this country in common and one or the other must withdraw. We cannot withdraw without checking the natural progress of Civilization." On another occasion, he asserted, "We must act with vindictive earnestness against the Sioux, even to their extermination: men, women, and children."

War against Native Americans characterized Sherman's long tenure as army head. At the same time, he found himself continuously at odds with Washington bureaucracy. The mutual animosity was so great that he journeyed to the capital only when specifically ordered to do so. Republicans wanted to nominate Sherman for president, but he replied curtly: "I will not accept if nominated and will not serve if elected."

Retirement from the military in 1883 made him one of the most sought-after speakers in the South as well as in the North. He could be expansive in his speeches. He stated at one commencement address, "War is at best barbarism . . . It is only those who have neither fired a shot nor heard the shrieks and groans of the wounded who cry aloud for blood, more vengeance, more desolation. War is hell."

With his wife a crippled recluse, Sherman gained a reputation for womanizing. He maintained a long affair with internationally known sculptor Lavinia "Vinnie" Ream.

Early in 1891, Sherman developed a cold. Erysipelas of the face and nose developed, so physicians painted his head with the standard antiseptic of the day, iodine. The general had difficulty talking. On February 14, a strong asthma attack proved fatal. He died in New York but was buried in St. Louis.

Not until the 20th century did historians (and novelists like Margaret Mitchell and her *Gone With the Wind*) turn Sherman into a callous conqueror of the South that he deeply admired. Yet he is remembered now as the general who altered war from a chess game of limited objectives into an open-season contest. The enemy was not to be found just on the field of battle but also in factories, barns, homes, and any other establishment that gave aid to its soldiers. The objectives of war had changed for good. The centuries-long age of sword-and-roses chivalry in war was now history. ❧

NATHAN BEDFORD FORREST

THE MOST FEARED CAVALRYMAN

FEW GENERALS IN THE CIVIL WAR were more celebrated and more feared than a premier horseman in the western theater, Nathan Bedford Forrest. Admirers called him "the wizard of the saddle" and "the world's greatest commander of mounted troops." Union General William Sherman labeled him "that devil Forrest" but later acknowledged the cavalryman to be "the most remarkable man our Civil War produced on each side."

Bedford Forrest was born to a dirt-poor Tennessee family and received no more than six months of formal education. In 1840 he survived a typhoid fever epidemic that claimed three of his sisters and two brothers. When he was a teenager, Forrest assumed responsibility for the family. He moved to Memphis and established one of the largest slave-trading businesses in the area. This prosperity enabled him to acquire extensive landholdings in Coahoma County, Mississippi. Success brought a number of public offices as well as a widely known reputation as a self-made man.

Forty years old when the Civil War began, the tall, strongly built man with gray hair and a fierce temper enlisted as a private in the Confederate Army. He became a brigadier general within a year because of a combination of intuitive genius and demonstrated leadership. Forrest's patriotism had a fierceness. He made war with driving rage, never wavering from a basic premise: "War means fighting, and fighting means killing."

His tactics were unorthodox. If surrounded by the enemy, he taught his men to "charge both ways!" Forrest initiated the concept of galloping deep into enemy territory, dismounting his troops to fight like infantry, and then dashing back to safety. When once asked for the secret of his success, the cavalry leader replied, "I get there first with the most." He had little use for leaders who fought by the book. "Whenever I run into one of those fellers who fit by note," he commented, "I generally whipped hell out of him before he could get his tune pitched."

Three times he organized independent cavalry units. On each occasion he made raids on isolated Union troops, command posts, and supply depots. His forays regularly disrupted Federal Army movements. The most famous, and controversial, of his raids was the April 1864 attack on Fort Pillow, Tennessee. Forrest's men easily overran the river earthworks and its garrison of white and black soldiers. The Confederates adopted a take-no-prisoners attitude, especially toward the black soldiers, and "Fort Pillow" thereafter became a synonym for "massacre."

While Forrest was a superb head of a large, independent cavalry force, he could never have commanded an army. Humorless and volatile by nature, he didn't get along with superior officers. (He once threatened to kill army commander Braxton Bragg if he ever saw him again.) Forrest did lead by example. Over the course of the war, he received four serious wounds, had 29 horses shot from under him, and personally killed at least 30 Federals in hand-to-hand fighting.

By the end of the war, in May 1865, Forrest's men gave up because they were used up. The general himself was crippled by war wounds and recurring boils. Forrest announced to his troops, "Men, you may all do as you damn please, but I'm a-going home."

He was physically broken and financially strapped, but he was determined to regain economic stability in his life. The slave-auction business no longer existed. Little was left of his Mississippi plantations. Yet many of his former slaves refused to leave, and with their help and the financial

An 1885 poster re-creates the chaos at the Fort Pillow Massacre.

assistance of seven former Federal officers, Forrest enjoyed a modicum of success in late 1865. Personally, he became a model of reconciliation.

The following year, however, Forrest was forced to sell the plantations and move to Memphis in search of other business opportunities. His personal struggles paralleled those of the South under Reconstruction. He was never able to readjust to the new realities of subjection. Paving streets and grading railroads were frustrating jobs that came and went.

Forrest joined the Ku Klux Klan because he believed it to be a defensive, vigilante-type mechanism to keep the peace in an atmosphere of lawlessness. He was with the organization for only a year, leaving when the Klan turned to intimidation and terrorism to achieve its goals. Yet he never wavered from his belief that blacks and whites were not—and could not—be equal. Thus, while Robert E. Lee became the symbol of a reuniting country, Forrest was the embodiment of white supremacy.

In July 1868 he finally received a pardon from the federal government. Forrest had by then become interested in the growing railroad industry.

Satirical sketches vilify four Democratic figures, three of whom were former Confederate officers, including Forrest.

He jokingly told a friend that during the war, he destroyed rail lines; now he wanted to build them. Scraping together sufficient funds, he purchased a controlling interest in a proposed line, the Selma, Marion, and Memphis Railroad.

He served five years as president of the developing rail line and in 1875 retired because of ill health. He mellowed with age and joined the Presbyterian Church. Although he lived comfortably, the general never recouped his prewar fortune. Bedridden toward the end, he came to weigh less than 100 pounds. Forrest was 56 when he died on October 19, 1877, of chronic diarrhea. The general was buried in his Confederate uniform in Memphis's Elmwood Cemetery. With his burial, legends about him began—and continue.

On one reported occasion, Forrest was working on his farm. He allowed his favorite horse, King Philip, to graze in the front yard. When a Union cavalry company rode past the home, King Philip dashed toward the group, "teeth bared and front feet flailing."

As Forrest fought to restrain the animal, the Union captain shouted, "General, now I can account for your success! Even your horses fought for you!"

Other legends had a more factual basis. William T. Sherman, who regularly complained about "that devil Forrest," supposedly said after the war, "Give me Union infantry and Confederate cavalry and I can conquer the world."

The Confederate cavalryman was the principal innovator of "mounted infantry." He predated modern strategies that require mobile staging of troops, such as the German Blitzkrieg of World War II, by advancing rapidly with mounted infantry and enveloping an enemy position in a surprise, usually overwhelming assault. Today's use of airborne infantry divisions is another extension of Forrest's principles. His tactics, one military analyst stated, were "a preeminent example of warfare's evolution from heavy columns and clashing armies to speed, stealth, and subterfuge." ↄ

RAPHAEL SEMMES

LAST OF THE GREAT PIRATES

THE GREATEST COMMERCE RAIDER in American naval history, and certainly the Confederacy's most exciting naval officer, was Maryland-born Raphael Semmes. Orphaned at the age of nine, he and a brother were raised by two uncles. One was in merchant shipping, and the other was a successful attorney. Hence, young Semmes acquired an early interest in the sea and the law.

At 16, he entered the Navy as a midshipman. That was a time of peace, and officers customarily received long furloughs without pay. Semmes used such periods to study law. Admitted to the bar in 1833, he established a practice in Cincinnati.

When the Navy recalled him to permanent active duty, Semmes moved to Pensacola, Florida. He took his family to nearby Alabama, bought property and three slaves, and declared himself an adopted Southerner. Survey duties, lighthouse inspections, and commanding various ships in the Mexican War all preceded an 1855 furlough. While practicing law again, Semmes published a highly received memoir of his Mexican War experiences and rose to the rank of commander.

Thanks to his 34 years of various experiences at sea, Semmes became one of the first volunteers accepted for the Confederate Navy. President Jefferson Davis named the 51-year-old naval veteran a commodore. Semmes immediately requested sea duty, and he and Secretary of the Navy Stephen Mallory agreed on a new venture. Semmes would command a

The coat Semmes wore when he took the Confederate cause to sea

commerce raider preying on loaded Northern merchant ships. This type of warfare would inflict heavy financial damage, disrupt the flow of supplies, and draw Union vessels away from blockading duties.

On June 30, 1861, Semmes steamed into the Gulf of Mexico aboard C.S.S. *Sumter,* a small and slow, five-gun, bark-rigged steamer. Still, given Semmes's daring, he sank 18 vessels in a year and eluded every interception by a Union warship. The *Sumter* experience brought him fame, but he learned two things: His tactics did not weaken the blockade, and many nations refused to let him bring a prize into port for adjudication.

Semmes's cruises accelerated after August 1862, when he took command of an English-built steamer simply named #290. The three-mast vessel was 220 feet long and carried eight guns and a 120-man crew. Under steam and sail, it could slice through the waves at 13 knots per hour. When Semmes became its captain, he renamed the ship C.S.S. *Alabama.* It proved to be the finest cruiser of her class in the world.

Her skipper looked the role of a swashbuckling sailor. Of medium height but erect bearing, with hard, dark eyes, Semmes wore his hair long and maintained a luxuriant mustache, which curled up and far outward to waxed points. It gave "Old Beeswax" a touch of flamboyance he had hitherto lacked.

The crew was an international mix that required constant attention. "I have a precious set of rascals on board," Semmes wrote, "faithless in the matter of abiding by their contracts, liars, thieves, and drunkards." Yet Semmes was a stickler for discipline and order. He was also opinionated and wordy, as well as extraordinarily lucky.

For 23 months, *Alabama* enjoyed spectacular success. It roved from one hunting ground to another, flying the American flag until close to a vessel, when the Confederate flag would suddenly appear along with shots fired across its victim's bow. Occasionally Semmes would have to run down a merchant ship. As he described one situation, "When the day dawned, we were within a couple of miles of him. It was the old spectacle of the panting, breathless fawn and the inexorable foxhound."

In all, *Alabama* captured 64 ships and boarded 447 others. It had cruised 75,000 miles when, in June 1864, it limped into the harbor of Cherbourg,

France, for refuge and repairs. Suddenly U.S.S. *Kearsarge* appeared off the coast. It was large, trim, and recently outfitted with guns far superior to those of *Alabama*. Semmes sent out a message to the *Kearsarge* captain, John Winslow, with whom Semmes had served on U.S.S. *Cumberland* during the Mexican War. "If you will give time to recoal," Semmes stated, "I will come out and give you battle."

The June 29 duel lasted 90 minutes. As *Alabama* was sinking, Semmes noted proudly that "we buried her at sea . . . safe from the polluting hands of the hated Yankees." Semmes made his escape to Southampton on an English yacht. He had the satisfaction of knowing that he was instrumental in driving insurance rates for American vessels to astronomical heights and toppling the American merchant marine from a once dominant position.

Semmes returned to Richmond and a rear admiral's rank. He took command of the ten-vessel James River Squadron, which was destroyed in the April 1865 evacuation of Richmond. He accompanied President Davis to Danville, Virginia, where a makeshift government sought to keep the dream alive. Because sailors made up most of the military party and manned the artillery defenses, Davis thought it appropriate that Semmes be appointed a brigadier general. No Senate existed to confirm the nomination, but Semmes has the distinction of being the only American officer to simultaneously hold the ranks of admiral and general.

On May 11, 1865, Semmes received his parole. He returned to Mobile and tried to find employment in a foreign navy. Yet nations were reluctant to incur the displeasure of the United States by hiring "the pirate Semmes." Seven and a half months after his parole, the admiral was arrested by order of Secretary of the Navy Gideon Welles. The charges were piracy and failure to surrender himself with the sinking of *Alabama*. Union authorities spent four months searching for incriminating evidence. When none materialized, Semmes was released. In April 1866 he again returned to Mobile.

His naval service was always a negative factor in the search for a job. Reconstruction prevented him from practicing law. Mobile citizens elected

Captain Semmes. on board. Conf. S. S. "Alabama"

Semmes rests atop the C.S.S. Alabama, *a much feared sight for Union vessels.*

him as a probate judge, but the secretary of war declared Semmes ineligible. When he gained a teaching position at what is now Louisiana State University, Northern newspapers howled at "a pirate" being allowed to teach a course on moral philosophy, and the appointment was withdrawn.

In 1867, Semmes became editor of a Memphis newspaper. This afforded him time to produce *Memoirs of Service Afloat,* published in England and filled with Southern romanticism and anti-Northern rhetoric. He moved back to Mobile in 1869 and eventually became its city attorney. He was at his cottage at Point Clear, across the bay from the city, when he died on August 30, 1877, of food poisoning after eating tainted shrimp. "The Poet-Priest of the South," Father Abram J. Ryan, conducted the funeral service at Mobile's Old Catholic Cemetery.

Semmes was the most successful of 19 Confederate privateers. He alone was responsible for a third of all captures of Union ships. In the North, his name became synonymous with that of Blackbeard. The South viewed him as a swashbuckling conqueror at sea. To merchants who sent goods abroad, Semmes was "a malevolent ghost, able to appear or disappear at will."

For all their dash and style, however, the privateers had little impact on the outcome of naval tactics. They were insufficient in number—a nuisance more than a danger. Yet American maritime trade fell so badly that it took three generations for it to return to normal levels. Later and on a more massive scale, German U-boat submarines prowling the Atlantic during World War II expanded the havoc caused by a lonely predator like Raphael Semmes. ↝

JONATHAN LETTERMAN

MOBILIZING MEDICINE

THE SEA CHANGE CREATED by one Civil War doctor can be shown in a single contrasting example: Following the 1815 British victory over Napoleon at Waterloo, it took ten days to treat the wounded scattered on the fields. In 1863, after three vicious days of combat at Gettysburg, a surgeon reported that "not one wounded man of the great numbers who had fallen was left on the ground."

That extraordinary development in medical care stemmed from the work of Jonathan Letterman, who remains one of the true heroes of the Civil War—and of mankind. He was the father not only of modern military medicine but also of today's emergency medical system.

Letterman followed in his physician father's footsteps. After graduating from Jefferson Medical College in Philadelphia, Letterman opted to bypass private practice and become an army surgeon. He spent 12 years at far-flung outposts stretching all the way to California. The experience proved highly beneficial. Compelled by his circumstances, Letterman discovered the value of ingenuity: to use whatever worked rather than to adhere to guidebooks that said what should work.

He was called east in 1861 and saw brief duty in western Virginia until July 4, 1862, when Letterman was appointed as a major and medical

*Saving countless lives, Letterman accelerated medicine's reach
with upgrades to quartermaster carts.*

director of the Army of the Potomac. He was 37, little known, slight in
build, and quiet by nature, with the earnest look of a student.

His new responsibilities appeared overwhelming. The entire army was
exhausted, emaciated, and dispirited. One of every three soldiers was
sick or wounded. Wagons for hospital use had to be requisitioned from
the Quartermaster Department and were always low on the priority list.
Teamsters had no medical skills; officers in the field paid scant attention
to the needs of the wounded. Any medical treatment was minimal.

The new major had long been filled with reform ideas. Now, with
complete control over an army's medical needs, Letterman went to work
on building a system where none had existed. Organization and common
sense were the keys.

His first accomplishment was the creation of an ambulance corps.
Letterman cast aside the old two-wheeled quartermaster carts capable of

Surgeons' field amputation kits evince a tragic necessity across battle lines.

carrying three men. Instead, he developed—solely for his department—a four-wheeled wagon with springs that could accommodate six men seated and three prone. Each wagon had a medical chest, and its teamsters were trained to handle injured soldiers.

Letterman next organized a chain of treatment centers. Wounded men were initially taken to a regimental first-aid station for examination. Those with serious injuries were carried to a nearby field hospital (usually a con-fiscated home, barn, or similar structure). After treatment, the soldiers were forwarded by wagon, rail, or ship to general hospitals in cities for care and recuperation.

This system of gradated medical care enabled Letterman to install a pri-oritized treatment based on the severity of the injury and the likelihood of survival. For ongoing care, he obtained and distributed medical supplies. Every brigade had a fully equipped medical wagon. When accused of overstocking materials, Letterman would reply gently, "Lost supplies can be replaced, but lives lost are gone forever."

While resting in western Maryland after the 1862 Battle of Antietam, Letterman met Mary Lee, of a prominent farming family. The couple wed the following year.

Letterman's brilliance was revealed most brightly at the Battle of Gettysburg. The Union Army numbered some 83,000 soldiers. The major gathered together 650 surgeons, 1,000 ambulances, and 3,000 drivers and stretcher-bearers. He oversaw the treatment and removal of 14,000 Federals and 6,800 abandoned Confederates with an efficiency that bordered on the miraculous. Whereas the mortality rate in the Army of the Potomac had been 33 percent during the Peninsula Campaign of 1862, it was only 2 percent at Gettysburg. And yet Letterman was not mentioned in a single official report of the battle.

Naturally, his sweeping reforms brought criticism from standpat diehards. His superior, General William Hammond, soon was undergoing censure en route to dismissal. Possibly Letterman felt that he had done all he could for army medicine. He certainly longed to be with his bride. Whatever the reason, Letterman resigned from the army in December 1864.

He wasn't unemployed for long. Thomas Scott, the railroad magnate who tutored Herman Haupt to success, knew of Letterman's organizational accomplishments and administrative skills. Scott offered the physician a job as general superintendent of a company doing oil exploration in California, and Letterman and his new family moved to the West Coast. The oil venture failed after a year's efforts, and in 1866 Letterman started a private medical practice in San Francisco.

A year later, he ran on the Democratic Party ticket for coroner. Joy over his election was short-lived, however. Three weeks before Letterman was to take office, his 38-year-old wife died of acute gastroenteritis. The brokenhearted physician was forced to send his two infant daughters to live with relatives in New York City.

Having lost his entire family, he tried to immerse himself in his work. Letterman practiced medicine during the day and remained on call when a body was discovered in suspicious or unexplained situations.

He performed autopsies and conducted inquests for as many as 600 cases a year. Through all his toil, he dwelled in loneliness and suffered from chronic dysentery.

In 1869 he won reelection as city coroner, but a broken leg the next year incapacitated him for five months. By 1871 the political and economic climate in San Francisco had undergone a change, and Letterman and his fellow Democrats were voted from office. With nothing to do but grieve over loved ones he could not see, the physician was beset by declining health. Letterman died March 15, 1872, of chronic dysentery at the age of 47.

He was originally buried in San Francisco, but in 1906 his daughters succeeded in having his remains reinterred in Arlington National Cemetery.

For 80 years thereafter, Letterman Army Hospital in San Francisco was a major medical center. His name is little remembered today, yet his ideas and implemented programs remain as fundamentals of all military medicine. In addition, his ideas also serve as a basis of civilian emergency medicine, disaster relief, and emergency management worldwide. The most enduring tribute came from General Paul Hawley, chief surgeon in World War II of the European Theater of Operations. In 1945 Hawley confessed, "There was not a day during [this war] that I did not thank God for Jonathan Letterman." ❧

JAMES EDWARD HANGER

MAKING STRIDES TOWARD
MODERN PROSTHETICS

AS A TEENAGER JAMES EDWARD HANGER wanted to be an engineer. Born at Mount Hope, a large home in the Shenandoah Valley community of Churchville, he attended local schools before enrolling at Washington College in nearby Lexington. Hanger was in his sophomore year when war interrupted his studies. The 18-year-old left school to join two brothers and four cousins in the "Churchville Cavalry," the first company organized for what became the 14th Virginia Cavalry Regiment.

Hanger was assigned to accompany an ambulance detail on the five-day trip to Philippi, a county seat in the western part of the state. A force of 750 Confederate recruits, including those from Churchville, was encamped there to protect the area from Federal threats. Most of the Southerners were unarmed; the rest carried "old flintlock muskets, horse pistols, a few shotguns and Colt revolvers."

On June 2, 1861, Hanger arrived in the pouring rain at the encampment. After formally enlisting in the army, he found his company occupying a barn near the Tygart River. At dawn the next morning, Federals delivered a surprise attack. Three artillery explosions preceded a charge of Union troops on the camp. Confederates bolted to the rear in what has since been called the "Philippi Races."

Cabinet Portraits.

STEPHEN PIPER, PHOTO. MANCHESTER, N.H.

*Union soldiers wounded at Petersburg, Virginia, are candidates
for Hanger's above-the-knee prosthesis.*

Hanger, in military service for less than 12 hours, recalled: "The first two [artillery] shots were canister and directed at the Cavalry Camps, the third shot was a 6 pound solid shot aimed at the stable . . . This shot struck the ground, ricocheted, entering the stable and struck me. I remained in the stable till they came looking for plunder, about four hours after I was wounded."

Using a stable door as an operating table, surgeon James Robinson of the 16th Ohio removed Hanger's shattered leg seven inches from the hip bone. Most authorities regard the surgery as the first amputation of the Civil War. Now a prisoner of war, Hanger received the usual peg leg, consisting of a wooden pole and a leather flap. Its characteristics were an ill fit, with its loud thumping sounds and lack of mobility.

Hanger was part of small group of captured soldiers transferred by train to Camp Chase, Ohio. During his short stay at the compound, he secured a crutch for better balance. Hanger and several others were moved to Norfolk, Virginia, and exchanged. His army career had quickly ended, replaced by disappointment in the present and despair for the future. "In the twinkling of an eye, life's fondest hopes seemed dead," Hanger declared. "What could the world hold for a maimed, crippled man?"

He painfully returned home, but an idea was already swirling in his head. For the next three months, Hanger secluded himself in his upstairs bedroom. Meals were left at his door. At his request, his widowed mother brought him a wide assortment of materials: barrel staves, strips of metal, scraps of lumber and rubber, a saw, a hammer, nails, screws, any type of hinge available, a plane, and sandpaper. Unknown to everyone, Hanger was creating an above-the-knee prosthesis with a joint at the knee and a hinge at the ankle. He used his other leg as a pattern.

The family was having dinner one night in November when, to the shock of all, the son came walking down the steps, holding on to the railing with both hands, and wearing a "Hanger limb"—the first articulated, double-jointed prosthetic leg. After his initial experiments, Hanger had to solve the rudimentary problem of keeping the prosthesis pointed straight ahead. Then he opened a shop in Staunton and produced several artificial limbs for wounded friends. Dr. Charles Bell Gibson, professor of surgery at the University of Virginia Hospital, tutored Hanger in design and technique. In March 1863, Hanger received Patent #155 from the Confederate government and opened a second store in Richmond. Virginia authorities soon contracted him to provide prostheses for disabled soldiers

By 1871, with Reconstruction waning, Hanger secured a federal patent for his creations. J. E. Hanger, Inc., expanded from one location to another. Its headquarters shifted to Washington. Meanwhile, from Hanger's 1873 marriage to Nora McCarthy of Richmond came six sons. Each of them joined their father in the family business. The elder Hanger's creative mind continued to turn out inventions. The one-legged executive invented a toy horseless carriage, the Venetian blind, an adjustable reclining chair, a water turbine, and a planography lathe for use in the prosthesis-manufacturing process.

Hanger stepped down from active management in 1905 but did not retire. In 1915 he traveled to Europe to see firsthand the manufactures of his competitors. The visit resulted in contracts with both England and France during and after World War I.

Not until the end of World War II did American armed forces begin to develop fully a prosthetic field. Significant advances continue to be made. With the use of plastics, silicon, and similar materials, artificial limbs are now lighter and stronger. That in turn has made the new limb easier to operate. Other materials make such items as hands more realistic. Electronics has entered the picture by converting muscle movements to electrical signals. Military research teams are working toward the creation of an artificial limb connected directly to the nervous system. This seems improbable, but then so did James Hanger's idea of carving a jointed wooden leg.

Today Hanger Prosthetics and Orthotics has 50 offices in North America and 25 in Europe. It produces 700,000 artificial limbs annually. Each— like its forerunner—brings mobility and hope to humans seeking the opportunity for a normal life.

Hanger died June 9, 1919, at the age of 76. He is buried beside his wife in Washington's Greenwood Cemetery. The gravestone is remarkable for its simplicity. It does not even contain the epitaph that he once suggested: "Here lies James E. Hanger—a man who made the best of a bad situation." ∽

THOMAS H. HOLMES

A NEW ERA FOR FUNERALS

THE YEARS BEFORE 1861 are known in the funeral business as "the ice age." Undertakers provided a coffin, funeral service, grave, and little else. What embalmers used in pre–Civil War times was crude, ineffective, and concerned more with appearance than with preservation. Bodies were usually placed on cooling boards or ice chests in the short interval between death and interment. This inadequacy, especially in the heat of summer, gave rise to a popular jingle: "Soon ripe, soon rotten / Soon gone, but not forgotten."

Thomas H. Holmes revolutionized the entire industry. Legend and fact are so intertwined in his story that it's impossible to separate the two. That he was born in 1817 to a Brooklyn merchant is certain. As is the fact that he attended the medical school at Columbia University and became fascinated with cadavers.

Then the story becomes murky. In medical school, he may have been searching for a better means of body preservation than the existing solutions, which were highly toxic. Or he might have just enjoyed using cadavers as playthings (one source claimed that Holmes was expelled from school for stealing a body and leaving it on a professor's desk). Still another source asserted that Holmes graduated from Columbia and started practicing medicine in Brooklyn.

Holmes's career took an upswing when he married the sister of William J. Bunnell, owner of a large funeral home in Jersey City. Holmes became a combination embalmer and pharmacist. In the late 1850s he perfected what was then believed to be a nontoxic embalming fluid of zinc chloride combined with arsenic. It had the remarkable effect of petrifying corpses. A body embalmed with Holmes's technique could be placed in a standing position with no ill consequences.

At the outbreak of the Civil War, Holmes owned an embalming shop at 80 Louisiana Avenue in Washington. On May 24, 1861, with the war barely a month old, young Elmer Ellsworth, a well-known Union officer, became one of the first public casualties of the Civil War when he was killed removing a Confederate flag from the roof of an Alexandria, Virginia, hotel. Ellsworth was a close friend of the Lincoln family, and as the story goes, Holmes visited the president and offered to handle the remains free of charge. Mrs. Lincoln was extremely touched when she viewed Holmes's work. Ellsworth "looks natural," as if he "were only sleeping," the first lady declared.

Holmes's prosperity promptly ensued after the outbreak of war. He served briefly as a contract embalmer for the Union Army, charging $50 for an officer and $25 for an enlisted soldier. With such high demand for his services, he left the military to devote himself full-time to his funeral parlor. His fee jumped to $100 per body.

In the neighborhood around Holmes, several embalming shops soon appeared. Like the city's hotels in wartime Washington, these shops became overcrowded. Restaurant owners began complaining of the mixed odors of death and chemicals. The number of "clients" in summer months led to a quick, natural decomposition of those awaiting preservation. Holmes was briefly arrested for operating a public nuisance. Yet he was unable—and probably unwilling—to stem the flow of customers.

Lincoln's son Willie was one of the 4,028 bodies, mostly soldiers, that Holmes claimed to have embalmed during the war years. He accumulated a fortune, but he also brought a public awareness of preserving bodies through his embalming technique. When President Lincoln was

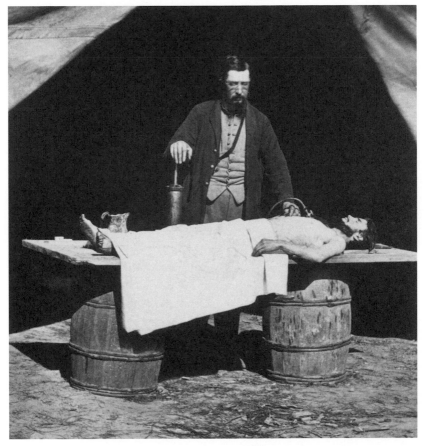

An embalmer uses a hand pump to infuse a deceased soldier with formaldehyde.

assassinated, Mrs. Lincoln asked that his body be embalmed. Holmes's fame—and fortune—was thus ensured. The murdered president's funeral trip to Springfield, Illinois, took 15 days, with 12 public viewings along the way. Thirty-six years later, when the body was exhumed for reburial in its present crypt, Lincoln's body was easily recognizable.

Embalming steadily became a popular new science in America. By the turn of the century, former undertakers, who usually also ran the local hardware store as a primary profession, had become funeral directors, and they could be found in every community of note.

An embalming establishment pictured in 1862 near Fredericksburg, Virginia, was one of many to come.

Thomas Holmes himself developed an eccentric turn of mind in the postwar decades. Specimens of his work filled his home—in halls, closets, and outdoors. He converted part of his funeral home into a pharmaceutical shop and another section of the building into a soda fountain featuring homemade root beer. In his storefront window could be seen, side by side, a corpse, advertisements for his embalming fluid, and bottles of root beer.

On his deathbed in 1900, Holmes made a single request: Under no circumstances was his body to be embalmed. Nine years later, the federal government outlawed the use of arsenic as a preservative. Still, Holmes's unique technique for embalming bodies gave rise to the American funerary industry as we know it. ❧

MONTGOMERY CUNNINGHAM MEIGS

REDEFINING WAR MANAGEMENT

MONTGOMERY MEIGS was thoroughly unlikable, but the Union war effort would have collapsed without him. He was a man of extreme qualities, once going so far as to steal the large estate of a friend and turn it into a cemetery to prevent anyone from ever living there again.

Although Georgia born, he grew up in Pennsylvania. He was but six years old when his mother termed him "high-tempered, unyielding, tyrannical toward his brothers, and very persevering in pursuit of anything he wishes."

Meigs attended the state university for a year before entering West Point. He graduated fifth in the Class of 1836. In a lifetime of service to the Army, the always stern engineer accomplished a number of projects still in evidence. Meigs was the chief builder of Fort Wayne on the Detroit River. He, along with fellow engineer and close friend Robert E. Lee, worked to keep the ever changing Mississippi River flowing past St. Louis. (At the time, Meigs considered Lee "the model soldier and the beau ideal of a Christian man.")

In the 1850s Meigs's well-known organizational and management skills led to his being placed in charge of construction of both the Washington aqueduct and a greatly expanded U.S. Capitol building. The aqueduct brought freshwater more than ten miles from the Great Falls of the Potomac River to downtown Washington. When it opened in 1859, Meigs

Among Meigs's earliest projects, the Georgetown Aqueduct brought fresh water to downtown Washington, D.C.

wrote to his father that his success was "for free use of the sick and well, rich and poor, gentle and simple, old and young for generation after generation, which will have come to rise up and call me sacred."

Enlarging the Capitol did not go as well. Meigs worked harmoniously with Secretary of War Jefferson Davis, but Davis's successor, John B. Floyd, awarded contracts to his friends and was careless in his oversight. This slovenly management ran counter to Meigs's meticulous honesty. Meigs and Thomas Walker, architect of the Capitol, had so prolonged a disagreement over matters that Walker refused to speak to Meigs for two years. In 1860, Floyd banished Meigs to duty in the Florida Keys. Yet the engineer returned to Washington two months before the onset of the Civil War.

By then, the six-feet-one-inch Meigs weighed 200 pounds. His dark hair and beard complemented a natural scowl. No one ever recorded seeing him smile. He was given to deep thinking and had a habit of picking his teeth with a small twig when in contemplation.

Meigs's hatred of the South knew no bounds. Confederate leaders, he proclaimed in 1861, "should be formally put out of the way if possible by sentence of death." He regarded both his pro-Southern brother and his longtime friend Lee to be unforgivable traitors.

Meigs looked in horror as the Northern capital sought to prepare for war. Quartermaster demands and contributions from individual states were creating chaos within the uncoordinated civilian infrastructure. Given his reputation for orderliness, it was almost natural that in May 1861, Lincoln appointed him quartermaster general of all Union armies, a post Meigs held for the entire war.

What followed was one of the logistical wonders of the Civil War. Prewar experience in dealing with contractors enabled him to bring order and reasonable honesty where chaos and corruption had held forth. Organizing national industry and agriculture along military channels, the quartermaster general made Union soldiers feel "prodigal of their provisions." A Union general remarked, "A French army of half the size of ours could be supported with what we waste."

Meigs increased the departmental staff from 60 to 300 personnel. He began issuing directives ranging from nails to wagons. Competitive bidding was mandatory. Every Union soldier was to be well clothed and fully equipped. An 1862 policy led to standardization of uniform color and the first range of clothing sizes (small, medium, large, and extra-large) in America.

Supply depots popped up in every military theater, and the supply lines formed a vast but orderly network. One of Meigs's greatest feats occurred in 1862, when General George McClellan advanced up the Virginia peninsula toward Richmond. The massive Army of the Potomac went by boat from Washington to Yorktown, Virginia, and then 70 miles by road. This force required a million pounds of supplies daily for 110,000 men and 25,000 animals. Meigs used 400 vessels and hundreds of wagons to maintain a steady flow of matériel. McClellan, 100 miles inside enemy territory, had all the weapons of war he needed to wage a successful campaign. Unfortunately, he lacked Meigs's forcefulness.

He "always had a bust look," one aide commented. His script was illegible. Once during the war, General William Sherman declared, "The handwriting of this report is that of General Meigs, and I therefore approve of it, but I cannot read it."

His loathing of the South blazed through all his efforts. To the contractors of a new prisoner of war compound at Rock Island, Illinois, in 1863, the general stated that the barracks "should be put up in the roughest and cheapest manner, mere shacks, with no fine work about them."

The following year, President Lincoln asked Meigs what to do with the 1,100-acre Lee estate overlooking the Potomac at Washington, which Federal troops had occupied at the outset of war. Meigs promptly replied, "The Romans sowed the fields of their enemies with salt. Let us make it into a field of honor."

In May 1864, Meigs began ordering that unknown and unclaimed Union soldiers be not merely interred on the estate; rather, all bodies were to be buried as close as possible to the house to ensure that it was uninhabitable thereafter. Meigs watched "with grim satisfaction" as 26 bodies from a military morgue were interred in the middle of Mrs. Lee's rose garden. Nearby, on a hot August day, 2,111 unknown soldiers were put in one gigantic pit.

A semblance of order soon took place. Meigs's son, killed in a Shenandoah Valley skirmish, was placed in Section 1, Grave 1. By war's end, 16,000 graves surrounded the ravished home. Until Meigs's retirement, Southerners were forbidden to enter the grounds.

Despite his personal nastiness, Meigs's accomplishments as quartermaster general cannot be overstated. He spent more than one billion dollars during the war. Not until the 20th century was so large a sum disbursed by order of a single individual—and Meigs could account for every dollar he spent.

In the quiet postwar years, undeterred by criticism, he oversaw construction of a new War Department building, an extension of the aqueduct, a hall of records, and the National Museum (now the Smithsonian Institution's Art and Industries Building). In a sign of his vanity, his initials appeared on girders, steps, and hydrants.

A sea of gravestones signals the unsought transformation of Robert E. Lee's estate to what would be Arlington National Cemetery.

His reputation took its hardest hit in 1879, when the Supreme Court ruled that the seizure of the Lee estate had been a gross violation of the law. The Court directed the government to return Arlington to the family. George Washington Custis Lee, the general's son, could have ordered the disinterment of 16,000 bodies buried there. Instead, the family accepted $150,000 for the property, and it was soon designated Arlington National Cemetery.

During 1882–87, Meigs was architect for the Pension Office Building. The red structure was widely ridiculed as "Meigs's Old Red Barn." One afternoon the quartermaster general led General Philip Sheridan on an inspection. Sheridan concluded that he found only one fault with the building. "What is that?" Meigs angrily inquired.

"It is fireproof," Sheridan replied.

Meigs died July 2, 1892, of pneumonia. Naturally, he was buried at Arlington. For reasons still debated, he decreed that his head be encased with hydraulic cement prior to interment. Perhaps he was worried that the ghost of Robert E. Lee would have his revenge. ☙

HERMAN HAUPT

WINNING THE WAR BY RAIL

ONE MAN WHO QUALIFIES as among the top dozen individuals responsible for Union victory was born in poverty. Herman Haupt went to work at the age of ten to help support his Philadelphia-based family. At 14, he became the youngest cadet ever to enroll in West Point. Haupt initially was too small to handle the musket when performing the manual of arms.

Following graduation in 1835, Haupt served for two months before resigning from the Army. He was fascinated by the burgeoning expansion of a new conveyance known as a railroad and served as a construction engineer for what became the Western Maryland line. His first patent was for a novel bridge construction known as the Haupt truss. So sturdy was his design that two of the spans still exist today.

In 1840, Haupt began a seven-year tenure as professor of mathematics and engineering at Pennsylvania College. The rail spirit beckoned again, and he became general superintendent for the huge Pennsylvania Railroad. In 1851 he published a highly respected manual, *The General Theory of Bridge Construction*. Haupt was hard at work on a new rail line and the five-mile Hoosac Tunnel in Massachusetts when the Civil War began. Financially prosperous, with a wife and 11 children, Haupt had little interest in volunteering for combat.

Both sides speedily realized how vital railroads were to military operations. Without trains, it was impossible to feed, equip, and move the large

A locomotive dubbed General Haupt honors the railroad virtuoso.

armies maneuvering over vast regions. The Federal government addressed the issue with the January 1862 creation of the United States Military Railroad—which, by war's end, became the largest rail network in the world.

On April 27 of that year, Secretary of War Edwin Stanton appointed Haupt chief of the bureau with the rank of colonel. The war secretary obviously did not know Haupt well. What he hired was a brusque, outspoken, no-nonsense individual who refused to wear a uniform, declined compensation because he was still working part-time on the Massachusetts project, and preferred not to work on the Sabbath unless "necessity imperatively requires it."

Worse for the Federal bureaucracy, the 45-year-old Haupt considered military officers to be intruders in civilian railroad work. He also dismissed the Quartermaster Department as incompetent from top to bottom. As superiors grumbled, Haupt embarked on bringing order out of chaos.

He started with the three war-damaged rail lines coursing through northern Virginia. Major repairs were the first order of the day. Haupt recruited civilian railroad workers and former slaves into construction teams. "The

*Orchestrating efforts off the battlefield, Haupt's contributions
to Union victory cannot be overstated.*

railroad is entirely under your direction," he told the employees. "No
military officer has any right to interfere with it."

The first and most noteworthy achievement was the rebuilding of a trestle
high above the chasm of Potomac Creek. Amid rain and mud, using green logs
and saplings, Haupt oversaw construction of a bridge 80 feet high and 400 feet
long—in nine days. When Abraham Lincoln visited the site, he termed the
trestle "the most remarkable structure that human eyes ever rested upon." The
president told his Cabinet, "Loaded trains are running every hour, and upon
my word, gentlemen, there is nothing in it but beanpoles and cornstalks."

Haupt also erected blockhouses to defend key bridges. He trained
workers to be soldiers when threatened. Crews restored damaged lines in
seemingly miraculous fashion. An awed contraband exclaimed that "the
Yankees can build bridges quicker than the Rebs can burn them down."

In addition to making prefabricated parts for his spans, Haupt ensured
that the trains ran on schedule. Boxcars no longer stood idly on sidetracks.

During the 1862 Fredericksburg Campaign, Haupt shipped 800 tons of supplies daily to the Union Army. His most spectacular feat for the Army of the Potomac came at Gettysburg. His trains daily carried 1,500 tons of matériel to the battle area—and then filled the empty boxcars with thousands of wounded soldiers bound for hospitals in Washington and Baltimore.

The colonel declined a brigadier's rank late in 1862 because he was still chief engineer for a New England rail line. In September 1863, Stanton demanded that Haupt accept promotion to general and devote his full attention to the military rail system. The railroad wizard, however, had no intention of becoming immersed in chain-of-command frictions. He resigned from the army to return to what he loved most: railroad construction.

First, Haupt gained a patent for a new rock-drilling machine. He superintended the creation and improvement of a number of lines, including major sections of the Southern Railway and the Richmond and Danville lines. He invested heavily in the Northern Pacific Railroad. Later, and in spite of opposition from both rail lines and Standard Oil Company, Haupt was instrumental in laying an oil pipeline stretching from the Allegheny Valley of Pennsylvania to the Baltimore seaboard. This endeavor proved the practicality of transporting oil by underground channels.

Such enterprises brought wealth. For one source of relaxation, Haupt and his wife purchased and refurbished a resort hotel atop a mountain in southwest Virginia. Named Mountain Lake, it was later the setting for the movie *Dirty Dancing*.

Haupt died December 14, 1905, of a heart attack. Appropriately, he was on a train bound for Washington at the time of the fatal seizure. He had the distinction of being the last living member of his West Point class. Funeral services were held at Laurel Hill Cemetery in Philadelphia.

"That man Haupt," as Lincoln termed him, was a civil engineer, railroad builder, entrepreneur, administrator, promoter, and investor. He, more than anyone else in the war years, showed both the potential and the rewards of smoothly working rail lines. Ahead of his time in technical thinking, quarrelsome but efficient, Herman Haupt was the Civil War architect who showed how "victory rode the rails." ❧

RICHARD JORDAN GATLING

THAT TERRIBLE WEAPON

RICHARD JORDAN GATLING, like Christopher Spencer, was an inventor of many implements. Yet where war was concerned, Gatling's major contribution included a central paradox. He was a peace-loving arms merchant—one who dreamed of making war obsolete by making it more terrible. By introducing the precursor to the machine gun, he achieved at least the latter.

Gatling was raised on a North Carolina cotton plantation, where his father and brother received patents for cotton and timber-harvesting machines. Gatling was 21 when he conceived the idea of a screw propeller for steamboats. His disappointment was acute when he learned that John Ericsson, who built America's first ironclad warship, had patented such an idea just months earlier.

Gatling, of solid build and with a round face, small eyes, and hair parted on the side, moved to St. Louis and worked in a dry goods store. On his own, he invented a rice-sowing machine and a wheat drill. Both instruments revolutionized agricultural systems in the South and Midwest. An attack of smallpox engendered his interest in medicine, and in 1850 he obtained a medical degree from Ohio Medical College, though he never went into practice.

Gatling was living in Indianapolis when the Civil War came. Some people regarded him as a crackpot eccentric, but he was a respected and socially connected businessman. He married a prominent physician's daughter and was a confidant of future president Benjamin Harrison.

The war stirred Gatling's inventive nature. He later wrote: "It occurred to me that if I could invent a machine—a gun—which could by its rapidity of fire enable one man to do as much battle duty as a hundred, that it would, to a large extent, supersede the necessity of large armies, and consequently, exposure to battle and disease [would] be greatly diminished."

Drawing plans for new weapons was a national hobby in the first years of the war. Throughout 1861, using his seed planter as a base, Gatling developed a prototype. He never thought of writing the War Department about his project and getting federal backing. Possibly his reputation as a Southern-born copperhead convinced him of the futility of such a course. In any event, Governor Oliver P. Morton became one of his strongest backers. The Gatling Gun Company manufactured ten weapons, but a December 1862 fire destroyed the production plant and the guns. Still determined, Gatling then contracted the Cincinnati Type Factory to produce 13 new weapons.

From afar, the Gatling gun resembled a cannon. Yet instead of one barrel, the gun had six barrels rotated by a hand crank. The public dismissed the weapon as "a coffee mill gun" because it was operated by hand and built on that principle, even to its separate steel chambers and hopper feed. On the remarkable side, Gatling's invention could fire 200 rounds per minute. Mark Twain observed, "It feeds itself with cartridges, and you work it with a crank like a hand organ; you can fire it faster than four men can count."

Critics of the gun considered it an unfair weapon. It took away "individual valor," one officer asserted. "One could not pin a medal on a weapon." Another skeptic declared that using the Gatling machine was like hiding a rock in a snowball.

Gatling persisted in getting his gun adopted by the Army. Lincoln's zeal for new weapons had long crested when, in February 1865, Gatling went to Washington and demonstrated the firepower of his gun to a group of senior officers. General Winfield Hancock was so impressed that he ordered a dozen for his corps in the Army of the Potomac.

Not until 1866, however, did the peacetime army make its first sizable purchase of the Gatling gun. The weapon had its most devastating effect on eliminating Indian resistance in the West. One historian wrote sadly, "Death could be reliably doled out in sweeps and clusters, in reeling multiples, instead of one by one . . . Civilization thus was irrevocably altered. Nothing—neither warfare nor diplomacy nor science nor business not technology nor literature nor art nor theology—would ever be the same."

In 1870, Gatling sold his patents to Colt's Manufacturing Company. "With an engineer's mind for the nuances of how things worked and a storekeeper's eye for the dollar," Gatling abandoned the arms business and sought other outlets for his inventive genius. A biographer stated, "He was the living embodiment of the journey the country had under-taken, shifting from a rural agrarian economy to an urban industrial one in only a few decades. He had moved from South to North, just as the money had."

Among his 43 patents were toilet improvements, bicycles, steam clean-ing of raw wool, pneumatic power, and motor-driven plow tractors. His entire career revolved around the idea of change. Like any good inventor, Gatling depended on the endless human appetite for the new.

Death came February 26, 1903, while Gatling was visiting a daughter in New York City. The cemetery where he is buried is now in a crumbling and troublesome neighborhood of empty storefronts, fast-food restaurants, and busy side roads. Gatling might not object, because of his respect and quest for change.

The Gatling gun remains his most famous contribution, in part because it has been modernized and incorporated into present wars. Although the machine gun of today operates on a different loading principle, using magazines, Gatling's original conception still lingers on. One of America's most feared weapons is the A-10 "Warthog" fighter. The entire plane was designed around a 30-mm rotary nose gun. The seven-barrel cannon has a firing rate of 3,900 armor-piercing rounds per minute. It is the most powerful aircraft cannon in the human arsenal. ∾

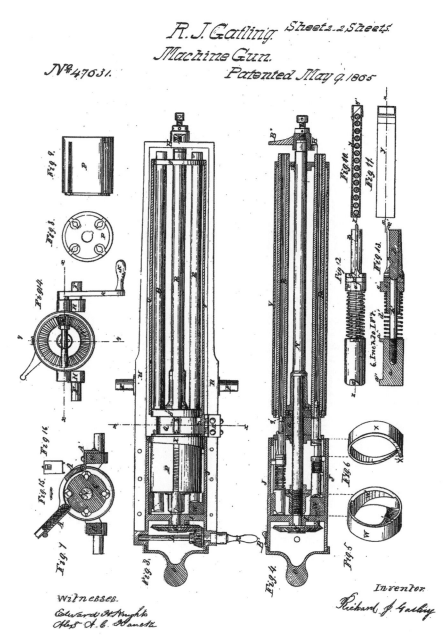

*Gatling's patent reveals the mechanics that would enable
innumerable future casualties.*

CHAPTER 4

AN

UNEXPECTED

MUSE

THE CIVIL WAR was the first great media event in American history. The public wanted to know all about it. Appetites of those back home grew for reports, illustrations, and personal observations. This led to the emergence of new voices inspired by the struggle across an array of fine arts, from photography and drawing to music and literature. These artists then continued their work well beyond the war to become figures that are immediately recognized today.

Mathew Brady brought the stark images of individual soldiers and the debris of battlefields into family parlors with the advances that he made in the new science of photography. His impressive collection of 10,000 portraits and group photographs now resides in the Library of Congress. Although he ruined himself personally, going deeply in debt to finance this prodigious body of work, he is considered the father of photojournalism.

Images of the war appeared in a more familiar guise as well: through drawings and paintings. One of the most famous American painters of all time, Winslow Homer, worked throughout the war to create field sketches

OPPOSITE: *Since 1800 the Library of Congress has housed some of the nation's greatest intellectual and artistic works.*

that were rugged and bold. He continued after the war to paint the same sorts of common folk, hardened by experience, that had appeared in his wartime portraits. Many of these works are now masterpieces that hang in museums around the country.

German immigrant Thomas Nast created a merger of art and politics in his sketches of the war. His wartime experiences formed the foundation of his satiric cartoons, which produced devastating results in the postwar era. The depictions of William Tweed and his Tammany Hall cronies helped bring down that entire corrupt political machine. Yet Nast was the father of not only editorial page cartoons but also America's most beloved individual, Santa Claus.

A lesser known artist today, Alfred Waud produced more battlefield sketches, and with more realism, than anyone else. His prolific drawings, sent back by courier to first *New York Illustrated News* and then *Harper's Weekly,* put a horde of woodblock engravers to work to reproduce the images on paper. During Reconstruction, he went on to create many vivid portraits of the ruined South.

Sculpture was slow to arrive in America, and the Civil War spurred a bonanza in the postwar years when veterans resolved to immortalize in statues their achievements in battle. Every major battlefield is decorated copiously with marble and granite monuments. Virginia-born Moses Ezekiel cast the most famous sculptures of this era—ironically producing all of them in his European studios.

Three days after the Civil War's opening shots, the first war song appeared. The conflict sparked no fewer than 2,000 new melodies. No other event in the history of music has inspired more compositions. At the top of dozens of composers stands George Root. His musical scores, most notably "The Battle Cry of Freedom," stirred deep emotions in generations of people who had known the war.

Throughout American history, the forge of war has produced great writers. Most people remember the seminal *Red Badge of Courage* by Stephen Crane, but a writer who actually experienced the war is one of our most beloved authors, Louisa May Alcott. She wrote a string of novels and stories that told of her time spent nursing at a military hospital. From there she moved on to write *Little Women,* which has never been out of print and is still widely read in schools today.

Another former army nurse was the eccentric poet Walt Whitman. Prior to the war, he had penned his greatest poem, *Leaves of Grass,* and his wartime experiences influenced his more mature work of nearly 200 poems. For good reason he was deemed America's poet.

All writers and artists benefited from the 1885 invention of the linotype machine and its attendant increase in newspaper publication. That evolution alone, however, wasn't sufficient for a word-hungry public. During that same period, public libraries assumed an increased importance in communities. Steel mogul and former Civil War armament supplier Andrew Carnegie contributed $60 million for the construction of 9,000 free circulating libraries all across the nation. The Library of Congress, which opened its doors in 1897, provided 13 acres of floor space and was the largest edifice of its kind in the world. In the arts, as in so many other facets of the nation's life, the figures impacted by the Civil War took part in the blossoming of the United States as it reached its full power. ∽

MATHEW B. BRADY

CAPTURING THE WAR ON CAMERA

THANKS TO MATHEW B. BRADY, Americans for the first time had a close look at the horrors of war. He not only introduced military photography as a new science but also became the father of photojournalism. Despite all his success, however, Brady paid dearly for the thousands of photos he took. Once the war was over, his business dwindled and he died alone and unwanted. He couldn't have known that the field he spawned would expand to the point that everyone who sits down for the nightly news expects the vivid images that fill our television screens.

Comparatively little is known of Brady himself. He kept no journals, wrote no memoirs, and paid little attention to business records. The son of Irish immigrants, he was born around 1822 in Warren County, New York. He left home, with no education, at the age of 16. Brady's first reason for traveling, to Albany and Saratoga, was an attempt to cure an eye affliction. Indications are strong that he was myopic, an impairment that proved permanent—and potentially dangerous on the battlefield.

In the late 1830s, Brady formed a friendship with Samuel F. B. Morse. The inventor was experimenting with the new medium of daguerreotype photography, whereby images were formed on a plate of chemically treated metal after ten seconds of exposure. Morse's attention soon shifted to the famous creation of the telegraph, but Brady continued to pursue the photographic trail. In 1843 he opened a studio in New York City.

Debonair and charming, with a melodious Irish brogue, a pointed beard and a large nose, Brady skillfully courted the rich and powerful. He became known as the photographer of politicians, millionaires, and visiting royalty. His business grew so steadily that in 1858 he opened a second studio at 352 Pennsylvania Avenue in Washington. Brady was the first and only photographer of statesmen like Daniel Webster, Henry Clay, and John C. Calhoun. With the exception of William Henry Harrison, who died after only a month in office, Brady eventually did portraits of every president between Andrew Jackson and William McKinley. One of his many likenesses of Abraham Lincoln adorns the U.S. five-dollar bill. To have your picture with the logo "Photo by Brady" was to have the most meticulous portrait available.

In the midst of his prewar success, Brady married Julia Handy. When she realized that her fashionable husband had little business acumen, Julia assumed management of the stores. The two dozen employees included several experienced photographers.

Business was soaring by the eve of the Civil War. The advent of *carte de visite* cameras allowed photographers to take multiple pictures. Exposed on paper and mounted on card stock, the inexpensive likenesses found great appeal among the general public. Volunteers rushed to enlist in the army, and many of them wanted images of themselves in uniform. Brady increased the demand with a newspaper advertisement that warned: "You cannot tell how soon it may be too late." Young men stood in line to be photographed.

That inspired Brady to undertake what no man had ever attempted: to make a photographic record of a battlefield. President Lincoln granted Brady permission to follow the Union Army into Virginia—with the proviso that Brady had to finance the project himself. The bushy-haired Irishman followed the army toward Manassas, armed with a camera and a wagonload of paraphernalia.

The result was a disaster. At the July 1861 Battle of Manassas, Brady was wearing a long white duster and straw hat that made him look more like "a French landscape artist than a war correspondent." And the violence of combat badly frightened Brady. In addition, he was unable to see any great distance because of his limited eyesight. He lost all his equipment and was later found wandering helplessly in the woods near Bull Run.

Brady's resolve to film the war remained unbroken. Now painfully aware of his nearsightedness, he had associates Alexander Gardner, Timothy O'Sullivan, George Barnard, and others do the actual photographing of war scenes. Brady shocked the North in October 1862 when he put on public display in New York a group of photographs taken of dead soldiers and horses scattered over the Antietam battleground. The *New York Times* stated, "Mr. Brady has done something to bring home to us the terrible reality and earnestness of war . . . [He] has brought bodies and laid them in our door and along the streets."

The visually impaired photographer contributed the most important visual documentation of the Civil War. Much of our understanding of the struggle comes from his images, which included individual soldiers in every form of uniform, camp scenes, groups of soldiers, battlefields, river crossings, field hospitals, armies on the march, railroads, seaports, naval vessels, executions, and scores of portraits of key figures, beginning with Lincoln and Grant. Through this mammoth body of work, Brady became the most important name in 19th-century American photography.

Not surprisingly, by war's end Brady's fame had spread far and wide. He had taken three-fourths of the known photographs of the Army of the Potomac. Financially, however, he was broke from accumulating too many loans and making a series of bad investments. Producing 10,000 plates had cost him $100,000. Cartes de visite had proved far more popular than formal portraits, and large-scale competition had cut into profits. Worse, the public had grown weary of wartime images.

By 1879 a deal to sell his collection to the New-York Historical Society collapsed, and Brady filed for bankruptcy. With some reluctance the federal government paid him $25,000 for all his images. That cleared his indebtedness for the time being. Still, he was forced to close down the Washington studio. He had continued to grant free admission to his New York gallery until a friend, P. T. Barnum, of circus fame, persuaded Brady to institute a ten-cent charge to see the photograph and to add the middle

*Photos made the aftermath of fighting, like this scene at Antietam,
visible to the world.*

initial "B" to his name for greater prestige. The fees did not offset a litany
of lawsuits, another bankruptcy, and the closing of the New York store,
which reduced Brady to poverty.

His wife's death in 1887 was a blow from which Brady never recovered.
He fell victim to depression and alcoholism, which in turn led to the
deterioration of his health. A traffic accident resulted in a broken arm
and leg. On January 15, 1896, the forgotten photographer died in the
charity ward of New York–Presbyterian Hospital. Although veterans of the
Seventh New York Zouaves paid for his funeral, Brady is buried beneath
the simplest of stones in Washington's Congressional Cemetery.

Late in life he stated, "My greatest aim has been to advance the art of
photography and to make it what I think I have, a great and truthful
medium of history." Despite his financial failings, he left a tremendous
legacy indeed. A huge block of his photographs formed the nucleus for

Brady went from portrait photographer to journalist with the onset of war.

1912's ten-volume *Photographic History of the Civil War,* and the bulk of the Brady Collection is stored in the Library of Congress.

The reportage of war had been changed forever. It had been brought home to the living rooms of all those awaiting the latest news. From that time forward, his photos inspired journalists in future wars, and when the media of film and television came along, every citizen could see the terrible price that soldiers must pay. Indeed, even today the sepia prints Mathew Brady produced show in stark terms the terrible scars war leaves behind. ✑

WINSLOW HOMER

BRINGING THE CONFLICT
TO LIFE ON CANVAS

PHOTOGRAPHY WAS NOT THE ONLY WAY that the folks by the hearth could experience the Civil War. Artists skilled at drawing roved the battlefields and camps of soldiers to produce illustrations of a soldier's life. Among them three men stand out: Winslow Homer was the most famous painter, Thomas Nast the leading artist, and Alfred Waud the most prolific battlefield sketcher. Homer is best known today for his marine subjects, but his series of Civil War scenes served as his "apprenticeship" and brought him national attention.

Homer was a Boston native whose mother, an amateur watercolorist, was his first teacher and always his best friend. At 19, Homer went to work for a Boston lithographer. For the next decade he toiled over sheet music covers and images of 40-odd state senators. In 1857, he set out as a freelance illustrator, composing both urban and rural drawings. He was 25 when he decided that what he really wanted to do was paint. He took five quick night-school lessons from an obscure French artist, and his talent did the rest. Within four years his paintings earned him full membership in the National Academy of Design.

The Civil War was a great boost in Homer's career. *Harper's Weekly* commissioned him to go to Washington, find the Union Army, and create portrayals of camp life and battles. His first sketch was of Lincoln passing through New York City en route to his inauguration. Homer followed the president-elect to the capital and did a two-page drawing of the inaugural ceremonies. The artist then joined the Army of the Potomac on the Virginia peninsula. He usually traveled with his cousin, Colonel Francis C. Barlow of the 61st New York.

Short and lean, Homer had a large nose, dark eyes, and an enormous handlebar mustache. He was somewhat of a dandy, preferring loud checks, high collars, and bowler hats.

While in the field, he penned a steady stream of illustrations, concentrating almost exclusively on genre scenes of soldier life in camp, which was where the soldiers spent 90 percent of their time. Homer had no interest in combat or bloody themes, and his paintings lack any patriotic call to duty. He was too objective and drily humorous to make a good propagandist. Rather, he sought to convey such feelings as loneliness, happiness, and endurance. After making his sketches, Homer returned to New York and developed some as woodblocks for *Harper's Weekly* to print. Others became detailed oil paintings.

Among the latter are "Sharpshooter on Picket Duty" (1862, his first oil painting), "Thanksgiving in Camp" (1862), "Home, Sweet Home" (1863), and "Young Union Soldier" (1864). The most famous of Homer's wartime art is "Prisoners From the Front" (1866), which depicts a young Union soldier (who bears a marked resemblance to Colonel Barlow) looking at four captured Confederate soldiers. The quartet reflects an array of youth, old age, defiance, and weariness. The painting suggests the difficult reconciliation that lay ahead for North and South.

During the Civil War, 35 of Homer's images appeared in *Harper's Weekly.* In all, he made 180 sketches, engravings, watercolors, and paintings related to the struggle. His next-to-last creation was "Veteran in a New Field" (1865), in which a former soldier, uniform coat lying to one side, has returned to the serene beauty of his farm and is depicted harvesting wheat with his scythe.

Following the war, Homer spent a year practicing landscape painting in France. On his return to America he accepted a job as a commercial artist to earn a living while he painted in his private time. Peasant life especially appealed to him. Throughout the early 1870s he focused on everyday life in America, especially rural scenes. He found in such settings "a sense of

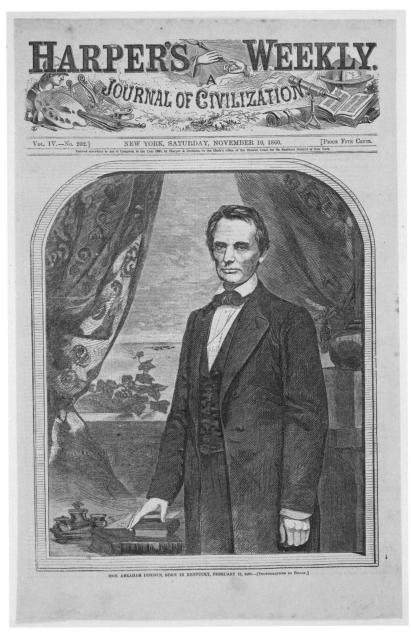

Among Homer's first Harper's Weekly *sketches was a solemn Lincoln en route to his Inauguration.*

*The increasingly withdrawn Homer appears for a rare photograph
with his "The Gulf Stream" circa 1899.*

the poetry of the earth." Although Homer lived in New York for 20 years, he painted a scene of the city only once.

One of his finest paintings of that era was "A Visit From the Old Mistress" (1876), which shows an encounter between four ex-slaves and their former owner. Women at leisure and children at play were regular subjects in the early 1870s, but then his feelings about women changed abruptly. In his subsequent paintings, women are no longer genteel figures enjoying society; rather, they are hardened, unattractive laborers cleaning fish, mending nets, or standing anxiously at water's edge awaiting the return of their men from the sea.

By 1875, Homer was financially successful and could devote himself full-time to his paintings and watercolors. He was reaching the apex of his career with his nautical scenes. The ocean fascinated Homer, and capturing its power on canvas became his greatest challenge. One of his first—and finest—oils was "Breezing Up" (1872). Critic Henry James wrote, "We frankly confess that we detest [Homer's] subjects . . . He has resolutely treated them as if they *were* pictorial . . . and, to reward his audacity, he has incontestably succeeded." Homer also began working with watercolors rather than oils, which led one reviewer to assert that "a child with an ink bottle could not have done worse." Homer remained immune to criticism, and time has proven his wisdom in persevering with his vision.

Never a social mingler, he grew increasingly reclusive. For two years he lived in an English coastal village. His paintings became larger and more ambitious. He returned home and, in the summer of 1883, purchased a small house in Prouts Neck, Maine, a few miles south of Portland. There Homer spent the rest of his life. Increasingly, he resembled an old sea captain with his rugged, deeply furrowed face.

The monumental sea scenes for which he is best remembered were painted there. "His epic of the sea and the wilderness," a biographer stated, "will always remain the classic expression of those elemental themes." He had several local friends but never courted new ones. He wrote little about his life and refused interviews. One of the few memorable quotations he made was "What they call talent is nothing but the capacity for doing continuous work in the right way."

In front of his property was always a sign: "Mr. Homer is not at home." He became known variously as "Robinson Crusoe, cloistered in his sea island" and "a hermit with a brush." Homer was camera-shy, but when making appearances, he retained his habit of always dressing with meticulous care.

In the summer of 1908, Homer had a slight stroke but slowly recovered. Two years later, recurring digestive trouble grew acute. Late that summer, while working on a painting titled "Shooting the Rapids: Saguenay River," Homer suffered internal hemorrhage and delirium. His mind cleared, but the attack left him blind. On September 29, 1910, the artist died peacefully at his home. His body was cremated and buried in Auburn Cemetery, Cambridge, Massachusetts. There Homer rests in good company with Henry Wadsworth Longfellow, Oliver Wendell Holmes, and James Russell Lowell.

Nurtured as an artist by the Civil War, Winslow Homer used striking backgrounds to underscore human feelings. One scholar concluded, "His subjects, often deceptively simple on the surface, dealt in their most serious moments with the theme of human struggle within an indifferent world." ⁂

THOMAS NAST

CARTOONS WORTH
A THOUSAND WORDS

ACCORDING TO AN APHORISM that predates the Civil War, "The pen is mightier than the sword." Thomas Nast proved its validity in his own fashion, and in the process he became one of the most influential figures in 19th-century America. His pen, mostly dipped into satire and often in tears, regularly aroused an apathetic public to indignation and action. He did not have to be a man of letters. His pen did the talking for him.

Nast was only ten years old when his German parents immigrated to America amid one of the human tidal waves from Europe. His father was a trombonist in an army band, and his son began drawing at an early age. In school, art was the only subject he enjoyed, which caused an exasperated teacher to say, "Go finish your picture. You will never learn to read or write."

After a year of studying art, Nash began his career with *Frank Leslie's Illustrated Newspaper,* a 16-page weekly publication in New York. The artist opened a new field of journalism with his caricatures. In 1862 he moved up to the staff of *Harper's Weekly,* a similar newspaper but with a national circulation of more than 120,000 readers. The tense atmosphere of wartime suited the young artist's strong moral convictions. In turn, his feelings matched the militant mood swirling through the North.

Nast never made any attempt to conceal his prejudices. He hated anything pertaining to slavery. Small and stocky in stature, he was bullied

*Nast's poignant "Christmas Eve" addresses the pain
of war-imposed family separation.*

as a child by Irish youths in the neighborhood. He also witnessed Irish
attacking freedmen. For these reasons, the Irish became Nast's symbol for
mob violence. And he was always on the lookout for dishonest politicians.

His first drawing in a 25-year association with *Harper's Weekly* appeared
September 20, 1862. "The Color Bearer" invoked sectional patriotism
and rage against a detested enemy. That the sketch appeared only three
days after the Battle of Antietam made it timely and more prized. Every
1862 drawing by Nast was an indictment of the Confederacy—save two.

For some reason he developed an affinity for Christmas. In his drawing
"Christmas Eve," a wreath of evergreens formed a scene of a wife praying
at home with sleeping children beside her, while a second wreath framed
a soldier seated at a campfire and gazing longingly at small pictures of his
family. Nast's subsequent creation of Santa Claus, the American spirit of
Christmas, won him worldwide acclaim. For a quarter century thereafter,
Nast annually produced Santa Claus in varying poses.

Nast blasts corrupt New York politics with his portrayals of Tweed as vulture.

His illustrations covered the Civil War from a variety of perspectives. From the bitter draft riots in New York to patriotic scenes of weary soldiers at rest after a long march, from lonesome women left behind at home to sharp-edged political attacks, Nast became the premier illustrator of his day.

He was one of the Union's staunchest supporters. Nast warned in 1862 that antiwar copperhead appeals for peace would permanently destroy the nation. He hailed the Emancipation Proclamation as almost God-given. In 1864, when Democrats approved a "peace platform" and nominated George McClellan for president, the party's battle cry was "Mac Will Win the Union Back!" Nast countered with a drawing, "Compromise with the South," depicting an arrogant Southern soldier holding a whip with a foot on a grave, symbolizing all the Federal soldiers who had already given their lives for the Union. Nast followed up that image with another harsh drawing in which Columbia—a precursor to Lady Liberty—wept at the grave of the Union as a weary Federal amputee shook the hand of a neatly dressed Confederate.

Lincoln, who had won reelection, always referred to Nast as "my best recruiting sergeant." Indeed, Nast was a key element in the elections of six presidents.

War's end found the 25-year-old Nast in the front ranks of the Radical Republicans. His drawings began to change from illustrations to cartoons. Recognizable drawings of public figures had an especial appeal in an age when photographs were still scarce, and when they were lampoons of well-known figures, the results were unforgettable. Nast pictured Andrew Johnson as Nero in his toga watching the "slaughter of the innocents." Horace Greeley, a favorite Nast target, always appeared as if hopelessly lost to reality. In 1868, Nast went after William "Boss" Tweed, the undisputed master of New York politics, always drawing Tweed and his associates as a flock of vultures on the prowl. At one point, Tweed dispatched some of his cronies on a mission: "Stop them damned pictures! I don't care what the papers write about me. My constituents can't read. But, damn it, they can see the pictures!" The Tweed ring collapsed the following year.

Grant attributed his 1868 presidential election to "the sword of Sheridan and the pencil of Nast." The artist's ridicule of Horace Greeley in 1872 was merciless. In political battles, a common sentiment among voters was "Let's wait and see what Tommy Nast thinks of it."

Nast embarked on a nationwide tour as a lecturer and sketch artist and returned a wealthy man. Photographs show a smiling, good-humored fellow, in sharp contrast to the savage attacks in his cartoons. As in the case of Rembrandt, Nast enjoyed self-portraits, yet they were unpretentious if not outright comical.

In the 1876 presidential campaign, Rutherford Hayes called Nast "the most powerful, single-handed aide" in his victory. However, Nast broke with Hayes over the president's conciliatory gestures to the South. At the same time, the new owners of *Harper's Weekly* stopped buying as many cartoons from Nast. As it happens, the magazine's greatest years had been Nast's greatest years as well. He switched to the Democratic Party in 1884 and helped Grover Cleveland gain the presidency.

The artist then lost most of his assets in a banking firm scandal. He made another cross-country tour, but many readers in a more relaxed America considered his sketches outdated. Moreover, years of drawing had left his arthritic hand in constant pain.

Nearly destitute by 1902, Nast sought government employment abroad. He wanted to return to Germany, but Theodore Roosevelt named him consul general to Ecuador. Nast arrived there just as an outbreak of yellow fever swept the country. He contracted the disease and died December 7, 1902. He is buried in Woodlawn Cemetery in New York City.

Nast's contributions to the American heritage are unprecedented. No other American cartoonist has ever made such a lasting impact on the public. He will always be "the father of American political cartoons." Modern illustrations on editorial pages are outgrowths of the seeds he planted. Nast bequeathed the Democratic donkey, Republican elephant, Uncle Sam, and Columbia, as well as personification of dirty politics Tammany Tiger. Yet to old and young alike, he is best remembered as "the man who made Santa Claus." ❧

ALFRED RUDOLPH WAUD

SKETCHES FROM THE FRONT LINES

I N 1864, a London *Daily Telegraph* correspondent traveling with the Union Army of the Potomac filed a long dispatch to his newspaper. At one point he stated: "There has galloped furiously by us, backward and forward during our journey, a tall man mounted on a taller horse. Blue-eyed, fair-bearded, strapping and stalwart, full of loud cheery laughs and comic songs, armed to the teeth, jack-booted, gauntleted, slouch-hatted, yet clad in the shooting-jacket of a civilian . . . He didn't look like an American; he was too well-dressed to be a guerrilla."

The British reporter was describing Alfred Rudolph Waud, the most productive battlefield artist of the Civil War. Often working under fire, he was able to record the action and the excitement of combat with an immediacy denied to Mathew Brady and other photographers. The quantity of his sketches was extraordinary; so was the quality of what he drew.

Born in London in 1828, "Alf" Waud began studying art at an early age. He came to America in 1850 because he had "a sentimental liking for republican institutions." He worked at various jobs in New York City before moving to Boston, where he learned to draw on wood blocks for engravers—the most common method by which a drawing could be reproduced on paper stock for mass circulation. He also began making scenic sketches, mostly of city life. In time he hoped to become a marine painter and made at least one oil painting of ships anchored in New York City.

On May 4, 1861, Waud agreed to become a "Special Artist" for the *New York Illustrated News* and made his way to Washington. His first Civil War image was of Colonel Elmer Ellsworth's New York Zouaves battling a blaze at Willard's Hotel. He was one of two artists allowed to accompany the Union Army to Manassas, where he did several drawings of the war's opening battle, notably one of an artillery battery moving into position. This was his initiation into four years of combat and military artwork, and the heavy detail of his drawings set Waud apart from the usual sketchers.

After Manassas, while General George McClellan built a new army, Waud joined a Union expedition to Forts Hatteras and Clark on the North Carolina coast. Unfortunately, only two sketches of the campaign have survived. Back in Virginia, Waud drew scenes of Fort Monroe and Newport News for a double-page spread that is stunning in its detail.

Along with his sketches, the artist wrote personal accounts of military affairs for the New York newspaper. He was pro-Union in sentiment and usually referred to Confederates in such terms as "rabble" and "devilish gray coats." As with his sketches, Waud's written dispatches to newspapers focused more on individuals and their activities than on statistics, troop movements, and other inanimate subjects.

Waud won national acclaim in the late summer of 1861 for what is considered to be the largest wood engraving ever produced in America: "The Grand Review of the Army of 70,000 Troops of the Army of the Potomac by Geo. B. McClellan." It folded into five sections in the newspaper.

That illustration led to Waud's joining the staff of *Harper's Weekly*, an association that lasted for 19 years. His first illustration for his new employer was a White House reception. By then his technique was firmly in place. He would rush a sketch to the New York office by mail or courier. Engravers would laboriously copy the drawing on boxwood blocks. Once finished, the blocks would be bolted together to form a completed picture for the printing press. As many as 40 blocks were used for a double-page spread. The journey from sketch to print took three

Behind enemy lines, Waud pens a sketch of the First Virginia Cavalry at a halt.

to four weeks. Naturally, the woodblocks failed to do full justice to the submitted sketch.

Waud intensely disliked fellow *Harper's Weekly* artist Thomas Nast because Waud claimed that the cartoonist tampered with his sketches when they arrived in New York and sometimes passed them off as his own creations. Nast vigorously denied these accusations.

In contrast, Waud seemed to make friends easily throughout the Union Army. Captain Oliver Wendell Holmes, Jr., informed his family that Waud was "quite a truthful draughtsman." The army's chief of staff, Colonel Theodore Lyman, wrote this in his diary in May 1864: "Friend Waud is along with us still and sojourns with the Engineers. He draws . . . very good sketches, and very poor woodcuts they make thereof. His indignation has long since given place to sarcasm; for W. is a merry & philosophic Bohemian!"

Waud found himself on one occasion "detained behind enemy lines." During his brief capture he did a sketch of men in the First Virginia Cavalry with the Confederate battle flag as the center of the drawing. The most famous of several wartime photographs of Waud shows him sketching while seated atop a boulder in Devil's Den at Gettysburg. The 35-year-old Waud also made the only eyewitness drawing of Pickett's Charge, the climactic assault of the three-day battle.

He appeared oblivious to danger. An 1864 news item from Petersburg, Virginia, told of Waud "cooly making his sketches under fire, whilst the enemy bullets were kicking up little columns of dust on the ground around him. His numerous adventures and narrow escapes would fill a volume."

No correspondent was allowed to attend the April 9, 1865, surrender conference at Appomattox. Yet Waud was outside the home and drew a hasty sketch of General Robert E. Lee starting the ride back to his defeated army. His sketch later that day of Federal soldiers sharing rations with starving Southern infantry is a poignant one. Waud also accompanied the Lincoln funeral train on the long journey to Springfield, Illinois. Those sad illustrations were the capstone of 344 sketches he made during the Civil War.

Harper's Weekly then sent Waud to record life in the defeated South. He sketched a fire in a Louisville opera house, found Cairo, Illinois, to be nothing but "dust, filth, and intrusive drinking-saloons," thought Memphis "the worst behaved city in the Union," and adjudged Vicksburg to be "in the hands of foreigners, the police being among the worst specimens."

Waud made a permanent picture of U. S. Grant's inauguration and captured part of the wrath of the Great Chicago Fire in 1871. The largest collection of printed Waud drawings were incorporated in *Battles and Leaders of the Civil War,* a four-volume work published during 1884–87.

His busy life ended at the age of 62. Waud died on April 6, 1891, of heart failure while visiting a friend in Marietta, Georgia, where he is buried in the Episcopal cemetery.

Waud led the procession of newspaper artists who witnessed and recorded scenes of the Civil War, the Reconstruction, and the growing union of the divided states. To untold thousands of Americans, the scenes of Alf Waud were their eyes to the past, present, and future. ∾

MOSES EZEKIEL

THE SCULPTOR WHO NEVER FORGOT

THOUGH MOSES EZEKIEL was only a teenage cadet in the final years of the Civil War, the North-South conflict was the springboard that elevated him to international fame as a sculptor whose creations are memorials of the war.

Ezekiel was the seventh of 14 children born to a family in a poverty-stricken neighborhood in Richmond, Virginia. His grandparents raised him, to ease the pressure of so many youngsters in the Ezekiel household. On September 17, 1862, the day of the Battle of Antietam, the 17-year-old became the first Jewish applicant admitted to the Virginia Military Institute (VMI) at Lexington.

He was a good cadet but not a good-looking one. A "brother rat," as freshmen are dubbed, later testified that Ezekiel "never could chisel himself into a pretty soldier. His head was as large as a Brownie's, his body thickset, and his legs were very short. In fact, he looked like a tin soldier that had been broken in the middle and mended with sealing wax."

Given the open anti-Semitism of that age, Ezekiel had to obtain permission from the board of governors to return home for the observance of Jewish holidays such as Passover. As though to underscore his difference from his fellows, his roommate was Thomas Jefferson Garand, a direct descendant of the man who had framed the Declaration of Independence.

One memory of VMI that Ezekiel did cherish was being corporal of the guard that stood watch over General Stonewall Jackson's coffin through the night before the former professor's burial. In May 1864, Ezekiel was among the 257 cadets who marched 89 miles down the Shenandoah Valley to confront a Union Army at New Market. Ankle-deep mud sucked the shoes off the charging teenagers. Ezekiel replaced his with a pair of boots taken from a dead Federal soldier. The green soldier had the unenviable task of caring for his mortally wounded roommate until his death three days later.

VMI cadets spent the last months of the war training the handful of recruits who came forth. When Ezekiel returned to VMI for his final year of study, General Robert E. Lee recognized Ezekiel's talents and encouraged him to pursue an artistic calling. Ezekiel spent a year studying anatomy at the University of Virginia and then journeyed to Europe with hopes of becoming a sculptor.

For a time he supported himself by serving as a correspondent during the Franco-Prussian War. His real break came when he was admitted to the Berlin Royal Academy of Art, where Albert Wolff, sculptor of the German royal family, became his mentor.

Ezekiel's first plaster, "Virginia Mourning Her Dead," was completed in Berlin. Now the most hallowed symbol at VMI, it faces the drill field. In front of the sculpture are the graves of six of Ezekiel's fellow cadets who were killed at New Market. Ezekiel himself described his creation: "The chain mail clad figure is seated mourning upon a piece of breastwork and her foot rests upon a broken cannon overgrown with ivy, and she holds a reversed lance in her hand."

Ezekiel moved to Rome, where he lived for the next 30 years. In his studio, located in the ancient Baths of Diocletian, he created more than 200 sculptures. His fame swept around the world. One set, consisting of 11 larger-than-life statues of famous artists, was installed in the Corcoran Gallery of Art. Among so many others, Robert E. Lee, Stonewall Jackson, and Thomas Jefferson were subjects for Ezekiel's creations. He even molded a tribute to dead soldiers at Johnson's Island Prison in Ohio.

Ezekiel divided his sculptures into three categories: works devoted to the Confederate cause, heroic poses, and religious subjects. His Rome

Ezekiel's experiences as a New Market cadet shaped his later artistic works.

studio, in the words of one admirer, was "a stupendous spectacle, strewn with the mighty monuments of the past, a wilderness from which nothing springs but grass, fever germs, and noble thoughts." The place became a must-see for American tourists. U. S. Grant, Mark Twain, John D. Rockefeller, and Theodore Roosevelt were among those who came to pay homage. By the end of the century, the sculptor had received

Ezekiel's "Religious Liberty" perpetuates a message of tolerance
and freedom from Independence Mall in Philadelphia.

commendations from four European heads of state plus dozens of high awards from America.

"Uncle Mosie," as family members affectionately called their bachelor kinsman, made periodic visits to the United States. His last trip, in 1910, was to dedicate the Jackson statue on the statehouse grounds at Charleston, West Virginia. He learned that the federal government had recently agreed to set aside a portion of Arlington National Cemetery for Confederate casualties and expressed strong interest in the movement. Back in Rome, he spent seven years creating a huge, intricate monument.

World War I slowed his production. Dampness and lack of coal in wintertime forced Ezekiel to close his Rome studio. He volunteered to assist the Red Cross Relief Agency by becoming an Italian ambulance driver. Fatigue and exposure led to pneumonia, and on March 27, 1917, Ezekiel died. One of his final wishes was to be buried with his Confederate comrades at Arlington. The European war delayed the return of his remains to America, and his burial did not occur until March 31, 1921. It was the first funeral service held in the large Arlington amphitheater, where formal ceremonies are now conducted regularly.

Ezekiel's gravestone, at the base of the soaring monument he sculpted, could have displayed for eternity some of his great statues, or international awards, or eminence in his field. Instead, the marker proclaims, "Moses J. Ezekiel: Sergeant of Company C, Battalion of Cadets of the Virginia Military Institute." ∞

GEORGE FREDERICK ROOT

SONGS OF THE CIVIL WAR

I F ANY AMERICAN DESERVES the title "musician of the people," it is unquestionably George Frederick Root of Massachusetts. Born with a talent for music, he could play 13 instruments by the age of 12. His first job was with a Boston piano instructor who introduced music curricula in local schools. Root pursued a career as a music teacher in elementary schools and professional institutions, including at the New York Institute for the Blind. There, he and Fanny Crosby, a lyricist, collaborated on numerous popular secular songs. He also wrote gospel music while collecting and editing volumes of choral tunes.

After a trip to Europe to study musical trends and styles, Root gained a national reputation by participating in musical convocations. In 1859, he joined his brother's music company in Chicago. When not writing music or helping to manage the company, he continued to travel and lecture at various musical festivals.

Sheet music by then had become all the rage, and Root contributed weekly to the output. The advent of war in 1861 brought out Root's leading assets: knowledge of instrumental music, improvisational skills, and absolute devotion to his country.

A week after the bombardment of Fort Sumter and the beginning of war, Root published "The First Gun Is Fired! May God Protect the Right!"

Next came a call to duty: "Stand Up for Uncle Sam, My Boys." In all his compositions, Root tapped into the emotions of soldiers and their families, expressing hope, grief, and inspiration that was individual and personal while sharing a widespread experience.

In April 1862, Root was reclining in a lounge chair at his brother's home when a song formed in his mind. He thought about it all afternoon, then drafted it on sheet-music paper the next morning. No other melody so stirred Union soldiers as did "The Battle Cry of Freedom." The tune was easy to sing, and the lyrics were inspiring: "Yes, we'll rally round the flag, boys / We'll rally once again / Shouting the battle cry of freedom! / We will rally from the hillside / We'll rally from the plain / Shouting the battle cry of freedom!"

The composition was a favorite throughout the war years and beyond. More than 350,000 copies of sheet music were sold in its first year. One Billy Yank asserted that "Battle Cry" put "as much spirit and cheer into the army as a splendid victory." Root himself confessed, "The song went into the army, and the testimony in regard to its use in the camp and on the march and even on the field of battle . . . made me thankful that if I could not shoulder a musket in defense of my country, I could serve her in this way."

One story that always touched Root concerned an Iowa regiment that made a charge at Vicksburg, Mississippi, and lost 50 percent of its strength in the fighting. The survivors retired from the field singing "The Battle Cry of Freedom."

Many of Root's wartime tunes may sound maudlin and melodramatic to modern ears, yet they touched the souls of the Civil War generation. "The Prisoner's Hope," also known for its chorus line "Tramp, tramp, tramp," offered hope to Union prisoners of war. "Just Before the Battle, Mother" was a mixture of fear and determination by a young soldier uncertain of his future. "The Vacant Chair" spoke of the empty place at the dinner table left by the death in some faraway place of a father or a brother. Root once explained his musical approach this way: "When anything happened that could be voiced in a song, or when the heart of the Nation was moved by particular circumstances caused by the war, I wrote what I thought would then express the emotions of the soldiers or the people."

Prosperity allowed Root to move his Chicago location in 1863 to a site four times larger. In all, he contributed 35 songs to the war effort. He gained national recognition and the appreciation of every Northern soldier who sang or understood music. After the end of hostilities, a Confederate officer told his former enemies, "Gentlemen, if we'd had your songs, we'd have whipped you out of your boots!"

Root was the most prolific composer of the Civil War. He rode that fame well into the postwar years by climbing aboard various bandwagons. A strong supporter of the temperance movement, he applied new lyrics to some of his Civil War tunes. "Just Before the Battle, Mother" was reissued with new verses as "Promise Me." The soldier song "Kingdom Coming" appeared as "The Temperance Sheep." For U. S. Grant's 1868 presidential bid, Root even changed "The Battle Cry of Freedom" to "The Ballot Box of Freedom."

Turning to hymns, Root made similar transitions. "The Prisoner's Hope" reappeared as "Jesus Loves the Little Children," while "The Vacant Chair" became "Life's Railway to Heaven." Root remained the nation's preeminent composer until the appearance in World War I of George M. Cohan.

At one point Root fell seriously ill, whereupon his physician diagnosed "a condition of the brain." A friend suggested weight lifting, and Root's health returned to normal.

The 1871 Chicago fire destroyed all his company's sheet music, but plates and copyrights survived. A year later, the University of Chicago bestowed on Root a doctor of music degree. He soon turned to writing cantatas and produced 28 in all. Decades before Walt Disney's *Snow White and the Seven Dwarfs,* Root and his daughter composed an operetta based on the same story.

In 1891, Root commented, "I cannot imagine a pleasanter life for myself than the one I now live." Four years later, on August 6, 1895, while going through a normal workday at his Bailey Island, Maine, home, Root died of a heart attack. He was buried in North Reading, Massachusetts. The following year, 20,000 people gathered in Chicago's Coliseum for a festival to benefit the George F. Root Monument Fund. Never was "The Battle Cry of Freedom" sung with greater fervor.

Root's battle songs rallied the nation and tugged heartstrings in equal measure.

The composer idolized music. "It is an interesting fact," he observed, "that some music, at every grade, from lowest to highest, has in it that mysterious quality which makes it live, while all the rest fades away and is forgotten." George Root died content. In the nation's darkest hour, he had contributed magnificently to the spirits of the brave men marching into battle. ∾

LOUISA MAY ALCOTT

RESILIENCE IN WRITING

No American writer benefited more—while suffering more—from the Civil War than Louisa May Alcott. Though she was a nurse, she herself became ill—and the cure proved worse than the disease. She suffered from mercury poisoning throughout the years of writing her finest books. In her case, war truly was the crucible of her works.

Born in the Philadelphia suburb of Germantown to Amos Bronson Alcott, an educator, and Abigail May Alcott, a social worker, Louisa spent her early life in near poverty and discouragement. After the family moved to Boston, she got her formal education from a father who stopped working in 1839 to contemplate and speak on "the sweetness of self-denial."

The Alcotts pursued transcendentalism, the credo that one can gain perfection through better spiritualism. This brought friendship with such established writers as Henry David Thoreau, Ralph Waldo Emerson, and Nathaniel Hawthorne. Her family's limited means forced Alcott to spend her teenage years as an occasional teacher, seamstress, and governess. In her spare time, she tried her hand at writing, which became a creative challenge as well as an emotional outlet for her unhappiness. Soon, she published her first book, *Flower Fables* (1849), and the first of her many short stories that would appear in the *Atlantic Monthly*.

The family struggled throughout the 1850s, and at one point in 1857, Louisa contemplated suicide. Neighbors soon converted the impressionable feminist to the abolitionist cause. The Alcott family became "station agents" for the Underground Railroad, helping runaway slaves to freedom. Late in 1859, Alcott wrote a poem, "With a Rose, That Bloomed on the Day of John Brown's Execution," and she referred to the abolitionist as "St. John the Just."

In her late twenties when the Civil War began, Alcott was tall and broad-shouldered, with dark eyes and hair. Her first work in the conflict was to sew uniforms and to act in theatricals for the humanitarian U.S. Sanitary Commission. She desired a more-fulfilling position and for six weeks in 1861–62 served as a volunteer nurse in one of Washington's military hospitals.

The 12-hour shifts exhausted her physically and mentally. An attack of typhoid fever ended her nursing duties and almost her life. Physicians plied her with calomel, a widely used purgative laced with mercury. Overdoses produced mercury poisoning, which, among other negative side effects, causes slow deterioration of the nervous system.

Alcott was near death when she reached home, and she remained a semi-invalid for the rest of her life. Her arms and legs ached, forcing her to frequently stand up from her writing table and walk around in an effort to stretch the discomfort from her limbs.

Her first postwar literary endeavor came with editing letters she had sent home while a nurse. The correspondence appeared in print under the title *Hospital Sketches*. Alcott freely described the filth and mismanagement of army hospitals as well as the indifference of many surgeons. The next year, she wrote a short story for children, "Nellie's Children," which related the experiences of a little girl who was moved by the wartime wounding of her brother to create a hospital for all the sick animals in her neighborhood.

A novel, *Moods* (1865), followed the success of *Sketches* and went into more detail about her war experiences. Another fictional work, *On Picket Duty, and Other Tales* (1866) was also set in the Civil War.

Under the pseudonym A. B. Barnard, the crippled Alcott stepped out of character and wrote two well-received novels of passion: *A Long Fatal Love Chase* (1866) and *Pauline's Passion and Punishment* (1868). She was 35 and graying when a New York publisher approached her to do "a girl's story." The offer meant returning to her childhood, which she did not want to

A book illustration brings Little Women's *heroines—*
Amy, Meg, Jo, and Beth—to life.

do, but it was an opportunity to earn money. And given that she'd grown up with three loving sisters, the writing assignment was easy. Alcott wrote continually and without excitement for two and a half months. The result was *Little Women* (1868), her most famous book.

It is a moving account of four sisters whose comfortable lives are disrupted by their father's absence in the war. She explained the base of her novel with the statement: "Very few letters written in those hard times were more touching, especially those which fathers sent home." *Little Women*—which parallels Charles Dickens's novels, in which every character is a caricature of some virtue or vice—has had an astounding ability to touch the hearts of readers and has never been out of print.

Alcott wrote two sequels, *Little Men* (1868) and *Jo's Boys* (1884). Her 33 books and essays made her the most famous female writer of her day. Pale and serious, dressed always in black or dark brown, she wrote at a steady pace. Her right hand eventually became cramped from overuse, whereupon she learned to write with her left.

Alcott never married. "I am more than half persuaded," she once confessed, "that I am a man's soul put by some freak of nature into a woman's body."

In 1882 a stroke paralyzed the father she adored and she became his constant companion as her own health deteriorated. She suffered from severe rheumatoid pain, trembling, irritability, and weakness. She wrote to a friend, "The [wartime] hospital experience was a costly one for me. Never well since."

She was 55 when she died of a stroke, two days after the passing of her father. It is traditionally believed that she died from the long-term effects of mercury poisoning. Revisionist theories of late attribute her death to autoimmune disease or spinal meningitis. Alcott was buried in Sleepy Hollow Cemetery in Concord, Massachusetts, near some of the great writers who had given her early encouragement.

One of her many biographers made this summation: "Her anxious and unhappy girlhood turned in the Civil War; and though physically stricken, she thereafter gained financial support and a source of both justification and satisfaction." ❧

WALT WHITMAN

AMERICA'S POET LAUREATE

IN THE FIRST HALF OF THE 19TH CENTURY, America was print-mad. Into the mainstream of that flood of ink appeared the works of Walt Whitman, whom one literary scholar has characterized as "the self-anointed poet of democracy, arguing for the dignity and meaning of ordinary labor."

Whitman endured ridicule and neglect in his early poetic endeavors, and his dismissal of conventional patterns of rhyme and meter drew early criticism worldwide. Praise came only in his older years, and today he is regarded throughout the literary world as "the father of free verse."

Born to a Brooklyn house builder in 1819, Whitman followed Benjamin Franklin's trail into the printing business. The self-taught youth loved the printed word and read voraciously. In 1841, after a five-year tenure as a teacher, Whitman turned to journalism as a full-time career. He edited a number of weekly newspapers in New York. A brief stint with a New Orleans periodical gave him a firsthand view of slavery's evils.

Meanwhile, he was developing an unorthodox style of poetry. His first collection of poems, *Leaves of Grass* (1855), contains a preface and 12 untitled poems, mostly lacking punctuation. The verses are filled with stories of the virtues and vices of common people—"the wildest players in American life," one critic snorted. Some literary analysts have suggested that in *Leaves of Grass,* Whitman came to terms with his homosexuality, then known as "free love."

Whitman persisted through early criticism to become one
of the nation's most revered poets.

With an endorsement from Ralph Waldo Emerson, Whitman released a second edition of *Leaves* in 1856, which had 33 poems—almost triple those in the first printing. Many reviewers denounced the collection for its blatant expressions of immorality; others praised Whitman as a great spokesman for brotherhood and equality. Human rights activist and former slave Sojourner Truth was so taken by Whitman's lines that she said the poems were messages from God.

Whitman spent the first stages of the Civil War as a freelance journalist and occasional volunteer in New York City–area military hospitals. In December 1862 he learned that his brother George had been seriously wounded at the Battle of Fredericksburg, and he hastened to Washington. He found his sibling only slightly injured, yet Whitman was shocked by the endless wagon trains bringing wounded soldiers to hospitals already crowded beyond capacity. "It is the most pitiful sight I think when first the men are brought in," he wrote to his mother. "I have to hustle around to keep from crying."

Whitman immediately decided to become a nurse, traveling among Washington's 40 soldier hospitals. His nursing duties were usually noon to 4 p.m. and 6 to 9 p.m., mostly in Armory Square Hospital, which had the most injured patients. He obtained a part-time job in the paymaster's department and supplemented his small salary by writing occasional war stories for newspapers. In his early forties, tall, good-looking, with clear blue eyes and an unhurried air, Whitman always wore Bohemian-style clothing and was a welcome sight and instant friend to everyone he met.

He came to know an extraordinary number of patients. During his three years of nursing, Whitman made an estimated 600 visits to as many as 80,000 incapacitated soldiers. As he viewed the human suffering from battle and disease, he became convinced that "future years will never know the seething hell and the bleak infernal background of minor scenes and interiors . . . of the Secession War; and it is best they should not. The real war will never get in the books."

Whitman's residency in the capital gave him opportunity to witness Abraham Lincoln personally and politically. He came to see the Great Emancipator as the all-seeking being the poet had long searched for. Lincoln's death in 1865 was for Whitman a grand tragedy that promised ultimate reunification for America. Two of his best known poems appeared as eulogies.

"O Captain! My Captain!" is a melodramatic poem in conventional rhyme and meter about a ship captain bravely guiding his vessel through

Whitman was deeply affected by mounting war casualties, such as this assembly of wounded at Savage Square, Virginia, in 1862.

a terrible storm. In "When Lilacs Last in the Dooryard Bloom'd," Whitman returned to free-flowing lines. Three images appear: the western star (Lincoln), a singing thrush (Whitman), and a lilac bush (the eulogistic poem). They interweave with meditations on the Civil War and death.

Yet his three years of hospital labor had taken a heavy toll. "I had to give up my health for it, my body, the vitality of my physical self," he stated. "O so much had to go!"

He took a job in the Department of the Interior and published a third, enlarged edition of *Leaves of Grass* in 1865. Secretary of the Interior James Harlan thereupon fired the poet for his "scandalous" writings. Whitman struggled to support himself by writing poetry full-time. In the next quarter century, he composed 194 poems, and at least 115 were published.

Typically when composing, he would tilt his big rocking chair back against a table and write with a mammoth quill pen as he held a pad on his knee. His followers regarded him as the nation's literary savior.

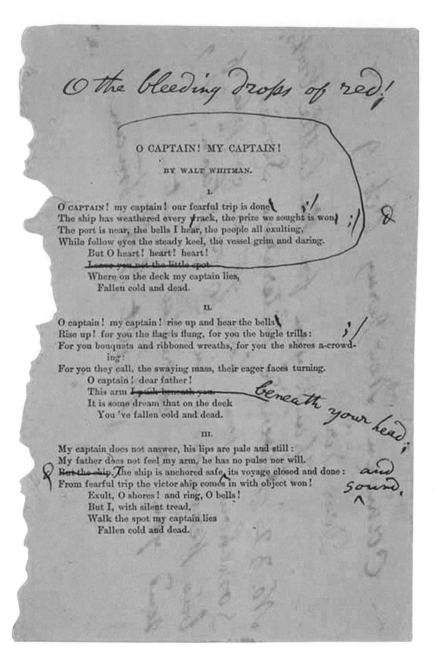

An 1888 proof sheet of "O Captain! My Captain!" bears the notes of a masterpiece in the making.

His critics—Henry James notable among them—never accepted his views or writing style. Another further enlarged edition of *Leaves of Grass* brought renewed praise—and criticism.

Whitman moved to Camden, New Jersey, to be near his brother and dying mother. In January 1873 he suffered a stroke that restricted the use of his left arm and leg. Recurring bouts of dizziness, vomiting, faintness, and slow locomotion further hampered his activities, and physicians were unable to ascertain a cause.

More and more he confronted in verse the meaning of the Civil War, his homosexuality, religion, the afterlife, and his place in culture. Toward the end, his once robust frame was slumped in a wheelchair. A series of ministrokes—"whacks," as he called them—increased his paralysis. His body—wasted, atrophied, and abscessed—became "a carnival ground of decay," a visitor noted. Whitman lived out his life in squalor. Death came March 26, 1892. Pathologists listed the causes as "pleurisy of the left side, consumption in the right lung, general miliary tuberculosis, and parenchymatous nephritis." Whitman was buried in Camden's Harleigh Cemetery, in a mausoleum whose construction he had overseen.

One authority wrote this summation: "No writer is regarded as more indisputably American than Whitman, yet no writer has reverberated on the international scene to the extent that he has. He was the democratic poet to an extent never heretofore recognized, gathering images from virtually every cultural arena and transforming them through his powerful personality into art." ∾

CHAPTER 5

WESTWARD HO!

Threshold the final echoes of the Civil War had barely faded into the distance when the nation's attention turned westward to the unspoiled Great West. This rough square of land measured about a thousand miles on each side. Plains, mountains, plateaus, and deserts lay for the taking. The region's only occupants were Native Americans and buffalo.

By 1890 the entire area was carved into ten states and four territories. "Men flung themselves greedily on this enormous prize, as if to ravish it," one historian stated. "Never before in human experience had so huge an area been reduced so rapidly to a semblance of civilization." This overnight transformation was the result of two factors: completing a transcontinental railroad and eliminating native tribes standing in the way of white settlement.

In the 1850s a rash of local companies had laid pieces of a rail network all along the eastern seaboard and the upper Mississippi Valley. The feverish years after the Civil War witnessed an unparalleled outburst of railroad construction. What had been 30,000 miles of track in wartime became 192,500 miles at century's end. American railroads eclipsed all of Europe's tracks combined.

The chief underwriter of the transcontinental line was the federal government. Only it had the necessary funds and executive power. Yet it took good men with firm determination to make the dream become reality. Grenville Dodge was the principal surveyor of the Union Pacific

OPPOSITE: *The completion of the transcontinental railroad*
in 1869 joins East and West.

Railroad, which built two-thirds of the transcontinental railroad. His route selections remain one of the wonders of modern railroading.

The coming of the "iron horse" changed virtually worthless land into valuable real estate linked in a chain of progress by rail tracks. Overlooked acreage became prosperous fields for a variety of crops. Frontier villages matured quickly into flourishing cities. A railroad took the farmer to his newly claimed land, carried the fruits of his toil to market, and brought him manufactured necessities.

Standing in the way of such progress were the original settlers of the West: Native American tribes. In the northern half of the region were principally the Sioux and Cheyenne; in the south were Comanche and Apache. As the railroads and more settlers approached in a tidal wave, the indigenous tribes found no solace. Solemn promises made by the government were broken; agents were corrupt; too many settlers treated tribes as unwanted animals. Murder, looting, and debauchery were common.

All too soon, these tribes found themselves fighting for survival. During the period from 1868 to 1890 the federal government engaged in almost incessant warfare from the Canadian to the Mexican borders. A printed list of the names of the engagements covers 100 pages. The fighting was fierce, with neither side inclined to take prisoners. The operations eventually led to ruthless subjugation of Native Americans and removal of the survivors to unwanted lands called reservations. This period of extermination remains one of America's most embarrassing.

On this new type of battlefield, the early efforts of the Federal Army were uneven. George Custer, known for being impetuous during the war, remained blindly unaware of the tactics his native foes used, including a reliance on deception. He rushed his men into a trap so disastrous that the battle at Little Big Horn has become legendary.

Far more stable was Winfield Hancock. One of the most proficient generals during the war, he, too, saw action on the Plains. Only in his case, he proved too magnanimous to the Native Americans for the liking of the more bloody-minded Republican Congress. He was reassigned so that the removal process could proceed apace.

Into the breech rushed Philip Sheridan. The short, ill-tempered hero of the Union cavalry became famous during the war for his scorched-earth policy that laid ruin to the Shenandoah Valley. He then turned his fierce disposition on a series of Western tribes, and his tactics against them amounted to wholesale slaughter of warriors and civilians alike. Under his direction the Cheyenne, Kiowa, Comanche, and Apache were brutally brought to heel.

Throughout the process of clearing the West, white settlers established the first towns and villages to resemble what they had left behind. The rawness of these outposts opened the way for all sorts of colorful characters, whether those breaking the law or upholding it. One Union officer, the leader of the ill-fated Irish Brigade, attempted to use the fear of Native Americans for his own personal and political gain. The story of Thomas Francis Meagher, who came to the Montana Territory to lay down his drunken decrees, strained the meaning of the word "governor" to its limits.

"Wild Bill" Hickok is a more familiar hero who migrated west. He fought for the Union in Missouri, and after the war he brought his murderous brand of law enforcement to the unfortunate frontier towns that hired him. In an era when might often made right, Hickok was unique even for the Wild West. ∽

GRENVILLE MELLEN DODGE

LAYING THE TRACKS FOR EXPANSION

JAY GOULD OWNED the Union Pacific Railroad, but the man most responsible for its creation was Massachusetts native Grenville Mellen Dodge. A Union general under Grant in war, and a confidant of Sherman in peace, Dodge lived longer and had a more active and varied life than any other prominent general in the Civil War. Indeed, his work on America's first transcontinental railroad outshines any of his fighting.

After graduating from Norwich University, Dodge put his civil engineering studies to practice by moving to Council Bluffs, Iowa, and surveying for the infant Union Pacific Railroad. With the onset of the Civil War, he began as colonel of the Fourth Iowa and advanced steadily through the army's chain of command. While stationed in Missouri, Dodge organized an intelligence service to gain information on enemy movements. His 100-man Corps of Scouts was the largest intelligence-gathering body in the war, and the agents were so effective that their names still remain unknown today.

In late 1862, at Grant's request, Dodge rebuilt a vital rail line connecting Nashville, Tennessee, with Decatur, Alabama. He rose to the rank of major general after being cited for gallantry during the campaign for Atlanta. With a full head of hair parted on the side and a bushy mustache and eyebrows, Dodge stood five feet eight inches tall and weighed only

In an 1869 engraving, Sioux riders pillage a Union Pacific train captured on the Great Plains.

125 pounds. He was an energetic man, nervous and high-strung. He spoke and wrote as if he could barely wait to finish his tasks.

At the end of the Civil War, Dodge's Department of the Missouri was expanded to include Kansas, Nebraska, and Utah. When Cheyenne and Arapaho tribes began raiding Bozeman Trail and other mail routes, Grant ordered Dodge, who had a strong bias against Native Americans, to end the nuisances. They must be relentlessly pursued and eliminated, Dodge felt, saying, "The Indian character is such that he will not stand continual following, pounding, and attacking." He thought peace treaties "not worth the paper they are written on." Yet Washington authorities preferred an uneasy paper peace. Dodge always believed that if he had been allowed to punish the tribes severely, "we would have conquered a peace that would have been a lasting one."

During an 1865 expedition in Wyoming, Dodge discovered a pass for the Union Pacific Railroad west of the Platte River. He resigned from the

Dodge (center, right) is shown mid-handshake in a crowd celebrating the "last spike" linking the Central Pacific and Union Pacific Railroads in Promontory, Utah.

army the following spring and, with the encouragement of Generals Grant and Sherman, became the Union Pacific's chief engineer in the renewed effort to build a transcontinental railroad.

Some 11 million acres of public-domain land were at the builders' disposal. Three rail companies began construction on a line connecting Council Bluffs with San Francisco. The Western Pacific labored on the Oakland-Sacramento sector, the Central Pacific toiled from Sacramento to Promontory Summit, Utah, and the Union Pacific laid track from Council Bluffs to Promontory Summit. The line extended 1,907 miles from the Great Plains across the Rocky Mountains to the Pacific Ocean.

Dodge did not "build" the Union Pacific. He was in charge of surveying and selecting the route of the line. Yet his strength in command and sense of direction were the bedrocks of the effort. Men laid track all day, then returned to portable towns that every few weeks were dismantled, packed on trains, and moved—stores, saloons, blacksmith shops, brothels, etc.—to another site to keep pace with the advance of the rail line. The towns became known as "Hell on Wheels."

At the height of construction, Dodge suddenly found himself immersed in the greatest political scandal of the century. He supervised track location and laying for a company known as Crédit Mobilier, in which Dodge himself had purchased stock. The company became involved in kickbacks, using routes to benefit its own landholdings, hiring subcontractors in return for under-the-table cash payments, and engaging in other acts of corruption.

For a time Dodge thought the firm was merely inefficient. "Like all roads," he said, the line "was managed a thousand miles away—the mere play thing for Wall Street, to be set up and down as a circus." Yet when the balloon burst, Dodge fled to Texas to avoid testifying before a congressional committee in Washington.

Late in 1866, Dodge defeated an Iowa incumbent for a seat in Congress. He was rather inconspicuous during his one term because he still had his old job as chief engineer for the Union Pacific and often worked at the ever shifting railhead. At the same time, Dodge tightened his political grasp in western Iowa in preparation for the time when he and his political colleagues would control the entire state.

On May 10, 1869, the transcontinental railroad joined ends at Promontory Point. Dodge is a central figure in the now famous photograph of locomotives standing nose-to-nose. He had a prominent role in linking East with West and in opening a vast new area for settlement and national prosperity. The places where he first created stops during railroad construction—Dodge City, Cheyenne, and Laramie—are living monuments to his influence.

He supervised a dozen different rail lines thereafter, with New York as his general headquarters. At one social affair, President Theodore Roosevelt told him publicly, "I would rather have had your experience in the Civil War and have seen what you have seen than to be president of the United States." On January 3, 1816, Dodge died of cancer. He had declined the offer of burial at Arlington National Cemetery in favor of being taken home to Council Bluffs.

Dodge and the country matured in step. In 1851, when he went west, Illinois was still on the western frontier. When he died in 1916, the United States stretched from sea to sea. Dodge's railroad was a mighty leap in that evolution. ℰ

GEORGE ARMSTRONG CUSTER

A FLAIR FOR DISASTER

N O AMERICAN OFFICER HAS KNOWN a more meteoric rise and meteoric fall than George Armstrong Custer. Fact and fiction swirl around him still, and perhaps always will. What is well known is his tendency to charge first and think later. As a result, he became famous for the U.S. Army's largest defeat in the West.

Ohio-born and named for a minister, Custer spent a stormy three years at West Point. He came close to expulsion each year because of poor grades and misbehavior. In addition, the illnesses he contracted ranged from diarrhea to gonorrhea. In the Class of 1861, which was commissioned a year early because the army needed officers, he ranked dead last. Allegedly he was under detention at the time of graduation.

He entered the army as a cavalryman and by the spring of 1863 had risen to company command. He was a protégé of the Army of the Potomac's cavalry chief, Alfred Pleasanton, who promoted Custer in one step from captain to brigadier general. Besides being so young, Custer lacked the aptitude for command. Nor did he look the part of a reliable general, despite being a broad-shouldered six-footer. Colonel Theodore Lyman, chief of staff to General George Meade, wrote at the time: "Custer is sight to behold, looking like a crazy circus rider! He had a faded velvet suit, with tarnished lace trimmings, a little gray felt hat and long boots. His head is garnished with soft flaxen curls, and he has a devil-may-care blue eye, very appropriate to his style."

No officer had more nicknames. "Fannie" originated at West Point; during the war he was called "Autie" from a loose pronunciation of his middle name; "Curly" came from his ringlets; and "Cinnamon" was for the spicy hair oil he used liberally. Custer had a passion for dogs, as well, and wherever he was camped, at least one dog was nearby.

In battle, he was aggressive but foolhardy, gallant but reckless. His attacks were always heavy; so were his losses. Custer's capstone came at Gettysburg in a July 3, 1863, charge on the Confederate cavalry. The flamboyant Custer later reported, "I challenge the annals of warfare to produce a more brilliant or successful charge of cavalry."

His February 1864 marriage to Elizabeth "Libbie" Bacon was a milestone for Custer. She would become his greatest publicist.

His rashness again surfaced on April 9, 1865, at Appomattox. While Lee and Grant were negotiating, Custer rode into Confederate lines and demanded that the Army of Northern Virginia surrender to him. A mini-battle almost occurred between Custer's troopers and General James Longstreet's infantry.

At the end of hostilities, Custer was a 25-year-old brevet major general. He wanted to stay in the military, but in February 1866 the army began down-grading officers who held brevet (temporary) rank. Custer suddenly found himself a lieutenant colonel, three steps below his wartime status. He took an extended furlough to consider his civilian options. In the end, Custer declined the colonelcy of the Tenth Cavalry (the all-black Buffalo Soldiers) and instead accepted appointment as lieutenant colonel of the crack Seventh Cavalry.

The American settlers pushing westward continually broke treaties and seized land, oftentimes aided by the Army. As resistance came from the native tribes, pressure arose to clear them out of the way. Custer joined in these efforts at suppression, but following his 1867 campaigns against the Sioux and the Cheyenne, he was court-martialed for taking an unauthorized leave to see his wife. General Philip Sheridan had the punishment ameliorated, and Custer returned to duty with a vengeance. His troopers gave him two more nicknames, "Iron Butt" and "Hard Ass," for the stern discipline he

The New York Daily Graphic's *"The Battle of Little Big Horn River— the Death Struggle of General Custer" reimagines the calamitous event.*

levied. Ambition fueled his new resolve, yet he never quite understood Native American tactics. He and his men were to pay dearly for this fatal drawback.

In November 1868, he was solely to blame for destroying an unoffending Cheyenne village on the Washita River. He explained his decision to army chief Sherman in this way: "I have to select the season when I can catch the fiends; and if a village is attacked and women and children killed, the responsibility is not with the soldiers, but with people whose crimes necessitated the attack."

Custer participated in a large 1873 expedition into the Yellowstone region. The following year, his regiment was part of a force dispatched to track down native warriors in the Black Hills of the Dakotas. American soldiers and the tribes fought one another in the rough country for two years.

Then came June 25, 1876, and the Little Big Horn. Custer had been ordered to take three columns and attack a large contingent of warriors in southeastern Montana. His force, in the center, arrived on the scene early. Instead of waiting for the support elements on either flank, and estimating there were no more than 500 to 600 enemies in front, Custer brashly galloped forward with 220 cavalry. Suddenly some 2,000 Cheyenne and Arapaho warriors assailed Custer from three sides.

Post-battle legend holds that Custer's men made a heroic stand on the side of a hill and fought to the death. Recent research has destroyed that myth. The Indian attack began at 4:30 p.m. and ended in a mere half hour. Bows and arrows were not used. Rather, the native braves were heavily armed with repeating rifles while Custer's troopers were using single-shot carbines. There was no "last stand." It was a running fight in which the men of the Seventh Cavalry were routed, chased down, and slaughtered. All 220 troopers were killed, and the only remaining survivor was a horse.

Custer's naked body was recovered two days later. He had been shot in the chest and the head. For a year his remains were buried alongside those of his troops.

The fame accorded to Custer came after his death. News of the Little Big Horn massacre did not reach Eastern cities until July 4, 1876—the 100th anniversary of the nation. Overnight, the heedless Custer became a heroic soldier who had sacrificed his life for his country.

Custer's body was reinterred with military honors at West Point. His widow, Libbie Custer, spent the next 57 years writing three books and giving countless lectures glorifying her husband. The distribution, by a national brewery, of an intricate battle scene titled "Custer's Last Stand" added to the myth of the great martyr. Henry Wadsworth Longfellow wrote an ode; Theodore Roosevelt gave public praise. On the other hand, professional soldiers such as Grant and Sheridan angrily denounced Custer's recklessness.

The Little Big Horn was the Army's most decisive defeat in the Indian wars. Yet it did serve to harden the mood of the nation. Thereafter, an all-out effort was launched to crush Indian resistance once and for all.

As in the case of George Pickett, with whom he shared a number of characteristics, George Custer was destined to give his name to a military disaster. His rashness within the Union Army during the war could be controlled. Left to his own devices, however, he earned the reward of any military leader who acts before he thinks. ❧

WINFIELD SCOTT HANCOCK

BELOVED SOLDIER

DUBBED "HANCOCK THE SUPERB" early in the war, Winfield Scott Hancock looked and acted like a man born to command. He was named, as were so many men of that time, for the hero of the nation's first two wars. Two distinctions marked Hancock's war years: He was the longest-serving corps commander in the conflict, and he never committed a major tactical blunder in the four-year struggle.

A month younger than Stonewall Jackson, Hancock was born to a Pennsylvania minister-lawyer father with strong Democratic ties. He was only 15 when he entered West Point, and he enjoyed the academy's discipline and the many friends he acquired with his genial personality. After he graduated in the lower third of his class, the Army became his life for the next 45 years—the last 17 of which were served with the Sixth U.S. Infantry.

Sickness and assignments kept him out of the Mexican War, and quartermaster duties did little to expedite promotion. For that reason Hancock was only a captain when secession came. His closest friend was a Virginia colleague, Lewis Armistead, and their 1861 separation to different armies was emotional for both men.

Hancock continued with the Quartermaster Department until his jump to become brigadier general of infantry. He attained fame in his first engagement: the May 5, 1862, Battle of Williamsburg, Virginia.

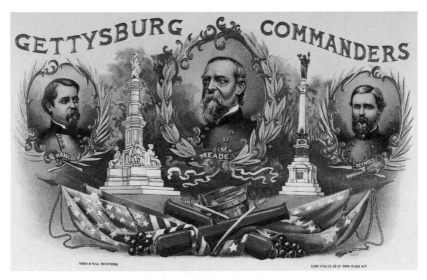

A cigar box label glorifies the Union Army commanders
at Gettysburg, with Hancock on the left.

General George McClellan praised him as "Hancock the superb," and the nickname stuck.

To meet Hancock was to see all the attributes of a good officer. He was six feet two inches tall, powerfully built, and with brown hair and "a military heavy jaw." He made a habit of personally getting to know every one of his field officers. In an army where leaders were generally profane, Hancock, with his full-bodied voice, was one of the best practitioners. U. S. Grant summarized Hancock as "presenting an appearance that would attract the attention of an army when he passed."

Promoted to major general between the battles of Antietam and Fredericksburg, Hancock continually displayed what one called "an inspiring fury in the hour of action." Offered command of the entire army on one occasion, he bluntly declined. He told his wife, "Give yourself no uneasiness—under no conditions would I accept the command. I do not belong to that class of generals whom the Republicans care to bolster up."

In the army's 1863 reorganization, Hancock assumed leadership of the veteran Second Corps. The pinnacle of his career came in July.

A ribbon honors Hancock's 1880 bid as the Democratic presidential candidate.

One military historian has declared, "No other general at Gettysburg dominated men by the sheer force of their presence more completely than Hancock."

On the critical third day's fighting, the Second Corps repulsed Pickett's Charge. Among the dead was Hancock's old friend, Confederate General Lewis Armistead. The Virginian went down at the same time that Hancock received a permanently crippling injury. Hancock was sitting on his horse when a bullet ripped through the saddle pommel and entered his upper thigh, carrying with it pieces of wood and a bent iron nail. A surgeon extracted as much of the material as his fingers could reach. Three months later, another surgeon managed to extricate the bullet. Yet the large wound festered intermittently for the remainder of his life.

Not until the eve of Grant's 1864 Overland Campaign could the army's best corps commander return to duty. A soldier noted that in the first engagement of the campaign, fought in the Wilderness of Virginia, Hancock's presence "was itself enough to inspire the troops to deeds of unmatched heroism." For much of the fighting to the outskirts of Petersburg, Hancock rode in an ambulance. The Second Corps took heavy losses at Cold Harbor and Ream's Station. By autumn, Hancock's wound had inflamed again. This ended his role in the Civil War.

The military's regard for Hancock showed when he was assigned to oversee the trial and execution of the four Lincoln conspirators. It was an ugly duty, especially since the general did not believe one of the condemned, Mary Surratt, was guilty.

In 1866, on Grant's recommendation, President Johnson placed Hancock in command of the Department of the Missouri, which included Missouri, Kansas, Colorado, and New Mexico. The general wished to pursue a moderate policy in negotiating with angry Cheyenne tribes. Hancock lived by the axiom "My politics are of a practical kind the integrity of the country, the supremacy of the Federal government, an honorable peace, or none at all." However, shortly after arrival at Fort Leavenworth, Hancock led an expedition to negotiate with Cheyenne and Sioux tribes. The "peace party" got off to a bad start by burning, for no reason, an abandoned Cheyenne village in central Kansas. The mission ended with relations worse than ever.

President Andrew Johnson, meanwhile, was embroiled in a personal feud with General Philip Sheridan. Late in 1867, Johnson transferred the volatile Sheridan to take Hancock's remote department, while Hancock was assigned to Sheridan's Louisiana-Texas district. Radical Republicans howled over Democrat Hancock's promotion. Hancock warned his friends that Radicals "will crucify me . . . I shall have [Johnson's] sympathy, but he is powerless to help me."

Sure enough, the following year Hancock was exiled to a virtual wilderness stretching from Minnesota to Montana. The general sought again to make peace with Native Americans. Yet a massacre of a Blackfoot band, plus settler encroachments in the Black Hills, in direct violation of the Treaty of Laramie, left both sides feeling contentious, with peace nowhere in sight.

This unhappy period for Hancock ended in 1872 with the death of General George Meade. Hancock became the senior major general in the Army. The war wound continued to be periodically infected, and he slowly mushroomed in size toward 300 pounds. He was assigned to duty in the populous Eastern states, which brought Hancock increasing attention as a potential presidential candidate.

Supported by Northern Democrats as well as Southerners who remembered his kindnesses during Reconstruction, Hancock became the 1880 Democratic candidate for president. His opponent, James Garfield, won by a scant margin of 7,000 votes out of 9,000,000 cast. Hancock refused to ask for a recount. "The true Christian spirit," he said, "is to forgive and forget."

In 1884, Hancock reinjured his bad leg and survived a large abscess. His last public act was to preside at Grant's funeral. A boil in the back of his neck developed into a carbuncle that resisted treatment. He died February 9, 1886, at Governors Island, New York. His death certificate listed malignant carbuncle and diabetes as causes of death. He was buried in Montgomery Cemetery in Norristown, Pennsylvania.

Hancock was an excellent soldier and gifted commander in the Civil War. Later, believing in the supremacy of civil over military government, he practiced a moderate rule in Reconstruction and paid a penalty for doing so. He seemed out of his element on the frontier and possibly too honest for high political office. Fortunately, "Hancock the Superb" is the image most remembered. As a Union private in the Second Corps wrote, "One felt safe when near him." ↝

PHILIP HENRY SHERIDAN

SCOURGE OF SOUTH AND WEST

AMID THE RAGING 1864 Battle of Spotsylvania in Virginia, a brigade of Union infantry stood motionless on a road behind the main line while regimental colonels speculated on what to do next. Suddenly a lone horseman galloped down the road from the front and began shouting orders for deployment of the units. The horseman was undersized and dark complexioned. He wore a funny felt hat with a floppy brim and talked brusquely. The infantry colonels snapped back, "Who are you, dictating orders like this?"

The horseman flipped up the brim of his hat so that his thick mustache and hard eyes could be seen. He barked, "Sheridan!" Immediately soldiers began forming into battle lines.

Philip Henry Sheridan possessed a belligerence in sharp contrast to his diminutive stature. He was unattractive, argumentative, and quick to anger, employing both profanity and fists. His pugnaciousness served him well during the Civil War, but his leadership during the Indian Wars displayed his merciless side in all its ugly coldness. He never made a secret of his sentiments about Native Americans: "The only good Indians I ever saw were dead."

Sheridan wanted to become a soldier so badly that he lied about his age to get into West Point. In his third year, he angrily attacked a fellow cadet, and the academy suspended him for a year. His hair-trigger temper earned him so many demerits that he almost failed to graduate.

Eight dreary years of frontier duty followed, in which Sheridan developed an intense dislike of the local tribes. He campaigned against them along the Rio Grande and into the Oregon Territory. Some sources claim that Sheridan developed diplomatic skills in dealing with the various tribes, but his taking an Indian mistress is the only clear evidence at hand.

By 1861 he had been a second lieutenant for eight years. He was initially assigned in the Civil War as General Henry Halleck's quartermaster. Then came action as colonel of the Second Michigan Cavalry. Sheridan's leadership in the western theater led five generals to petition the War Department: "Brigadiers scarce; good ones scarcer. He is worth his weight in gold." Sheridan received promotion to brigadier and transfer to the infantry.

His valor at Perryville, Stones River, and Missionary Ridge established a solid reputation for dependability. In 1864, Grant made the major general his cavalry chief in the Army of the Potomac. Sheridan promptly remolded the mounted brigades into a mobile and hard-hitting command that reflected his own temperament.

The 33-year-old general, at only five feet four inches tall, did not quite fill the normal model of a commander. Lincoln thought him "a brown, chunky little chap, with a long body, short legs, not enough neck to hang him, and such long arms that if his ankles itch he can scratch them without stooping."

In command of Grant's horsemen, Sheridan led a force around Lee's army and, in a running fight, killed Lee's cavalry chief, Jeb Stuart. Then Grant dispatched Sheridan to take 37,000 soldiers and neutralize the Shenandoah Valley, the "breadbasket of the Confederacy." Sheridan fought three major battles, and he used his superior numbers to roll over the opposition. The devotion of his soldiers shone brightly when they turned potential defeat into smashing victory at the Battle of Cedar Creek in October. Sheridan then followed orders to reduce a large portion of the Shenandoah to a wasteland where "a crow would have to carry his own" rations to survive the trip. He laid waste a portion of the valley with a methodical effectiveness that even Sherman could not claim.

Sheridan's reputation for ruthlessness invoked the fear and respect of troops and fellow officers.

A conspicuous figure in the final campaign against Lee, Sheridan broke the Southern position at Five Forks before placing his forces astride Lee's line of retreat south of Appomattox. That ended the fighting in Virginia.

The career of "Little Phil" thereafter entered an even stormier phase. In 1862 France had seized control of Mexico and installed Ferdinand Maximilian as emperor. With the end of the Civil War, the United States could finally turn its attention to this problem. Sheridan and 50,000 veteran soldiers were dispatched to the Rio Grande. Their object was to threaten the Maximilian government, and they succeeded. The French withdrew their troops, and in 1867 revolutionaries captured and executed Maximilian.

Sheridan next commanded the military department of Louisiana and Texas. He so harshly enforced Reconstruction policies that President Johnson had to replace him. Sheridan responded, "If I owned both Hell and Texas, I'd rent out Texas and live in Hell!"

In 1871 his regiments arrived to help contain the Great Chicago Fire. Sheridan acted the role of a dictator throughout the calamity, and his lack of personal feeling alienated many afflicted citizens.

Sheridan was then assigned command in the West. He applied to frontier warfare the total-war philosophy he had employed in 1864–65. He relentlessly pursued and killed warriors, burned villages, and sometimes left dead women and children in his wake. He ordered the senseless slaughter of four million buffalo to deny Indians both food and clothing. Survivors were herded to lands no settler wanted and converted into reservations.

In 1868–69, Sheridan waged a winning campaign against warring Cheyenne, Kiowa, and Comanche. Custer's death spurred Sheridan to full fury. He went after the Plains Indians and captured Chief Joseph. In 1886, Sheridan oversaw the surrender of Geronimo and the humiliation of the Apache. These brutal wars left a legacy of hatred on both sides.

Despite his extermination of the proud natives, Sheridan accomplished one positive good for the nation. The general blocked a large tract of highly desirable land from being sold to developers. Today the property is Yellowstone National Park.

Sheridan made frequent trips east to party with women. He married in 1875 and fathered five children. In 1883, William Sherman's retirement enabled Sheridan to become general in chief of the Army, but physical ailments soon forced his retirement. Excessive eating and lack of exercise contributed to his first heart attack at age 57. Subsequent seizures left him frail and emaciated. In August 1888, three days after completing his rather transparent memoirs, Sheridan died at his seaside home in Massachusetts. The attending physician put the cause of death as "disease of the mitral and aortic valves, originating in the line of duty." He was buried in Arlington National Cemetery.

One of his officers commented: "He was a wonderful man on the battlefield, and never in as good humor as when under fire. This presupposes, however, that everyone about was doing his duty as he deemed it should be done. If he judged the contrary, one might as well be in the path of a Kansas cyclone." ❧

THOMAS FRANCIS MEAGHER

IRISH TO THE END

H E CARRIED TO EXCESS the traditional Irish fondness for fighting and drinking. His military success peaked midway through the Civil War and declined rapidly thereafter. Yet his wayward efforts to tame part of the Wild West proved to be his final downfall.

Of aristocratic background, Thomas Francis Meagher studied law in England before joining the Irish revolutionary movement in the 1840s. He fought the English, designed the Irish tricolor that remains the country's flag, and came to America after escaping from a British prison. In steady progression, the young hero married the daughter of a wealthy merchant, edited a newspaper, and became the leader of New York City's Irish community.

Meagher viewed the Civil War as a threat to his adopted country. He began a wide-ranging recruitment of Irish immigrants who, like himself, envisioned service in the Union Army as training for a war to free their homeland from English rule.

In February 1862, Meagher received an appointment as brigadier general in command of the Irish Brigade, which was easily recognizable. The men wore sprigs of evergreen on their hats and bore emerald flags embroidered in gold and decorated with shamrocks as well as harps. The general himself

The Irish Brigade advances toward the Sunken Road
in the Battle of Antietam.

was a sight to behold. Heavyset, with a trimmed mustache and imperial, he wore a uniform of dark green with silver stars on black epaulets, plus a yellow silk scarf around his waist. He looked the part of a dashing Irish soldier, but he was also a heavy drinker. He bored easily and turned to whiskey often.

The Irish Brigade gained praise at the July 1862 Battle of Malvern Hill. Two months later came the bloodiest single day of the war at Antietam Creek, Maryland. Meagher was ordered to assault the Confederate center (known later as "Bloody Lane"). He mounted his white horse and bellowed, "Boys! Raise the colors and follow me!"

The Irishmen charged into a withering fire. Their assault collapsed after 940 soldiers had been killed or wounded. In the middle of the fighting, Meagher fell off his horse. Whether his mount was shot or he was drunk was never determined. One soldier observed that the general "regained his feet and floundered about, swearing like a crazy man."

In the lopsided Union defeat at Fredericksburg, only 280 of Meagher's troops survived the attacks. His brigade was down to 10 percent of its strength. Even so, his request to return to New York to rebuild his brigade was denied. The general angrily resigned from service. Meanwhile, criticism mounted that his drunkenness had produced the heavy casualties at Antietam and Fredericksburg. Meagher received further denunciation for being the only prominent Irish American to support Lincoln in the 1864 presidential election.

Among the postwar problems of the federal government was what to do with the Montana Territory. As the northernmost region of the Louisiana Purchase, the area held no attraction until the early 1860s. Then the discovery of gold and abundant grazing lands brought a small flood of settlers and in 1864 designation as a territory. For its first 16 months Montana did not have a territorial secretary to sign federal warrants. Hence, no funds could be spent.

President Andrew Johnson, sympathetic to Meagher's military and political exile, appointed him secretary and acting governor of Montana. What resulted, a state historian declared, was "one of the most chaotic periods in Montana political history."

Meagher arrived in Helena with an appetite for greater glory. What he found were hostile Native Americans, vigilante justice, and a legislature so dishonest that members were known to go out into the street and sell their votes to the highest bidder. What the region needed, Meagher confided to a friend, was "a strong infusion of . . . Celtic blood to counteract the acidity and poverty of its present population."

Initially, both political parties viewed Meagher as a friend. The secretary sided at first with Republicans; he then shifted to the more Irish-dominated Democratic Party. The Democrats wanted quick statehood. Republicans opposed the move because it was obvious that Montana lacked sufficient population.

Meagher and the Democrats held two legislative sessions and passed several measures. The legislation, one editor sneered, was "sired by the Acting One and damned by the people." Then the state's supreme court declared all the legislation null and void. Meagher responded by ignoring the court's decision whenever it suited him.

The governor spent hours in efforts to improve territorial affairs. He also spent hours in a drunken stupor. Late in 1866 a local attorney concluded, "Among decent men of all parties, [Meagher] is dead beyond hope of resurrection."

A possible escape from his woes came with the killing of a prominent settler by renegade Sioux warriors. Meagher thereupon concocted the illusion that murderous Indian raids were taking place all across Montana. This would draw soldiers to the area, and with a strong military arm present, Meagher would regain his military status while quelling his political opposition.

He secured permission to raise 800 volunteers. "Not an hour to be lost! . . . Danger is imminent!" he stated time after time in a steady stream of dispatches to departmental commander William Sherman in St. Louis.

In the months that followed, no fighting occurred, but Meagher's "army" ran up bills in excess of $1.1 million for uniforms, supplies, and equipment for scouting purposes. Disgusted, Sherman began to ignore Meagher's telegrams. A Montana editor called Meagher's war "the biggest humbug of the age."

By 1867 the state administration was floundering. Twice Meagher "lost" his father and required an "Irish wake" each time. The minutes of a House session stated, "The Legislature met today. The Governor very drunk." Another critic called the governor's office "a place of rendezvous for the vilest prostitution."

Meagher met a fitting end when in late June 1867 he boarded a vessel to go to Fort Benton for supplies. The Missouri River was swollen by spring rains and melting snow. On the night of July 1, Meagher was seen running wildly around the deck in his nightshirt. Presumably he fell overboard and drowned. The body was never recovered.

An equestrian statue, paid for mainly by Irish settlers, was erected in 1905 in front of the Montana Capitol. He is still considered a hero in his homeland and in many Irish-American communities. Yet the monument still stands alone. ✺

JAMES BUTLER HICKOK

"WILD BILL"

GOLD, SILVER, FERTILE LAND, and unlimited opportunities lured thousands of Americans to the West. As Federal troops cleared the indigenous tribes, towns appeared along trails spanning the Great Plains. Villages marked every mountain pass and road junction. In all of them, lawlessness ruled.

Such "earthly terrors" as Abilene, Dodge City, Tombstone, Deadwood, Tucson, and Santa Fe were stepping-stones for Western development. To those towns came "gunslingers": outlaws and killers whose raucous and cruel behavior has been liberally embellished by Hollywood movies and television series. For example, few of those gunmen were accurate shooters. Most were bullies who would never lay themselves open to a middle-of-the-street confrontation. Not one is remembered by his contemporaries as a fast draw who shot from the hip.

Nor were they the builders of the West, but rather the lawless rogues who preceded civilization. When the real builders—legitimate merchants and enterprising farmers—arrived and became the majority of the citizenry, the criminal element disappeared.

Two of the most notorious of this tough breed were the fictionalized creations of a pair of newspaper writers. Ned Buntline made a living legend of "Buffalo Bill" Cody. Buntline believed every story and took down every

A colorful rendering of "Wild Bill" immortalizes his renegade legacy.

word the self-promoting Cody said. Cody became an overnight sensation with his traveling circus, when in reality he never shot a man and was known mostly for his wanton slaughter of buffalo.

In like fashion, George W. Nichols manufactured the legend of "Wild Bill" Hickok. The gambler-gunman may have been "a wheezy old phony," as one critic labeled him, but Nichols crafted and recounted exploits that made Hickok one of the most feared names in the West. His habit of wearing two Colt revolvers with handles pointed to the front to permit "cross-draw" was his most familiar feature.

So much fiction surrounds James Butler Hickok that sifting truth from the passel of folklore is difficult. Born in Illinois in 1837, he moved to the

Kansas Territory while a teenager and began farming. He joined a free-state vigilante group—the Jayhawkers—and slowly gained a reputation for his hot temper and fast gun. He served briefly as a town constable and drove a stagecoach until the coming of the Civil War.

His first alleged killing of note was an 1861 encounter in which Hickok reputedly took on ten desperadoes of the McCanles gang and killed them all in an exchange of gunfire. In reality, the McCanles boys were simple farmers who had come to town to discuss a debt. Hickok shot Old Man McCanles and two passersby who got in the line of fire. Even worse, Hickok killed the three men not in an open fight but in an ambush.

Exactly what Hickok did in the Civil War is unclear. Turmoil raged in the Missouri-Kansas borderland throughout 1856–65. Hickok served first as a wagon master for Union forces near Sedalia, Montana, followed by a short stint as a lawman in Springfield, Missouri. Other sources assert that Hickok during 1862–64 was a Federal scout and spy. Only half that assertion could be true.

Wild Bill was too conspicuous in appearance to ever be an espionage agent. At a full six feet tall, with a heavy mustache and thick hair extending to his shoulders, he literally stood out in any crowd. The two revolvers worn backward would also have revealed his identity.

As for being a scout, Union patrols were always in search of guerrilla bands roaming at will. The most notorious was that of William Quantrill, called "the bloodiest man in American history" because of his take-no-prisoners policy toward soldiers and civilians alike. Hickok was familiar with the country and would have been a reliable scout.

By June 1865, Hickok was working as a gambler in Springfield. One observer at the time described him as "by nature a ruffian . . . a drunken, swaggering fellow, who delighted when 'on a spree' to frighten nervous men and timid women."

Despite his personal habits, Hickok spent several years as sheriff or marshal of various settlements in the Kansas-Missouri region. He wasted little time in verbal disputes before whipping out a gun. He shot men with disturbing frequency for violations of the law or simply because they made him mad.

In his first month as sheriff of Hays City, Kansas, the lawman killed two drunks for reasons that several witnesses claimed were unjustified.

Stories of his fighting prowess, planted by Nichols and embellished by others, multiplied with time. Hickok himself did nothing to diminish the attention. In one tale, he killed a large bear with his bare hands and a knife. And no man could match him in a gunfight.

Hickok was still serving as marshal when, in 1871, he became involved in a gunfight in which he accidentally shot his deputy in the stomach. That ended his career as a gunslinger. Thereafter, Hickok lived off his reputation of having slain 100 men without suffering a single injury.

By 1876 he was in the gold fields of the South Dakota Territory. There he met and had a relationship with Martha Jane Cannery, whose riding and shooting skills had earned her the name "Calamity Jane."

As his fame began to fade, so did his eyesight. Hickok displayed signs of glaucoma or ophthalmia, although his disclaimers claimed he was suffering from venereal disease. He was reduced to roaming the West as a traveling gambler. Several times he was arrested for vagrancy.

When Hickok played draw poker, he insisted on sitting with his back to the wall to observe all the action around him. Yet on August 2, the drifter joined a poker game already in progress, and the only available seat put his back to the door. Hickok was about to display a winning hand when former buffalo hunter Jack McCall walked up behind Hickok and shot the 39-year-old gambler in the head. Hickok's hand contained pairs of dark eights and aces, and today such dealt cards are known as a "dead man's hand."

For decades most Western movies were cartoons of real life. Indians attacking an encircled wagon train are killed but their horses ride safely away. The "bad guy" is shot by a large-caliber bullet and slumps slowly to the floor. The "good guy" fires a dozen rounds from a six-shot revolver and hits a target every time.

Much of this distortion stems from legends. Wild Bill Hickok was the first dime-novel hero of the Western era. As for the 36 men he actually killed, Hickok supposedly was confronting challengers of law and

The quintessential cowgirl "Calamity Jane" visits Hickok's grave.

well-being. Newspapers and pamphlets elevated him to a modern-day Robin Hood: a brave man eliminating evil in the taming of the West.

Hickok was a skilled gunfighter and gambler, and he achieved fame as a hard-nosed law enforcer. However, he provided more color than order to the towns he policed. People back East did not want to hear about the extermination of native tribes. They did not want to see the vicious cruelty of men scrabbling for whatever could be grabbed. Instead they wanted men like Wild Bill Hickok, a shining hero of the Wild West. ᴄͻ

CHAPTER 6

ONLY
THE GLORY
REMAINED

ONE CURIOUS PHENOMENON of any war is how many leaders during the struggle subside into obscurity afterward. History seems to call them forth for their moment in the limelight and then hurry them off the stage. Some of the most famous Northern figures in the Civil War fall into this category. Several were victims of circumstances, while others simply couldn't measure up to expectations. Several were wayward, while others were the souls of steadiness. Some had a long record of success before the war started. Whatever the reason, their moment of glory came—and went.

None of them suffered more than Mary Todd Lincoln. Widely disliked during the war, "the martyr's wife" found little comfort in the postwar years. She careened from one irrational outburst to another. The nadir of Mrs. Lincoln's life came when her son committed her to an asylum.

Timing worked against Winfield Scott. In 1861 he was considered America's second greatest soldier, just behind George Washington. Scott painstakingly devised a strategy for winning the war. Public opinion vetoed it as too elaborate for what was certain to be a short conflict. "Old Fuss and Feathers" was too aged and infirm to take any field command, yet three

OPPOSITE: *A composite illustration places Lincoln among the Union Army commanders.*

years later, General U. S. Grant adopted Scott's suggestions and squeezed the South from all sides.

Falling in this same camp is David Farragut. Already a dominant figure in the Navy, he would conquer all obstacles before him. He ran the forts at the mouth of the Mississippi and captured New Orleans. He would "damn the torpedoes!" at Mobile. Yet after the war, he quietly faded into his good night.

Sometimes it mattered not whether a general was erratic or stable. Falling in the former camp, "Fighting Joe" Hooker was one of the best of the Union corps commanders despite his debauched personal life. Yet his weakness of character ruined his one chance at leading an army with the disaster at Chancellorsville. Pride led to his resignation from the army, and he died in virtual obscurity 14 years after the war.

In contrast, George Meade was one of the most stable personalities in the war. He succeeded Hooker as head of the Army of the Potomac and led that force to the end of the war. Yet Meade was enduring the drudgery of departmental duties when he succumbed to pneumonia in 1872.

Another steady hand, George Thomas, may have been overly accustomed to taking orders to attain greatness. When the Virginia native remained in the Union Army after his state's secession, his relatives cut his limb from the family tree. Thomas knew no other occupation but the military. In the postwar years, he avoided avenues of potential fame to remain loyal to his duties.

It has been said that every person has but one chance to shine in his or her life. In the same way that certain individuals rise to a challenge, they can feel left without a purpose once the crisis has past. For these half-dozen individuals, the war represented a culmination of all that had come before, never to be matched afterward. ∽

MARY TODD
LINCOLN

THE WOES OF WIDOWHOOD

THE DEATH OF ABRAHAM LINCOLN wounded a nation, but far more so the woman who endured the fatal shooting. Mary Todd Lincoln had relied on her husband to withstand the tides of instability that frequently overwhelmed her. No person in the Civil War era had a higher climb—or deeper plunge—than she. During the last 20 years of her life, the losses she suffered proved too much.

Mary Todd was a member of the Kentucky slaveholding aristocracy. Twelve years of schooling made her one of the most educated women of the 19th century. She could be witty and vivacious, but she also had a stubborn streak, a passion for clothes, and outbursts of temper. Some later historians claimed she had bipolar disorder.

In 1829 she went to live with a sister in Springfield, Illinois. Future senator Stephen A. Douglas became one of her suitors, but she fell in love with Abraham Lincoln, a popular attorney nine years her senior. They wed in 1842, had four sons (one of whom died in infancy), and lived comfortably at the state capital.

At every step of the way, Mary encouraged her husband's ambitions. Any victory he won was a gain for her. He knew this. On the night in 1860 when he learned of his election as president of the United States, Lincoln rushed home and shouted, "Mary! Mary! We are elected!"

Mrs. Lincoln intended to be a first lady in every respect. Her clothing set the standard for women's fashions. Shopping expeditions to Philadelphia and New York produced a large wardrobe. To distract from her plainness, she wore overly elaborate gowns. One hostess remarked, "She stuns me with her low-necked dresses and the flower beds which she carries on top of her head." Her habit of overdressing, another socialite concluded, made her "the laughing stock of the town."

The dilapidated condition of the White House was not what a Kentucky blue blood expected, or what a president's wife should tolerate. Seeking the advice of no one, she bought custom-carved furniture, ornaments, carpets, and imported draperies. She oversaw wallpaper hanging and major carpentry. Staggering bills were casually forwarded to the Treasury Department. When Lincoln learned of the cost overruns, he was furious. There will be "a stink in the land" at such extravagance, he exclaimed, "when the poor freezing soldiers could not have blankets."

Mary reigned on an unsteady pinnacle of arrogance. Washington society never warmed to her for reasons other than her exorbitance. She was widely suspected of Southern loyalties because she had a brother and two half-brothers in Confederate service. The deaths of all three elicited no sympathy from Northerners.

Her strongly expressed opinions on political matters earned her the reputation of meddling in affairs that were not her business. She shocked people with indiscreet remarks, speaking out on policies and personalities with a cheerful disregard for consequences. She distrusted every member of the presidential Cabinet; to her, Secretaries William S. Seward and Salmon P. Chase were "little brief authority people."

Worst of all were her wild, sudden outbursts of temper, which seemed uncontrollable and, of course, were widely reported. The angry explosions that were pitched at the president exceeded all accepted decorum. As the war ground on, Mary became less assertive and thus terribly jealous of her husband. She could be a flirt around men, but she flew into a rage when a woman paid more than passing attention to the president. People came to dislike being in her presence. The only real friend she

A Brady photograph captures Mrs. Lincoln in her much criticized finery.

Booth pulls the trigger on a shot with epic reverberations.

had in Washington was Elizabeth Keckly, an ex-slave who was her maid and seamstress.

The question naturally rises: How did Lincoln endure it? Playwright Mark Van Doren suggested, "He did so by being the man he always was—reasonable, charitable, and very intelligent, with a deep longing for peace."

In February 1862, the Lincolns' 11-year-old son Willie died of typhoid fever. It was a crushing blow for Mary. Starting that day, she began to display true mental instability. She became an avid devotee of spiritualism, eagerly seeking to make contact with the lost child and believing that she did reach him on occasion.

Then came the evening of April 15, 1865, and a comedy staged at Ford's Theatre. Because Mrs. Lincoln had been so erratic of late, a dozen people declined invitations to sit in the presidential box. A young couple agreed to accompany the Lincolns. They were witness to the nation's first assassination of a chief executive.

Diarist Elizabeth Blair Lee wrote of the first lady two days later: "Mrs. Lincoln's condition is very pitiable—she has hysteria & has sometimes been very delirious." Anguish and unreality would fill the remaining 17 years of Mary Lincoln's life. Although Lincoln left a personal estate in excess of $100,000, and gifts of money flowed to the widow, she became obsessed with the idea that she was destitute.

Six weeks after the murder of her husband, Mary left the White House unnoticed and took refuge in a Chicago boardinghouse. She complained loudly about her homeless condition, the oversight of Republicans, honors going to other wartime heroes, and friends she thought were conspiring against her. Two years later, she created a scandal when she offered her wardrobe and jewelry for public sale.

Her son Robert, a rising young attorney in Chicago, took his mother abroad for three years. While she was gone, Congress (by a narrow margin) voted her a $3,000 pension. On the heels of that news came word of the death of her son Tad. Staggering from another crushing blow, Mary thereafter became even more unpredictable and sometimes wild. Laudanum often was her crutch. On one occasion, she arrived panic-stricken in Chicago from a trip to Florida. Robert was dead, she screamed. Someone had tried to poison her on the train, and "a wandering Jew" had stolen her purse. None of the charges was true. In 1875 she attempted to jump out a window to escape a nonexistent fire, forcing Robert to have his mother declared insane. She was institutionalized for three months.

Mary Lincoln returned to Springfield to live with her sister. She made aimless trips to Europe before settling into a paranoid state at home. Usually she could be found in a darkened room, dressed in widow's clothing. Cataract problems restricted her vision, and a fall from a ladder injured her spine and limited her movements. On July 16, 1882, she died from a stroke suffered the previous day.

From an exuberant girlhood, through the unhappy war years, to the bleak meanderings of her widowhood, Mary Lincoln experienced the full range of emotions life has to offer. In the end at least, she had the comfort of being placed beside the man who had loved her most. ✑

WINFIELD SCOTT

"OLD FUSS AND FEATHERS"

WINFIELD SCOTT WAS THE FIRST truly professional soldier in the American military establishment and the hero of two wars, the War of 1812 and the Mexican War. By 1861 he was a lieutenant general, a rank attained by only one other man, George Washington. That spring, with another war beginning, the lumbering general in chief was actually older than the half-built federal capital he was trying to save.

Scott was born on a farm near Petersburg, Virginia, a year after the Constitution was ratified. He briefly attended the College of William and Mary and spent another year studying law. A quest for glory led him to the Army. In 1808, President Thomas Jefferson appointed Scott a captain of artillery. The War of 1812 offered him an opportunity for leadership, and he won national attention for his exploits. One came in the Canadian Campaign at the Battle of Chippewa, when the Virginian led a bayonet charge that shattered the British line. He emerged from the war as the youngest general in service.

For the next two decades Scott sought diligently to instill more professionalism in the Army. He wrote the first comprehensive set of Army regulations as well as America's first infantry tactical manuals. Yet his professional knowledge was of limited value in the military campaigns against the Seminole and Cherokee tribes. Scott was also in charge of the "Trail of Tears," when Native Americans in the East were driven to barren reservations in the Oklahoma region. In 1841, he was promoted to the rank of general in chief of the nation's military forces.

The Mexican War was his crowning achievement. He displayed skillful planning and execution as he led his numerically inferior army from one victory to another. More than 100 Civil War generals served under him in the conquest of Mexico. Robert E. Lee and George B. McClellan were members of his staff.

By then Scott was known as "Old Fuss and Feathers," a nickname earned from his strict adherence to discipline, frequent disputes with subordinate officers and civilian superiors, and his ornate uniforms replete with gold sash, gleaming sword, sprawling shoulder epaulets, and cocked hat.

His fame catapulted him toward the presidency. For the 1852 election, Democrats nominated dark-horse candidate Franklin Pierce. The Whigs split into Northern and Southern wings. Scott won the nomination on the 53rd ballot, but he was so badly defeated that the Whig Party thereafter ceased to exist. Into the vacuum stepped the Republican Party.

When the Civil War opened with the April 1861 bombardment of Fort Sumter, South Carolina, the General was asked to cast his lot with his native Virginia. He thundered, "I have served my country . . . for more than fifty years, and so long as God permits me to live, I will defend that flag with my sword, even if my native State assails it!"

Those were high-flown words from an incapacitated source. By then Scott was Washington's most imposing monument: a mountain of a man eroded and crumbling with age. He stood six feet five inches tall. Age, infirmities, and an epicurean appetite had ballooned his frame beyond 300 pounds. In addition, after decades of field service, he had a fractured collarbone, bruises from a spent cannonball, a broken shoulder, yellow fever, and protracted bouts with dysentery. In 1861 he was also afflicted with vertigo, gout, rheumatism, and dropsy. Scott couldn't walk even a short distance without effort. He was unable to ride a horse to inspect soldiers, much less to lead them into battle. His sterling reputation and his stout old heart were all he could place at the government's disposal.

For 16 hours a day, Scott sat at his desk while trying to corral an army together and to find a way to suppress what he considered a serious rebellion. He soon developed a wide-ranging plan. Naval forces would blockade three sides of the Southern states; Union armies would mass all along the northern border of the Confederacy. Constant pressure on all sides would suffocate the enemy and bring an end to the uprising.

When newspaperman Horace Greeley heard of Scott's strategy, he sneeringly dismissed it as the "Anaconda Plan." The idea of a huge snake slowly squeezing the life out of the seceded states struck many Northerners as tedious, ungallant, and unnecessary. The strategy had no dash in it, nothing to stir the pulse. Its execution would take too long in a war that, many believed, one battle was going to decide.

Scott's proposal was shelved. Three years later, though, General U. S. Grant resurrected and implemented the plan. The strategy of using its superior numbers forcefully won the war for the North.

Public clamor for battle in the late spring of 1861 forced the general against his will to send an unorganized army into northern Virginia. After the debacle at the Battle of First Manassas, it was ironically Scott who picked and called General George McClellan to come to Washington to take command of the army. McClellan's vast reorganization left no place for Scott. The new field commander warned openly that if "the old General in his dotage . . . cannot be taken out of my path, I shall ... resign and let the administration take care of itself."

In October 1861, Scott submitted his resignation. "I have become an encumbrance to the army as well as to myself," he told Lincoln. Following a brief trip to Europe, Old Fuss and Feathers settled in New York City. He worked diligently on his memoirs. Unfortunately, his recollections of events 50 years earlier were clearer than those of recent years. An imbalance of material and faint pomposity marred the two volumes that were eventually published.

Steadily declining health ended with his death on May 29, 1866, two weeks short of his 80th birthday. President Johnson ordered all flags nationwide lowered to half-mast on the funeral day. Scott was buried at West Point, a school he always wished he could have attended. ∾

"The Hercules of the Union," Scott slays "the great dragon of secession" in an 1860 cartoon.

DAVID GLASGOW FARRAGUT

BETTER AT SEA

N INETY PERCENT of David Glasgow Farragut's life belonged to the U.S. Navy. Born in eastern Tennessee, he spent his early years in New Orleans. The death of his mother from yellow fever compelled his father, a naval officer, to search for someone with whom he could place his young children. Commodore David Porter answered his friend's request and became the boy's guardian. In 1812 the lad—whose first name was James—adopted the name David in honor of his foster father.

At the age of nine, Farragut entered the Navy as a midshipman. His first duty was that of a powder monkey. He saw action in the War of 1812 and was slightly wounded while a crewman on the well-known U.S.S. *Essex.* Farragut received additional battle experience against West Indies pirates in the 1820s and fought in the Mexican War. In 1853, Commodore Farragut oversaw construction of a naval station on Mare Island in the San Francisco Bay. It became the port for all ship repairs on the West Coast.

For 30 years Farragut made his home in Norfolk, Virginia. He was a kindly man whose conversations and sense of humor won him many civilian as well as military friends. On his birthday he would customarily do handsprings to demonstrate that he still retained his youth.

The Civil War uprooted Farragut from his longtime home. Before he left, he warned his neighbors, "You fellows will catch the Devil before you get through this business." He moved his family to a New York City suburb and awaited orders.

He received a disappointing assignment to the Navy Retirement Board. Government officials harbored doubts about Farragut's loyalty, given his long residency in Virginia. Yet Secretary of the Navy Gideon Welles had long admired Farragut for his unorthodox amphibious attack against Veracruz in the Mexican War. Welles recognized the self-confidence and audacity in the man, asserting that Farragut "will take more risks to obtain great results than any officer in either army or navy."

In December 1861, Farragut received orders naming him flag officer of the West Gulf Blockading Squadron. He departed Hampton Roads on his flagship, U.S.S. *Hartford,* a 24-gun screw steamer. With 16 other vessels, he was ordered to attack New Orleans, the largest city and most important port in the Confederacy.

Farragut welcomed the challenge. A half century in the Navy had in no way rendered him a fossil. He was supple and buoyant, possessing both an old man's understanding of the use of sea power and a young man's willingness to be daring. Farragut never considered the possibility of losing. "Any man who is prepared for defeat," he wrote to his wife, "would be half defeated before he commenced. I hope for success, shall do all in my power to secure it, and trust to God for the rest."

A newspaperman with Farragut at the time described him as "about five feet eight inches high, slightly inclined to corpulency and evidently of a strong physique. His complexion is florid, face round and beardless . . . his forehead high and broad; head large and partially bald; eyes hazel gray with a strabismus in one, which lends additional fire to the other, and features regular and pleasant."

Farragut was a good executive and careful planner. The naval expedition began in mid-April 1862, when his ships blasted their way past two Confederate bastions near the mouth of the Mississippi. One officer likened the roar of exchanging artillery fire as "all the earthquakes in the world and all the thunder and lightning storms together, in the space of two miles, all going off at once."

The flotilla successfully ran the gauntlet and steamed unmolested to New Orleans. On April 26, 1862, Farragut accepted the surrender of the town. His triumph came at a time when the North badly needed a victory. Gaining control of both the "Father of Waters" and the South's largest port brought Farragut promotion to rear admiral, a rank never before used in the Navy.

His attempt two months later to gain control of the Confederate stronghold of Vicksburg failed in great measure because his seagoing vessels had deep drafts and kept running aground in the often low river. For the next two years, the new admiral provided naval assistance to army operations along the Mississippi. Farragut was cooperating with General Nathaniel Banks in the siege of Port Hudson, Louisiana, when the two officers held a conference. Over a bottle of wine, Farragut raised his glass and said, "General, we came here to die. It is our business and must happen sooner or later. We must fight this thing out until there is no more than one man left, and that man must be a Union man. Here's to his health."

Farragut experienced his greatest success in the summer of 1864. Mobile, Alabama, was the Confederacy's last major port on the Gulf of Mexico. It was heavily defended by three strategically planned land forts, "torpedoes" (mines) at the entrance to the harbor, the ironclad C.S.S. *Tennessee,* and a half dozen small gunboats. Farragut's fleet of 14 wooden warships formed a double column, with four *Monitor*-type ironclads in the van. The admiral had little respect for metal-armored vessels, which he dismissed as "damned tea-kettles." But they operated better than wooden vessels did in shallow water.

On the windless, hot morning of August 5, the Union fleet attacked. The ironclads passed through the breakwater as Farragut's warships dueled with shore batteries. Suddenly ironclad U.S.S. *Tecumseh* struck a mine and sank swiftly. The advance of the entire fleet, now under fire, began to slow. Farragut, lashed to the rigging of the *Hartford,* where he could observe better, saw the lead vessels floundering. "What's the trouble?" the admiral yelled through a megaphone.

"Torpedoes!" came the reply.

"Damn the torpedoes!" Farragut shouted. "Full steam ahead!"

Farragut's flotilla pushes through wreckage in this rendering of the battle on the Mississippi River.

Union ships pounded their way into the harbor, overpowered the *Tennessee* and its consorts, and seized the port, while Federal soldiers occupied the three abandoned forts. The success came dear: 145 sailors killed, 174 wounded, a monitor lost, and several vessels badly damaged. In the general Northern discontent of that summer, what Farragut had done did not seem as impressive as it would when combined with the fall of Atlanta the next month and the destruction of the Shenandoah Valley in October.

Honors came steadily to Farragut thereafter. In December 1864, he received another newly created rank—that of vice admiral. Cheering crowds greeted him whenever he appeared in public. The admiral served as a pallbearer at Lincoln's funeral. On July 26, 1866, Farragut became the first American naval officer to hold the rank of full admiral, a lifetime appointment. He never retired from the Navy.

Dispatched in 1867 to command the European Squadron, he was feted with honors by several heads of state. On August 14, 1871—a month after performing his annual handsprings, Farragut was inspecting facilities at Portsmouth, New Hampshire, when he died suddenly of a heart

A Navy man for life, Farragut was the first to earn the noble rank of full admiral.

attack. President Grant led an estimated 10,000 soldiers and sailors who marched in the funeral procession. Farragut was buried in New York City's Woodlawn Cemetery.

Unknowingly, the 19th century's most famous naval officer wrote his own epitaph. In a letter to his wife just prior to the attack on New Orleans, he stated, "He who dies doing his duty to his country, and is at peace with his God, has played out the drama of life to the best advantage." ℘

JOSEPH HOOKER

THE MANY BATTLES
OF "FIGHTING JOE"

BY HIS 1837 GRADUATION from West Point, Joseph Hooker had already gained a reputation for being independent and outspoken. The Massachusetts native went on to display aggressive leadership in fighting the Seminoles in Florida and then the Mexicans. Unluckily for him, that pugnacious side extended into his dealings with his superiors. During the Mexican War, he sided with General Gideon Pillow in an argument with General in Chief Winfield Scott.

Scott also disliked Hooker's well-known fondness for heavy drinking and frequent womanizing, a feeling shared by Civil War notables Henry Halleck, U. S. Grant, and William Sherman. Hooker did not get an Army commission until after Scott retired in the autumn of 1861.

Instead he left the Army in 1855 to pursue farming in California. It was a failed venture, and as one authority wrote, Hooker "descended almost to the level of beachcomber." Nonetheless, newly appointed General George McClellan assigned him a brigade in the Army of the Potomac. Hooker's regiments subsequently became known for valor and high casualties. Reporters dubbed him "Fighting Joe," a title Hooker loathed because, he said, "people will think I am a highwayman or a bandit." He continued to be a first-rate combat officer until he was shot in the foot at the 1862 Battle of Antietam.

Hooker's scheming side emerged once again during his four months of convalescence in Washington. Openly seeking command of the army, he plotted against first McClellan and then Ambrose Burnside, McClellan's successor. At one point Hooker even asserted, "Nothing will go right [until the country] has a dictator, and the sooner the better."

Simply because Lincoln had no one else to put in the hapless Burnside's place, Hooker in January 1863 was given the command. A Michigan soldier made an astute remark about the choice: "We all feel that General Hooker will be like the poor man that won the elephant at the raffle. After he got the animal he did not know what to do with him."

At least Hooker looked the part, with an "Apollo-like presence." Six feet tall, strongly proportioned, with an unshaven face and large blue eyes, he smiled often and acted with boldness. However, a fellow officer added, "his defects, like evil angels, walked by him always."

The major general still had an insatiable appetite for whiskey and women. At no time was he a favorite among his fellow officers. Grant thought him "ambitious to the extent of caring nothing for the rights of others." A stuffy New Englander stated that Hooker's headquarters was a place to which no gentleman cared to go, and to which no lady would go. (Contrary to myth, Hooker did not give birth to the word "hooker" as a synonym for "prostitute." The meaning was in popular use years before he became a public figure.)

Yet Hooker's command breathed new life into the Army of the Potomac. Furloughs, back pay, good equipment, unit badges, and other moves to create higher morale turned the North's premier army into a finely tuned, 130,000-man force. His brilliant strategy to attack Lee's Confederate Army from two directions in May 1863 came to within the doorstep of triumph. Then Hooker inexplicably paused at Chancellorsville, a crossroads junction in the densely wooded Wilderness of Virginia.

Lee the flanked abruptly turned into Lee the flanker. A surprise, overwhelming counterattack by General Stonewall Jackson's corps rolled up the Union Army. When the smoke cleared four days later, Hooker had been soundly beaten.

Transfer to the western theater followed. In spite of the distrust of his superiors, Fighting Joe again proved a skillful corps commander in the

*Columbia, the early Lady Liberty, lambastes Lincoln and Stanton
for appointing Hooker to command in an 1862 Nast cartoon.*

campaigns from Chattanooga to Atlanta. After the fall of Atlanta, however, Sherman promoted General Oliver Howard—whom Hooker pointedly blamed for the disaster at Chancellorsville since his wing was the one Jackson had overrun—to army command over Hooker. In a rage, Hooker resigned from Sherman's forces. General George Meade's chief of staff, Colonel Theodore Lyman, saw Hooker at this low period: "Was much disappointed in his appearance; there is a great want of character about his mouth, and, in addition, he was shaky about the legs, red in the face and had a boiled eye, like one who had been on a great spree."

In September 1864, Lincoln named Hooker commander of the Northern Department. It embraced the states of Ohio through Michigan, with headquarters in Cincinnati, and consisted of scattered reserve troops. This gave Hooker ample opportunity to defend his indecision in the Chancellorsville calamity. His efforts were successful, for in the spring of 1865, the Congressional Committee on the Conduct of the War found

Hooker blameless in the defeat. Hooker felt exonerated, but public opinion never agreed.

While "pursuing justice," the 50-year-old general wed Olivia Groesbeck, from one of Cincinnati's most prominent families. Their marriage was short-lived because of mutual ill health. Hooker suffered a stroke a month after his marriage. His wife's health deteriorated steadily thereafter, and she died three years later, in 1868.

Hooker had charge of the Lincoln funeral train, and he led the procession at the May 4 interment in Springfield, Illinois. In November of that year, while at a reception for Grant, Hooker had a stroke, which reduced him to a cripple who could sign his name only by guiding the pen with both hands.

A second stroke forced his retirement from the Army. Assisted by attendants and a cane, he traveled frequently to address veterans groups. He put on weight, his hair grayed, and he displayed his worst fault by publicly criticizing his army superiors. Grant "had no more moral sense than a dog"; Sherman was "crazy" and "possessed of no more judgment than a child"; Oliver Howard "would command a prayer meeting with a great deal more ability than he would an army."

Hooker followed trend by beginning to write his memoirs, but they were never completed. On October 31, 1878, he died of "paralysis of the heart" and was buried in Cincinnati's Spring Grove Cemetery.

For all his efforts to clear his name, Hooker had made a telling admission only a few weeks after the debacle at Chancellorsville. One of Hooker's few friends, General Abner Doubleday, asked Hooker what really went wrong in the battle. Hooker paused for a moment, and then answered: "I lost confidence in Joe Hooker, and that is all there is in it."

For once, the man was sincere. ∾

GEORGE GORDON MEADE

THE UNINSPIRED COMMANDER

THE DAY AFTER SURRENDERING HIS ARMY at Appomattox, General Robert E. Lee was riding to his headquarters when he met a mounted Federal party. At its head was General George Gordon Meade, commander of the Army of the Potomac. Lee at first did not recognize his longtime prewar friend. "What are you doing with all that gray in your beard?" Lee asked.

Meade shot back, "You have to answer for most of it!"

That was one of the few recorded exhibitions of wit on Meade's part.

He was the last commander of the North's premier Army of the Potomac, and he had the longest tenure of those who led the host. In the climactic 1864–65 fighting, he was overshadowed by the presence of General In Chief Ulysses Grant. Still, he was the "Old Reliable" of Union commanders.

The son of an American merchant, he was born in Spain on New Year's Day 1815. His widowed mother secured him a free education at West Point, from which he graduated in the middle of his class. Meade devoted himself to being a professional soldier and served as a topographical engineer to General Zachary Taylor in the Mexican War. In succeeding years, Meade built a solid reputation for engineering work on lighthouses, breakwaters, and coastal surveys. This led to early appointment in 1861 as a brigadier general at the head of a Pennsylvania brigade.

On June, 30, 1862, at the Battle of Glendale, Virginia, Meade received a wound from which he never recovered. A bullet entered the right side of his body. Hours later, a surgeon probed for the projectile, but this proved too painful for the general. The bullet was never removed and thereafter gave him periodic discomfort. His recurring bouts of pneumonia suggest damage to a lung.

Meade displayed underpublicized gallantry at Antietam and again at Fredericksburg, where his division alone temporarily punctured General Stonewall Jackson's line. Six months later, in the middle of the night, Meade was awakened and told to take command of the army. He tried to refuse the directive, claiming that other generals were more capable than he. Reminded that the directive was an order, not a request, Meade acquiesced. "Well, I've been tried and condemned without a hearing, and I suppose I shall have to go to execution."

Though a steady combat officer, Meade lacked the ability to inspire his troops. Tall, thin, bespectacled, he reminded soldiers of a clergyman or a college professor. His sad eyes were sunken and large. A habitual frown caused bagginess under his eyes. His deep streak of humility contrasted with a violent, uncontrollable temper. His chief of staff once observed, "I don't know of any thin old gentleman . . . who, when he is wrathy, exercises less of Christian character." Down in the ranks, the enlisted men called him "a damned old goggle-eyed snapping turtle."

Three days after his appointment to army command, the Union Army was drawn into the bloodiest battle of the war: Gettysburg. The fighting lasted three long days, and the army suffered more than 23,000 casualties before gaining victory. It was an exhausting experience for Meade. "From the time I took command till today, now over ten days," he confided to his wife, "I have not changed my clothes, have not had a regular night's rest and many nights not a wink of sleep, and for several days did not even wash my face and hands, no regular food, and all the time in a great state of mental anxiety."

Lincoln criticized Meade for not pursuing Lee's crippled forces, whereupon the testy commander tendered his resignation. The president moved speedily to placate his general, and Meade dutifully continued to lead

Meade's professorial mien failed to stir enthusiasm among troops.

the army. That lasted until the spring of 1864, when the new general in chief, Ulysses Grant, opted to lead the main army into battle rather than operate from behind a desk in Washington. Grant's arrival contracted the chain-of-command structure. To Meade's credit, of the four generals who led the Army of the Potomac, he was the only one who quietly accepted the subordinate role to which he was relegated. He wasn't even present at Lee's surrender in the McLean House.

Philadelphians nevertheless gave Meade a lavish welcome on his 1865 return home. Harvard presented him with a doctorate in law. He remained silent as the exploits of Grant and Sherman filled newspapers, magazines, and public attention. He refused to write his memoirs. During the war he had made too many enemies among Republicans and the press to hope for charity from either. (His prickliness reached a peak in the war years when he had a newspaperman drummed out of camp wearing a large sign around his neck with the word "Liar!" in bold letters.)

As the nation's fourth-ranking general in the postwar years, Meade commanded several military departments. One was the Division of the Atlantic, with headquarters in Atlanta. Meade worked hard to bring reconciliation

*Meade's blouse, hat, sword belt, sash, and presentation weapons
appear well preserved.*

between North and South. Former Confederate generals William J. Hardee and John B. Gordon became close friends. As Meade prepared to depart for home, an Atlanta congregation saluted him with a resolution declaring, "We shall remember you as an honest, merciful, and liberal Christian gentleman."

Meade's old battle wound continued to plague him. He survived two attacks of pneumonia in the postwar period. A third onset, coupled with jaundice, led to his death on November 6, 1872. After a huge military funeral, he was buried in Philadelphia's Laurel Hill Cemetery. His tombstone reflects his modesty: "He did his work bravely and is at rest."

His most enduring monument is Fort George G. Meade, midway between Washington and Baltimore. Established in 1917, the installation is headquarters for the National Security Agency, Defense Information Systems, and U.S. Cyber Command. These installations, like Meade himself, perform dutifully and without fanfare. ∽

GEORGE HENRY THOMAS

"THE ROCK OF CHICKAMAUGA"

GENERALS GEORGE HENRY THOMAS and James Longstreet had a great deal in common. Both were Southern-born graduates of West Point (Thomas was two years ahead of Longstreet), massive in size, senior corps commanders in their respective armies, and controversial in their Civil War careers. That's because the two officers were methodical rather than aggressive. While each was outstanding on defense and showed little predilection for offensive maneuvers, each was also capable of a hammering assault at the appropriate moment.

In 1831, Thomas was a teenager with a widowed mother and four siblings when Nat Turner's bloody slave uprising swept toward his home in Southampton, Virginia, near Norfolk. The family managed to flee to safety. However, the massacre had no effect on the boy's opposition to human bondage.

At the advanced age of 20, he entered West Point, where William T. Sherman was one of his roommates and "Sam" Grant and Braxton Bragg were among his close friends. Upon graduation, Thomas was assigned to the artillery. He gained three brevet promotions for gallantry against the Seminoles and the Mexicans. In 1853 he returned to West Point to teach artillery and cavalry tactics. Thomas's large size led cadets to refer to him as "Old Slow Trots"—the first of several nicknames he would receive.

Secretary of War Jefferson Davis determined in the mid-1850s to create an elite unit in the Army, the Second U.S. Cavalry. A. Sidney Johnston was appointed colonel; Robert E. Lee, lieutenant colonel. Thomas was picked to be major. He termed the duty as the happiest of his life.

In November 1860, the major was traveling through Virginia on a nighttime train when it stopped at Lynchburg for water. Thomas disembarked to stretch his legs. He thought he was stepping down to the roadbed when, in fact, a deep depression yawned below him. He tumbled some 25 feet and badly wrenched his back. He never fully recovered from the injury.

During his period of recuperation Thomas had to make the same critical decision about his future as other Virginian officers. His close colleague, Robert E. Lee, opted to follow his home state into the Confederacy. Thomas chose to remain with the Union. His sisters at home immediately turned his portrait to the wall, destroyed all correspondence with his name on it, and never made contact with him again—except to request that Thomas change his name.

His Southern background initially created distrust among some Federal authorities. Thomas was passed over more than once for assignments and promotions. A strong feeling existed that no Southerner should ever hold a general's rank in the Union armies.

Nevertheless, in the summer of 1861 he received appointment as a brigadier general and an assignment to Cincinnati. "With a deceptive air of unhurried calm," Thomas organized a well-trained and confident force. His soldiers called him "Old Pap." In January 1862, in spite of mud and freezing temperatures, the general gained a victory over a small Confederate force at Mill Spring, Kentucky. It was the first Union success since the Federal rout at Manassas. Thomas emerged with the reputation as a commander who could win.

Promotion to major general followed. Thomas led one wing of the Union Army under General Don Carlos Buell. That autumn, Lincoln removed Buell for indecisiveness and picked Thomas as the successor, but the Virginian declined. Buell's offensive plans were well advanced,

*The Army of the Cumberland's triumph is hard-won
at the Battle of Chickamauga.*

Thomas explained, and it would be inappropriate to replace him on the eve of battle. Lincoln withdrew the order.

Thomas's courtesy was not widely praised. Some thought him of the same mold as his army superior. A Chicago reporter wired his editor, "Thomas is a slower man than Buell. It takes Thomas half an hour to say no." Throughout the war Thomas was known as a general who shunned self-promotion but was methodical to a fault—going so far as to assign seats to staff officers at dinners. Even Grant laughed at a popular camp statement: "Thomas is too slow to move and too brave to run away."

The general spent a year molding a force that became the Army of the Cumberland. His soldiers displayed gallantry at the battles at Stones River and Chickamauga, where Thomas's immovable stand caused General James Garfield to give him his most lasting sobriquet: "The Rock of Chickamauga." Thomas continued his triumphs the following year by all but destroying the Confederate Army of Tennessee at the battles at Franklin and Nashville.

*Commanding in stature, Thomas is considered one of the Union's
great—but underrated—strategists.*

Public and press hailed Thomas, but the high command did not. As
the battered Confederate Army limped away from Nashville, Grant complained that Thomas's "sluggishness" prevented him from "going for the
kill." A permanent chasm developed between the two men.

In peacetime, Thomas sought to reconcile with his family in Virginia,
to no avail. He declined several offers to enter the political arena. Because

of a short temper and devotion to honesty, he announced, "I have no taste for politics."

Thomas commanded the Military Department of Tennessee for two years and worked hard to protect freedmen from white abuses. He similarly created a military commission to enforce labor contracts that local courts were ignoring.

In a political move, President Johnson submitted Thomas's name for promotion to lieutenant general to replace Grant in 1868. Thomas refused the offer. "My services since the war," he replied, "do not merit such a compliment, and it is now too late for it to be regarded as a compliment if conferred for services during the war."

Thomas sought and received command of the Department of the Pacific. He not only made no attempt to record his wartime memoirs but also destroyed his private papers because he did not want his "life hawked in print for the eyes of the curious."

By 1870, he had clogged arteries from overeating and underexercising and his weight had ballooned to 245 pounds. That's when Thomas read a *New York Tribune* article in which General John Schofield was credited with winning the Battle of Nashville. At last, Thomas took pen in hand to make a strong rebuttal. On March 28, halfway through writing his letter, Thomas said calmly, "I want air." He then slumped to the floor, dead from a stroke.

Among the huge assemblage at his funeral in Troy, New York, were Generals Grant, Sherman, Sheridan, and Meade, although no member of the Thomas family was in attendance. A sister told her neighbor, "Our brother George died to us in 1861."

His legacy has never died, however. His staunch bravery and well-trained troops prevented disaster at several of the most momentous battles of the war. Some rank him as the third greatest Union general, behind only Grant and Sherman. He never would have accorded himself that honor, however. Thomas was content in the postwar era to keep on carrying out his duties in the same self-effacing manner with which he had served his country so well. ᘓ

THE WORKING-MAN'S BANNER.

FOR PRESIDENT. FOR VICE-PRESIDE

TANNERY

ULYSSES S. GRANT HENRY WILSO

"The Galena Tanner" *"The Natick Shoemaker"*

CHAPTER 7

FROM THE

FRONT LINES

TO THE CAPITOL

W inston Churchill once observed: "Politics are almost as exciting as war, and quite as dangerous. In wartime one can only be killed once, but in politics many times." While Ulysses Grant proved this adage most consistently during his two terms as president, a host of other Union veterans fit the bill after the war. That may be because the qualities required by a commander do not work as well in the more nuanced art of persuading voters.

That divide was not on the minds of the citizens in the North when their soldiers returned home. Each state had heroes with well-known exploits, and their instant name recognition worked as well back then as it does today. How well they served in public office proved to be another matter altogether.

A prime example of a soldier turned politician is George McClellan, who created the North's premier army and then was fired for not employing it more in battle. He did not even wait until after the war to switch his coats. Disgruntled by his dismissal, he became the Democratic candidate who ran unsuccessfully against Lincoln in the 1864 presidential election. He went on to serve an unimpressive stint as the governor of New Jersey.

OPPOSITE: *Grant's Republican presidential poster signals the start of a new career.*

Affable Ambrose Burnside followed a lackluster Civil War career by serving three terms as governor of Rhode Island. He eventually gained election to the U.S. Senate but died after a few months at the post. The likable "Old Burn" might have risen higher had he possessed more faith in his own abilities. In contrast, Daniel Sickles was a Tammany Hall politician in every negative sense of the phrase. He contributed a leg to the Civil War, which should have made him a hero, but spent his last years as a suspected embezzler.

The path did not always lead from the battlefield to the podium. Abraham Lincoln appointed a number of high-ranking political figures as generals in the army. The rationale was that the war would be short and the political generals thereafter would feel indebted for receiving generals' stars. Lincoln's selections in almost every case proved to be liabilities.

Benjamin Butler had a terrible war record, but he was a powerful Lincoln ally, so he was continually sent to battle. He went on to serve a postwar term in Congress, where his futility held steady. He ran for Massachusetts governor 11 times before winning election.

Judson Kilpatrick's Union cavalrymen called him "Kill Cavalry" for good reason. His insatiable sexual appetite made him unelectable to public office. Yet presidential appointments as ambassador to Chile kept him in politics—albeit at a healthy distance from Washington. Another political appointee, Oliver Howard, could not have been more different. The highly religious general wasn't so successful in war, but his stewardship of the Freedmen's Bureau after the war was admirable. Among all the corruption of carpetbaggers in the South, Howard earnestly tried to secure the rights to land and education for freed slaves.

One of the most quoted of Union generals was Lawrence Chamberlain. The militarily untutored college professor gained fame several times in the war. Afterward, Chamberlain won landslide victories as governor of Maine. In his case, unhealed war wounds and academic feuds during his presidency of Bowdoin College prevented him from rising higher in the political constellation.

*The Army of the Potomac marches along Pennsylvania Avenue
in Washington, D.C., to celebrate the end of war.*

Though all were tested on the same anvil of battle, these men showed colorfully different fortunes in higher office. Sometimes they brought the same virtues or vices to war as they did to peace. Sometimes what made them failures in war made them successful in peace. Either way, their fame would vault them in public office, where they were put on public display. ☙

GEORGE
BRINTON
MCCLELLAN
MORE TALK THAN ACTION

N O CIVIL WAR GENERAL INSPIRED MORE passion and controversy than George Brinton McClellan. None augured more
promise and delivered fewer results.

Born to well-to-do parents in Philadelphia, the intellectually gifted
McClellan attended the University of Pennsylvania for two years. He
did so well in his studies that West Point waived the age requirement
and admitted him as a cadet at the age of 15. The teenager graduated
second in the famous Class of 1846, which eventually contained 21
general officers.

Engineering skills brought McClellan two brevets in the Mexican
War. For a decade thereafter he was one of the Army's most brilliant
minds. He invented the McClellan saddle and the pup tent, in addition
to translating two French manuals on bayonet techniques. The War
Department chose him to observe the Crimean War and to record his
observations and suggestions for American army use. When military
life contained no other challenges, McClellan resigned from service.
By 1860 he was living in Cincinnati and working as president of what
became the Illinois Central Railroad. When the Civil War began,
McClellan accepted the governor's offer to take charge of all the Ohio

volunteers. He was given a brigadier general's rank and command of the Department of the Ohio.

McClellan won a couple of minor scraps in the mountains of western Virginia. The successes were ideally timed, because they coincided with the defeat of General Irvin McDowell's army at Manassas. The North needed a hero, and McClellan stood in the wings. Lincoln summoned the young general to Washington and placed him in charge of the thousands of troops flocking to the capital. McClellan set to work, using organizational skills matched only by his vanity. "By some strange operation of magic," he wrote his bride, "I seem to have become the power of the land."

He looked the part. Only 34 years old, he was handsome as well as charming when he needed to be. His gray eyes were steady; his thick hair, mustache, and goatee imparted a look of wisdom. While average in height at five feet eight, he had a 42-inch chest that hinted of sturdiness and self-assurance.

McClellan was aware that his generalship could be a political path to the White House, so he carefully molded his 120,000-man Army of the Potomac. It received everything it needed, including organization, morale, and affection for and by its commander. McClellan was contemptuous of any civilian interference. (He once referred to Lincoln as "the original gorilla.") He considered it *his* army, and he never stopped believing that it should remain his.

While McClellan was energetic in organization, he proved timid in battle. He thought too long and hard about a campaign he was going to make at some point. As a perfectionist, he was never quite ready to commit the army to battle. In fact, Lincoln in 1862 had to order McClellan to take the offensive. His three-month Peninsula Campaign failed, not from McClellan's delays, uncertainties, and halfhearted tactics, but because—in his mind—heartless villains in Washington would not send him reinforcements for his army. He overlooked the fact that it already heavily outnumbered its opponent.

His second encounter with Robert E. Lee's forces came in September of that year at Antietam Creek, Maryland. McClellan's piecemeal, uncoordinated attacks resulted in the bloodiest single day in American history. It was his refusal to pursue the badly wounded Confederate Army, however, that was the last straw for the ever patient Lincoln. In November, McClellan was removed from command.

The administration did not know what to do with him, so McClellan was ordered to Trenton, New Jersey, to await further instructions. His army career was over, but crowds cheered his return home. His appearance on a New York City hotel balcony, according to one reporter, "was the signal for an outburst of enthusiasm simply impossible to describe."

McClellan was convinced that the nation couldn't be successfully reunited under Republican rule. To all who would listen, he blamed the failure of his 1862 Peninsula Campaign on a government that "shamefully ignored" his pleas for more soldiers. He was making these observations while still in the Army, and his $6,000 salary as a general was his only income. The federal government chose to ignore his public remarks.

Throughout 1863 and into 1864, McClellan was vigorously entreated to run for the presidency—if for no other reason than to seek vindication for his mistreatment. He resisted such inducements by making the altruistic declaration that "no man should seek the high office, but no true man should refuse it." He followed his own advice.

The 1864 presidential race was a referendum on the war and emancipation. The Democrats opposed both, but McClellan repudiated a plank in the party platform that peace negotiations would immediately follow Democratic victory at the polls. McClellan also dismissed the slavery issue by proclaiming, "The Civil War should be a war for Union and Constitution and no other object." The party was far from unified; hence, voters were given a ticket with a war candidate for president and a peace candidate (George H. Pendleton) for vice president.

Lincoln won the electoral vote by a 10–1 landslide. Ironically for McClellan, Lincoln's margin in the popular vote was provided by Union soldiers. With no business prospects before him, McClellan went on a tour of Europe and did not return until after the 1868 election.

Presidential hopeful McClellan is the mediator in a symbolic tug-of-war between Lincoln and Davis.

He remained out of politics for almost a decade. In the interim, McClellan served as chief engineer for New York City's Department of Docks, established a consulting firm, and journeyed again to England, this time to promote his company. In 1877, to the surprise of many, he was nominated and elected governor of New Jersey. His stabilization of the uncoordinated bureaucracy and his financial frugality brought public praise.

McClellan campaigned arduously for Grover Cleveland in 1884, with the expectation of being named secretary of war. Cleveland won, but McClellan did not get the post. Another setback followed. McClellan had been composing his war memoirs and was two-thirds done when a fire destroyed his manuscripts. Undeterred, he started anew.

Early in 1885, McClellan suffered an attack of angina pectoris; the recurring chest pains sapped his strength. On the morning of October 29, he murmured, "I feel easy now. Thank you," and then died. Funeral services were held at Madison Avenue Presbyterian Church in New York City,

*"Little Mac" lives on in a campaign button that failed
to get him to the White House.*

followed by burial in Trenton's Riverview Cemetery. His book, *McClellan's Own Story,* appeared two years later. Unfortunately, criticism outweighed praise. "It was better for his memory," one reviewer concluded, "had he left his story untold."

"Little Mac," as his soldiers had affectionately called him, has long been an enigma. Grant remarked that McClellan "is to me one of the mysteries of the war." A master of planning, a failure in execution, he was a military genius crippled by insecurity. A Pennsylvania veteran commented a few years after the struggle, "Grant did not know how to retreat; McClellan did not know how to fight." That could be said for both their military and political undertakings. ‿

AMBROSE EVERETT BURNSIDE

OVERCOMING WARTIME FAILURES

AMBROSE EVERETT BURNSIDE was a likable fellow. He made friends easily, smiled often, and remembered names. His successes were many; his failures, disastrous.

Born in an Indiana log cabin in 1824, Burnside received a West Point education. For two years he served on the western frontier as a member of the Third U.S. Artillery, and his captain was Braxton Bragg. In 1853, Burnside left the Army and settled in Bristol, Rhode Island, where he designed a breech-loading weapon known as the Burnside carbine. Secretary of War John B. Floyd contracted with Burnside for the production of a large number of the carbines. Yet no sooner had Burnside constructed the Bristol Rifles Works then another arms manufacturer bribed Floyd to break the Burnside contract. Burnside had to sell the patent to cover his debts. To compound his futility, he ran for Congress in 1858 and was soundly defeated.

The dual setbacks sent him westward. He settled in Cincinnati and became treasurer of the Illinois Central Railroad. There a strong bond developed with an old West Point friend and fellow railroad executive, George McClellan.

Burnside still retained a brigadier general's commission in the Rhode Island state militia. At the onset of war, he returned east and accepted the colonelcy of the First Rhode Island Infantry Regiment. He displayed more confusion than action at the 1861 Battle of First Manassas. Nevertheless, he received promotion to brigadier general of volunteers. The following winter, he gained rave notices for an amphibious operation at Roanoke Island, North Carolina. In truth, the Confederates lost the coastal toehold because of inferior numbers and inept leadership.

Serious questions about Burnside's ability arose after the Battle of Antietam, where his attacks were unimaginative and tardy. Despite that background, Lincoln named Burnside in November 1862 to command the North's major force, the Army of the Potomac. Burnside openly confessed his unfitness for the post but obeyed the order out of a sense of duty.

In appearance, "Old Burn" was a striking figure. He compensated for his premature baldness with a fantastic set of whiskers that made a double parabola from in front of his ears, down over his jaws, and up across his mouth. The whiskers were so unique that the fashion was thereafter called "sideburns"—Burnside's name in reversed. He customarily wore a high, bell-crowned hat with the brim turned down, plus a double-breasted, knee-length coat that made him resemble the caricature of a beefy policeman in the 1880s.

While one general described Burnside as having "a hearty and jovial man-ner, [with] a good-humored cordiality toward everybody," those qualities did not bestow success as a leader of men. Another colleague said of him, "Few officers have risen so high upon so slight a foundation." This was only partly true. One reason for the affection given Burnside was his lack of ambition. He recognized his limitations even if he was never able to surmount them. Put another way, he did his best, but his best was usually not good enough.

A month after taking command of the Army of the Potomac, Burnside led it to the most lopsided defeat it ever suffered at the Battle of Fredericksburg. Seven times Burnside attacked Lee's line. Concentrated Confederate fire easily repulsed each attack. Union losses were nearly 13,000 men. Lee had fewer than 5,000 casualties. A newspaperman wrote, "It can hardly be in human nature for men to show more valor or generals to manifest less judg-ment." Critics quickly dubbed Burnside the "Butcher of Fredericksburg."

He and his IX Corps were transferred to the Department of Ohio. Late in 1863, Burnside gained a measure of redemption by outmaneuvering

The distinctive appearance of "Old Burn" preceded his tepid leadership.

General James Longstreet's forces and defending Knoxville, Tennessee, against Confederate probes. Tying down Longstreet at Knoxville contributed substantially to Bragg's defeats in the November battles at Chattanooga.

Burnside settled back into his usual bumbling in 1864. His supporting assaults at the Wilderness and Spotsylvania were disappointing, and his downfall came with his mismanagement of the 1864 Battle of the Crater at Petersburg, Virginia. Grant pronounced him "unfitted" for command and relieved him of all duties.

The general settled in New York City to be near his railroad affairs, but he refused to take dismissal quietly. After a court of inquiry found him responsible through negligence for the July 30 massacre, he spent months in a futile effort to present his case personally to Lincoln or to Grant. Neither would agree to a meeting. In February 1865, the Joint Committee on the Conduct of the War shifted the blame for the Crater disaster from Burnside to Army commander George Meade.

Though exonerated, he found the military wanted nothing more to do with him. A month later, a humbled Burnside sent a letter to Secretary of War Stanton. "If I can be of any service . . . as a bearer of dispatches from you to either [Grant or Sherman], I am quite ready." Stanton never acknowledged receipt of Burnside's willingness to be a messenger boy. On April 15, 1865—four years to the date of his joining the First Rhode Island, Burnside resigned from the Army.

His ineptitude fortunately remained on the battlefield. By contrast, the amiable general's popularity with civilians was surprisingly high. In 1866, having switched to the Republican Party, he won election as Rhode Island governor by a threefold majority. Two reelections followed. Because governing so small a state was a part-time job, Burnside was able to serve as director of numerous industrial and railroad corporations. That Union veterans liked him is evident from his election as third commander in chief of the 450,000-strong Grand Army of the Republic veterans organization. In 1871 he was elected the first president of the National Rifle Association. By then his waistband far exceeded the width as his shoulders.

When bad investments caused Burnside financial difficulty, the state senate appointed him to the U.S. Senate for two terms. He sat alongside former president Andrew Johnson and former vice president Hannibal Hamlin. Burnside chaired the Foreign Relations Committee in his second tenure. Brown University added luster to his career with an honorary degree.

Burnside retired from public life and became a "gentleman farmer," raising stocks of horses and cattle. He died December 14, 1881, of "enlargement of the heart," according to the death certificate. His burial took place in Swan Point Cemetery in Providence.

Today, on the statehouse lawn, is the usual equestrian statue, with Burnside on top. He wrote his own epitaph with this wartime comment: "I have simply to do my duty. I can safely leave any claim I have to the judgment of future years and the justice of my fellow countrymen." That reliance on "justice" was his greatest flaw, Burnside's biographer concluded. Old Burn spent a lifetime with "blind trust in the essential goodness and honesty of men." ❧

DANIEL EDGAR SICKLES

A RASCAL IN EVERY ARENA

WHETHER IN POLITICS OR WAR, granite monuments or easy women, Daniel Edgar Sickles was never accused of hesitation. His early years as a Tammany Hall lawyer presaged the bombastic course of his entire career. As one writer stated, "If history had not produced Sickles, a novelist would have had to invent him."

Sickles attended New York University, gained admittance to the state bar, and quickly earned a reputation as an attorney who toed and occasionally overstepped the legal limits. As a member of the notorious Tammany Hall political machine, he was a corporate counsel at the age of 28. Sickles served briefly as a state senator before his 1857 election to Congress. His only positive contribution over the next four years was introducing a bill to make George Washington's birth date a national holiday.

That was lost in the smoke of an 1859 scandal that attracted wide attention. Possessed of a brisk gray beard, dashing air, and good manners, Sickles had a well-known and widely practiced appetite for sex. To everyone's surprise, the 32-year-old congressman married the 16-year-old daughter of an opera director. The young bride failed to curb Sickles's lust, and he consorted openly with fashionable prostitutes. Yet when the neglected Mrs. Sickles had an affair with Philip Barton Key (the nephew

A friend looks on as Sickles exacts his revenge on Key.

of the author of "The Star-Spangled Banner"), Sickles shot Key to death in Lafayette Square, across the street from the White House.

His defense attorney, Edwin M. Stanton, had Sickles acquitted on the novel plea of "not guilty by reason of temporary insanity." The well-publicized affair spelled the end for Sickles in politics, but he viewed the episode as a momentary setback. An influential New Yorker once observed, "One might as well try to spoil a rotten egg as to damage Dan's character."

The Civil War opened a new field of opportunity. Authorized by the New York governor to raise a 1,000-man regiment and be its colonel, Sickles organized a 5,000-man brigade and demanded a brigadier general's commission, despite the fact that he was lacking in military experience.

Limited action without making mistakes led to a promotion to major general and corps command under General Joseph Hooker, with whom Sickles shared a number of personality traits. Sickles then demonstrated that his military incompetence matched his personal vanity. At the 1863 Battle of Chancellorsville, he left open a gap in the lines that contributed directly to the Union defeat. Two months later at Gettysburg, Sickles, without orders, shifted his corps from the safety of Little Round Top to a defenseless peach orchard in front of the Union lines.

In the July 2 fighting, Sickles lost a third of his men as well as a leg. He was directing his troops when he was struck by a cannonball that left his right leg dangling below the knee by a few shreds of flesh. As Sickles was borne to the rear, he lit a big Havana cigar and puffed it ostentatiously to the cheers of his men. ("Good Old Dan" proudly donated the severed limb to the Army Medical Museum in Washington and visited the shattered bones periodically for the rest of his life.)

A rumor spread through the army that had not Sickles lost his leg, he would have been court-martialed. Certainly no army commander desired his services thereafter. Rather than retire gracefully from the scene, the fiery Sickles used his political connections in an effort to regain his corps. Failing in that, Sickles and his cohorts launched an attack on army commander George Meade. Sickles brazenly asserted that Meade was preparing to retreat from Gettysburg, but Sickles's courageous action in the peach orchard forced Meade to stay and fight to a victory.

When reports spread that Sickles was being considered for head of the army, pious General Oliver Howard wailed: "If God gives us Sickles to lead us, I shall cry with vexation . . . and plead to be delivered." In fact, Sickles spent the remainder of the war jockeying in vain for a field command.

The postwar years were equally tumultuous. President Andrew Johnson placed him in command of the military department of the Carolinas, but then had to fire the general for acting like a dictator. Sickles promptly joined the Radical Republicans seeking Johnson's impeachment.

In 1869, newly elected President Grant wanted no part of Sickles. He appointed the one-legged general as ambassador to Spain with the sole task of acquiring Cuba. Instead Sickles engaged in an open and wild affair with exiled Queen Isabella, the hereditary ruler of Spain. Apparently her sexual vitality equaled that of Sickles.

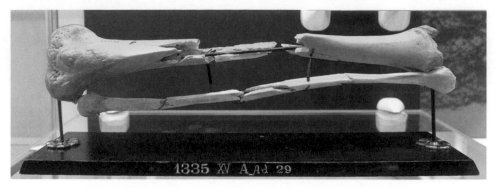

Shattered by canon fire, what remains of Sickles's leg is on display at Maryland's National Museum of Health and Medicine.

The hobbling general—he preferred crutches to an artificial limb—returned to America in 1874 still fully energized. He won a term in Congress and ironically, considering his part in the battle, spent much of the next quarter century working to get the Gettysburg battlefield turned over to the federal government as a national park. Then chairman of the New York State Monuments Commission, Sickles toiled arduously for state and unit monuments to blanket the hallowed grounds. He was a man who rarely took no for an answer.

Once when he was asked at Gettysburg where his own monument stood, Sickles snapped back: "Hell! They're *all* my monuments!"

In 1912, Sickles was forced off the New York commission when an audit revealed $28,000 in arrears. No charges were brought against him, in deference to his age and position. His last years found him separated from family and reality. He had squandered an estimated five million dollars in the postwar period.

Sickles lived to be 94, irresponsible and cantankerous to the end. He died May 3, 1914, of a cerebral hemorrhage at his New York City home. His burial in Arlington National Cemetery was a far more formal ceremony than "Good Old Dan" merited. However, he would have felt fully deserving of the honor. ⟆

BENJAMIN
FRANKLIN BUTLER

HATED FROM ARMY TO OFFICE

"A SHIFTY, CROSS-EYED Massachusetts politician," they called
him before he became the first volunteer major general in the
Union Army. Thereafter, he was the most hated man in every
corner of the Confederacy. Mean-spirited, egotistical, and self-serving,
Benjamin Franklin Butler fairly earned his nickname "Beast."

His father was a privateer who died in the West Indies from either yellow
fever or hanging (sources vary). Butler managed to graduate from Colby
College and established a large criminal law practice in Boston. He was
initially a Democrat who, at the party's 1860 presidential convention,
voted 57 times for the nomination of Mississippian Jefferson Davis. The
disgruntled Butler then supported the state rights candidate before trans-
ferring his allegiance to the Republican Party.

President Lincoln named Butler a major general solely because of the
New Englander's political influence. He proved to be a man of many
talents, but being a soldier wasn't one of them. In his youth, Butler had
applied for admission to West Point and been rejected. During the war he
always resented the academy graduates with whom he had to associate. Yet
he would have profited by learning some lessons from them.

Only weeks after war began, and totally without orders, Butler and a
contingent of troops seized the pro-Southern city of Baltimore. General

in Chief Winfield Scott angrily relieved Butler from command. Yet the North applauded the action. Lincoln, politically calculating, gave Butler command of the military department along Virginia's seacoast.

He immediately precipitated another crisis. Three slaves escaped into Union lines, and in spite of the 1850 Fugitive Slave Act, Butler refused to return the bondsmen to their owner. Instead, he declared them "contraband of war": property of men in rebellion and hence usable by the federal government.

Butler's June 10, 1861, attack at Big Bethel was embarrassing for its ineptitude, and he was shifted off the battlefield to a position where he hopefully could do no more harm.

In the spring of 1862, he became military governor of New Orleans. Butler's grotesque appearance matched the ruthlessness he unleashed. Tall, paunchy, and bald-headed, he had a set of arms and legs that—to a staff officer—"look as if made for somebody else, and hastily glued to him by mistake." A left eye, noticeably out of alignment, drooped as heavily as his mustache. A Billy Yank remembered Butler coming out of his tent, "looking in all directions at once."

Butler's dictatorial rule of New Orleans was as efficient as it was distasteful. One man who defiled the American flag was instantly hanged. Shop owners who refused to sell to Federal soldiers had their businesses shuttered and then sold. Theft and corruption became the order of the day, and Butler was given the sobriquet "Spoon" for the family silver that was regularly confiscated.

The most remembered of his directives came after local women repeatedly snubbed or insulted Union soldiers. General Order No. 28 announced that henceforth, any female who "by word, gesture, or movement" displayed disrespect to a Union soldier could be "treated as a woman of the town plying her avocation." Butler, in short, officially condoned sexual assault.

A negative outcry came from Europe as well as from Southerners. President Davis branded Butler "an outlaw and enemy of mankind," which meant that he could be executed without benefit of trial. As it turned out, the order was more smoke than fire. No Federal soldiers were insulted, and no New Orleans women were assaulted.

Butler was returned to the battlefield because he was so popular with both Radical Republicans and War Democrats. In 1864 he somehow gained

Lincoln and the widely loathed Butler are painted as Don Quixote and Sancho Panza in a shrewd Confederate cartoon.

command of the newly created Army of the James. His assignment was to march westward up the James River and approach Richmond from the underside. What resulted was one of the most mishandled campaigns of the entire war. Butler let inferior numbers drive him into a broad peninsula jutting out into the James. Confederates quickly dug in across the neck of the peninsula, leaving the Union Army locked up as securely as cattle in a corral.

The hapless general still retained his political influence with Lincoln, however. Though he was a key ally of Lincoln, for the upcoming election he not only allowed Radical Republicans to consider him as an opponent to Lincoln in the presidential race but also agreed to be Lincoln's running mate if chosen. Lincoln did toy with the idea of designating Butler as his running mate, but fortunately, it was a passing thought.

In December, Butler's bumbling attempt to seize Fort Fisher on the North Carolina coast finally brought an end to his military career. A Union corps commander dismissed him as "helpless as a child on the field of battle and as visionary as an opium eater."

His military failures did not mar his political standing. After the war Butler served nine years in Congress. He chaired the House Committee on Reconstruction, which framed the military occupation of the Southern states. Ever in the limelight, he was one of the prosecutors in Andrew Johnson's impeachment trial. Butler flew into a rage when Senator Edmund Ross cast the deciding vote against impeachment and shouted, "Tell the damned scoundrel that if he wants money there is a bundle of it here to be had!"

He ran for governor of Massachusetts 11 times before winning the office. By then he was grossly fat and immensely wealthy, but he still enjoyed a good political fight. He was so nearsighted that he had difficulty signing the oath as governor. Butler campaigned in vain to get the Republican presidential nomination in 1884.

A few years later, the retired general and politician had a surgical procedure to remove a section of his left eyelid because the eye had almost closed. Surgeons cut a wedge from the lid and attached the remainder to his eyebrow so it would be "wide open tight" to allow maximum light. Butler endured the entire operation without anesthesia and then entertained the physicians at dinner.

Two years later, Butler published his memoirs. The 1,100-page narrative explained away—at least to Butler's satisfaction—every charge of failure and corruption in a half century of public life.

On January 10, 1893, a day after arguing a case before the U.S. Supreme Court, Butler suddenly developed heavy breathing and coughing. He died before the day's end of what was diagnosed as pulmonary congestion and heart failure. Butler was buried in his wife's family cemetery in Lowell, Massachusetts.

Constantly motivating Butler were the demands of soaring ambition. He was unpredictable because he was an opportunist to every shift in the wind. Always suspected of misdeeds but never convicted of any lawbreaking, he was all that one dislikes in a politician. ✧

HUGH JUDSON KILPATRICK

KILLER OF CAVALRY

ARANKING STAFF OFFICER DECLARED that it was difficult to look at Union General Hugh Judson Kilpatrick without laughing. Wiry and undersized, with stringy side whiskers, he had a lantern jaw and seemingly no upper lip. Kilpatrick wore carefully tailored uniforms, thigh-high boots, and a felt hat tilted to one side to achieve an urbane effect. He seemed woefully out of place in an army of grown men, and in this case, appearances did not lie. In no other Civil War officer was valor more overcome by vices.

Born on a New Jersey farm in 1836, Kilpatrick determined early to make himself a good soldier en route to a governorship and the presidency. He performed well at West Point, despite a proclivity to settle cadet arguments with his fists. Playing leading roles in school dramas made him such a good speaker that he gave the valedictory address at his 1861 graduation.

Kilpatrick married on the same day he left for war. Trained officers were badly needed for the thousands of recruits answering their country's call. He was a captain in the Fifth New York when wounded in a June 10, 1861, skirmish at Big Bethel, Virginia. Supposedly Kilpatrick was the first regular army officer injured in action. He submitted his official—and somewhat exaggerated—report of the action not only to the War Department but to the *New York Times* as well. The published account brought him national attention.

Promotion to lieutenant colonel and colonel of the Second New York Cavalry followed. During 1862, Kilpatrick conducted a number of independent raids in northern Virginia. He spent much of his time engaged in contraband, confiscating horses from farmers and setting aside the best ones to sell for himself in the North. Similarly, he stole tobacco stockpiles and sold them to army sutlers. After he was caught stealing a team of mules, Kilpatrick's other thefts came to light. He was arrested and put in Washington's Old Capitol Prison. Secretary of War Edwin Stanton stated, "The affidavits . . . leave no question of his guilt."

Those crimes should have ended Kilpatrick's military career. Yet the army was desperately in need of experienced cavalry leaders. Kilpatrick won restoration to duty after a three-month jail stay and subsequently rode with General George Stoneman in a raid on Richmond. The campaign threw the Confederate capital into momentary panic but gained no military fruits.

At Brandy Station, the largest cavalry battle of the war, Kilpatrick performed capably, though, as usual, incurring high losses. Shock ran through the Union ranks a week later when Colonels George Custer, Elon Farnsworth, and Kilpatrick were promoted to brigadier generals. Kilpatrick was 27 and, in the words of General George Meade's chief of staff, "an errant knave and impostor, not capable of commanding even a battalion."

Kilpatrick confirmed that judgment a week later at Aldie, when he recklessly made piecemeal attacks that brought stunning casualties. Thereafter, he was known as "Kill Cavalry." The same overly aggressive leadership came to the forefront on the third day's fighting at Gettysburg. Kilpatrick sent a brigade in a mounted charge through woods and across rocky terrain. The assault was bloodily repulsed. Kilpatrick blamed defeat in his official report on a lack of infantry support.

His negative reputation was now fully established. He boasted that he was afraid of nothing in battle and that heavy losses were the cost of victory. Yet his results were never equal to his bragging. Further, while Kilpatrick did not gamble or drink, his pursuit of women was notorious. Females of loose virtue frequented his headquarters.

Kilpatrick shows his horseback prowess during his raids as colonel in northern Virginia circa 1863.

In the spring of 1864, desperate to regain his status as a hero, Kilpatrick received permission to make another raid on Richmond. The expedition failed so badly that Army commander George Meade demoted him. Kilpatrick requested transfer to the western theater, and surprisingly, General William Sherman welcomed him. "I know that Kilpatrick is a hell of a damn fool," Sherman stated, "but I want just that sort of men to command my cavalry."

Kilpatrick served well with Sherman in the advance on Atlanta, the March to the Sea, and a push through the Carolinas. Yet his recklessness was replaced by ruthlessness. His men "committed every kind of devastation," a Southern diarist wrote. Soldiers even robbed slaves of their clothing. In one instance, Kilpatrick needed horses to replace worn-out mounts, and his men collected 500 more animals than necessary. To solve the problem, Kilpatrick ordered the horses slaughtered in the front yard of a plantation.

The blustery Kilpatrick and his destructive Third Division staff gather for a picture.

Meanwhile, the general had at least two mistresses accompanying him, and one bore him a child. He and the other were frolicking at his headquarters when a band of Confederates made a surprise attack. Kilpatrick escaped—clad in only his underwear.

A major general at war's end, he resigned from the Army in August 1865 to campaign for the Republican candidate in the New Jersey gubernatorial election. "I am not willing to see the Rebels of the South, whose hands are yet red with the blood of our fallen brave, restored to their old rights and privileges," he said. But when Kilpatrick's man failed to gain the Republican nomination, he went to work for his opponent. The general's rhetorical skills led to the man's election.

President Andrew Johnson rewarded Kilpatrick's party loyalty by appointing him ambassador to Chile. On board the ship bound for Santiago, Kilpatrick met another passenger, a Mrs. Williams, the young, attractive wife of a naval officer stationed in Panama. The two immediately began an affair that continued a month into his Santiago residency. At state dinners, Kilpatrick introduced Mrs. Williams as his wife.

When this news reached Washington, Kilpatrick came close to losing his post. He forced his consort to leave the embassy, and she ended up as a street prostitute who freely recounted her previous experiences when soliciting. Kilpatrick, in turn, married Louisa Valdivieso, cousin of a future Chilean president and niece of the Catholic archbishop of Chile. The new Mrs. Kilpatrick was five feet tall, with hair so long that it tumbled all the way to the floor when not braided around her head.

Kilpatrick's one notable proposal as ambassador was an effort to persuade England, France, Russia, and Italy to form an armada and destroy the Spanish fleet. The four nations reacted with disgust.

After returning to America in 1868, Kilpatrick saw the futility of running for public office. His opponent had only to make reference to Mrs. Williams and Kilpatrick's candidacy was dead. President James Garfield reappointed Kilpatrick ambassador to Chile (probably because of his wife's connections). It was a short-lived assignment. In the scant months he had left, Kilpatrick gave most of his attention to a verbal war with the American legate in Peru, General Stephen Hurlbut. The feud ended November 4, 1881, when Kilpatrick died of nephritis in Santiago. His remains were buried at West Point.

At least one of his bad deeds was rectified. Two years later, having learned of the Mrs. Williams affair, Kilpatrick's mother-in-law had her daughter's body and headstone removed from next to Judson Kilpatrick's grave and sent to New York City for reinterment. ✌

OLIVER OTIS HOWARD

PIOUS CRUSADER

OLIVER OTIS HOWARD WAS AN ENIGMA. He left much to be desired as a military commander but proved to be a devoted albeit frustrated humanitarian in the years of peace that followed. "No officer entrusted with the field command of soldiers, a historian recently concluded, "has ever equaled Howard's record for surviving so many tactical errors of judgment and disregard of orders, emerging later with increased rank." Yet his pious efforts both for former slaves and for education in general did much to offset his checkered record as a career soldier.

Born in Maine, he graduated from Bowdoin College and spent an additional four years at West Point. In 1857, while on duty in Florida, Howard converted to evangelical Christianity and gave serious thought to entering the ministry. The coming of the Civil War erased that idea. Howard accepted the colonelcy of the Third Maine and led one of the Union brigades that was driven in confusion from the Manassas battlefield. In spite of the disorderly retreat, Howard received promotion to brigadier general.

In his next battle—Seven Pines, Virginia, in May 1862—a wound necessitated the amputation of his right arm. Howard accepted the loss fatalistically. His only known witticism came from a meeting with General Philip Kearny, who had lost his left arm in the Mexican War. Howard commented, "There is one thing we can do, General: We can buy a pair of gloves together."

A portrait taken in Brady's New York studio shows Howard
before the loss of his right arm at Seven Pines, Virginia.

The amputation brought elevation to major general—and later a Medal
of Honor. Reorganization of the Army of the Potomac early in 1863 put
Howard in command of the newly formed XI Corps. The 12,000-man
unit contained a large number of German-American regiments that had
seen no action of note. Jingoism was strong at the time, and the XI Corps
was widely ridiculed as "Dutchmen" of second-class status.

Howard's home, now known as Howard Hall, stands strong on Howard University's campus in Washington, D.C.

Howard's penchant for strict military and moral discipline collided with the soldiers' Continental-style freethinking and heavy drinking. Corps and corps commander had difficulty accepting one another. A staff officer noted: "Howard would be a decidedly handsome man, were he a little taller, having a high, projecting forehead, with a comely beard and very thick head of hair . . . He has been placed in an unfortunate position, being given the 11th Corps, a body of very inferior material."

At Chancellorsville these "outcasts" were placed on the far right of the Union line. Late on the afternoon of May 2, 1863, Stonewall Jackson's Confederate corps slammed into Howard's flank "like the eruption of a volcano," as one Billy Yank exclaimed. Federals broke from the field in the first stage of what became a decisive Union defeat.

Two months later, on the first day's fighting at Gettysburg, Howard's corps collapsed again under fire. Some 4,500 Federals were captured, in addition to those killed and wounded. Howard fell back through town to a position atop Cemetery Ridge, where he engaged in an untimely argument with Union General Winfield Hancock over seniority of command.

"The Christian Soldier" was not above enlisting God in defense of his actions. He ended his official report of Gettysburg with this statement: "No candid mind can review those scenes of horror, and doubt, and ultimate joy, without feeling constrained to acknowledge the Divine hand which controlled and directed the storm." For his role in the battle, Howard received the thanks of Congress.

Many soldiers did not feel the same. Following Gettysburg, they openly referred to the general as "Uh-Ho" Howard. He and his troops were transferred to Sherman's command in the West. The pious, straitlaced Howard seemed out of place in an army of loosely disciplined midwestern farm boys. Yet under Sherman, Howard performed well for the remainder of the war.

The years after Appomattox were more fulfilling. On March 3, 1865, Congress enacted the Army Bureau of Refugees, Freedmen, and Abandoned Land Act. It was the Northern government's first welfare agency: a War Department–controlled experiment to help both blacks and whites readjust to a post-racial society. The Freedmen's Bureau, as it came to be called, was designed to feed the poor, establish schools and hospitals, find jobs for the unemployed, negotiate labor contracts, and allocate land to freedmen in a wide-ranging redistribution process.

In May, President Andrew Johnson appointed Howard as the bureau's commissioner, a post he held until the agency's 1872 disbandment. Howard's many efforts were conscientious and impeccably honest. Because he considered education as the best route for freed slaves, he kept the bureau focused on building schools. Yet the agency's overall success was limited.

From start to end of his tenure, Howard waged an uphill battle. A moderate antislavery man before the war, he assumed his new duties with the best interests of ex-slaves at heart. The problem was, he had the power to exercise only the government's wishes. Johnson gave him no support, congressional appropriations were inadequate, and white Southerners opposed all reforming efforts. Inside the bureau, many of the employees engaged in an orgy of fraud and corruption. In the end, and despite his efforts, Howard failed to gain landowner status for freedmen. In addition, the legal and physical protection that the Freedmen's Bureau provided ex-slaves became short-lived.

In his longest-lasting effort, Howard in 1872 began serving as president of a college he had created as an institution to train future black ministers. Although his tenure as president of Howard University was short, and he encountered continual opposition to educating former slaves, the college went on to become one of the preeminent black institutions of higher learning in the United States. It trained generations of black professionals during the long years of de facto segregation and lent strong support to the civil rights movement.

Two years later, the one-armed general went west to counsel with warring Indian tribes. He was able to broker an uneasy peace with the Apache and Nez Perce. When West Point's first black cadet committed suicide, Howard was named superintendent to restore calm at the academy. His greater achievement, many said, was improving the quality of food the cadets received.

Thereafter came command of various military districts for Howard. While commanding at San Francisco, he became prominent in religious circles. Much of his time was devoted to preaching, finding positions for clergy, and organizing revival meetings—and reminding people that he was not an ordained minister.

Service in New York City strengthened his friendship with General Sherman, and Howard was put in charge of the commander's 1891 funeral. He was also instrumental in the establishment of Lincoln Memorial University, a school for indigenous mountain residents in Kentucky, Tennessee, and Virginia. Now respected and applauded, Howard lived "to try every day to make somebody happier and better." His memoirs, published in 1907, are highly embellished and rarely quoted.

On October 26, 1909, Howard died of a heart attack. He was buried in Lake View Cemetery, Burlington, Vermont. The guard of honor was a contingent from the Tenth U.S. Cavalry, an all-black regiment.

Near the end of his life Howard observed, "My glory, if I ever have any, consists in results attained, and the results in the case of the Freedmen's Bureau, are, for me, more marked than those of the war." Such also is the judgment of history. Piety is not needed for a military command, but it served Howard well at a crucial juncture in our history when his crusade for racial fairness was roundly opposed. ❧

JOSHUA LAWRENCE CHAMBERLAIN

FROM TEACHER TO HERO

EDUCATION ALSO FEATURED PROMINENTLY in the career of another general from Maine. Joshua Lawrence Chamberlain underscored the old adage that sometimes the pen is mightier than the sword. He was relatively unknown until the 1975 appearance of Michael Shaara's novel *The Killer Angels*. The 20th Maine—Chamberlain's regiment—was blessed with a good regimental historian, and that book, plus Shaara's imagination, turned a college professor into a folk hero. Two movies and a PBS documentary catapulted Chamberlain into almost idolatrous fame.

The tide is now receding with the knowledge that Chamberlain overly publicized his accomplishments, which were not as singular as they appeared, and he memorialized at times rather than reported accurately.

Born in 1828 in Brewer, Maine, Chamberlain was a descendant of a long line of soldiers. He also received his first education at a military school. These two facts debunk his claimed lack of martial knowledge when he entered the Civil War.

In 1852 Chamberlain graduated from Bowdoin College. Three years later he received a degree from Bangor Theological Seminary. He returned to Bowdoin as a professor of logic and theology, a position that had previously been held by Calvin Stowe, whose wife wrote the powerful novel

Uncle Tom's Cabin. Chamberlain's professorship carried academic tenure and a two-year sabbatical leave to study in Europe. The tall, heavily mustached academic hardly seemed destined to be a heroic soldier. He was soft-spoken and philosophical, perfectly at home in his academic cocoon.

Patriotism disrupted Chamberlain's serenity. In 1862 he applied for his sabbatical leave and left Bowdoin, not for a European tour but to become lieutenant colonel of the newly formed 20th Maine. He worked earnestly to learn the rudiments of command.

The regiment reached the Army of the Potomac too late to participate in the Battle of Antietam. Its baptism in battle came in December with the murderous slaughter of the army at Fredericksburg. The Maine unit was engaged in one of the final, useless assaults. Chamberlain and his men spent the night pinned down on the field by Confederate fire, using dead Union bodies for cover.

A smallpox quarantine prevented the 20th Maine from taking part in the 1863 Chancellorsville action. Instead, its most publicized fight came July 2 at Gettysburg. Desperately anchoring the Union left flank against attack, and out of ammunition, Chamberlain ordered his troops to counterattack with only bayonets and cheers. Confederates, suffering from heavy losses and a lack of water, fell back in retreat. Chamberlain's leadership earned him a Medal of Honor.

For a year the colonel alternated between regimental and brigade command. Court-martial duties held him back from the first battles of Grant's 1864 Overland Campaign against Richmond. Yet on June 18, at Rives's Salient near Petersburg, Chamberlain led a charge. When the color-bearer fell dead, Chamberlain seized the flag and held it aloft for his men.

A bullet slammed into his right hip, sliced at least one artery, nicked his bladder, fractured his left pelvic bone, and exited behind his left hip joint. Bleeding heavily, Chamberlain thrust his sword into the ground for support and continued shouting orders until he collapsed. Surgeons on the scene pronounced the wound fatal.

Chamberlain's brother rushed him to a field hospital, where two physicians pulled together as much of the complex damage as possible. As he

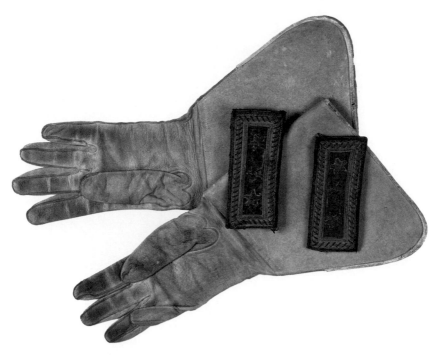

*Chamberlain's well-worn leather gauntlets and shoulder straps
are typical of the Union Army uniform.*

clung to life, the colonel sent a farewell letter to his wife. The Army issued an obituary, and General Grant promoted Chamberlain on the spot to brigadier general—one of only two such battlefield promotions in the Civil War.

His health slowly improved, although the widespread injury plagued him for the remainder of his life. In February 1865 he rejoined the Army, limping badly but with his usual determination.

On March 29, in a sharp fight at Lewis's Farm on the outskirts of Petersburg, he was wounded again. A bullet passed through his horse's neck, struck Chamberlain just below the heart, and passed out his coat. The wound from the spent bullet was more painful than severe. Grant recognized Chamberlain's valor by recommending him for promotion to major general and accorded him the honor of receiving on April 12 the official surrender of Lee's army.

Chamberlain (right), identifiable by his white beard, and his 20th Maine, pictured in 1889

The general returned home a crippled hero. Without discounting his bravery, part of the reason Chamberlain was so lauded is because he insisted throughout the war years that any exploit he accomplished be widely publicized in the press. His war experiences expanded the professor's ambitions. After serving for a year as acting president of Bowdoin College, he ran for governor and won 70 percent of the votes. He was reelected three times—twice by the largest margins in Maine history.

Although Chamberlain sought higher office than the one-year governorship, the opportunity never came. Debate over his support of temperance and opposition to capital punishment cost him popularity. He left politics in 1870 when he became the unanimous choice for president of Bowdoin. He was head of the school for 12 years, and in those more rudimentary days of higher education, he taught every subject in the curriculum except mathematics and physical science.

So long a presidential tenure inevitably spurred dissatisfaction among professors and alumni. In Chamberlain's case, he was too far ahead of his time. He overmodernized the curriculum, often in the face of strong opposition. What proved the largest bone of contention was his institutionalization of a military program and drill system for all students.

Future wars were inevitable, the general firmly believed. Younger generations should be more prepared for military duties than was the nation at the outbreak of the Civil War. A student uprising on campus brought the issue to a head. In the end, Bowdoin adopted the policy but abolished it a decade later.

The military curriculum battle, plus a flare-up of his war wound, produced ongoing stress with his wife that led to the rim of divorce. Chamberlain resigned the college presidency in 1883 and underwent major surgery on the still unhealed hip wound. He almost died as a result, and his pain and disability continued.

Chamberlain spent his remaining years in various business ventures, nationwide lectures, and active participation in veterans organizations. His gift of articulation made him one of the most quoted veterans of his age. He was a star attraction at the 50th anniversary of Gettysburg, when thousands of veterans gathered for a reunion.

By then, with the war injuries inflamed and his rejection of any further treatment, Chamberlain described his days as "unspeakable agony." He managed to complete his memoirs of his last year of army service. *The Passing of the Armies,* published posthumously, was more a lawyer's brief, defending the removal from command of his friend General G. K. Warren and laced here and there with snide comments about Grant and Sheridan.

The wound eventually overcame Chamberlain altogether. By January 1914, he was bedridden. He wrote to his sister, "I am passing through deep waters. The Doctor thinks I am going to land once more on this shore."

On January 24, Chamberlain died of chronic cystitis and chronic posterior urethritis. Although he wanted a simple service, a huge number of mourners attended the funeral in Brunswick's Pine Grove Cemetery. Maine citizens still regard him as their most famous soldier. ∾

CHAPTER 8

AN
UNSTEADY
WHITE HOUSE

THE LONG-HELD BELIEF that good generals instinctively make good presidents has been discounted by history. George Washington was the first military commander to lead the nation, and numerous others followed in his wake during our first full century. Seven American presidents are associated with the Civil War, and Abraham Lincoln towers over all. While he would be a giant in any age, the latter half of the 19th century was littered with one-term presidents whose legacies are mostly negative. Indeed, they seemed to be mere bystanders as the gathering forces of industrialization propelled America to the world's foremost economic power.

Three rank among the least-admired presidents. The worst of the bunch was also the first: James Buchanan. He maintained a lawyerly dispassion while the country disintegrated around him. After Lincoln came such slim pickings that Congress remained more in the spotlight than the White House. Andrew Johnson, a square peg trying to fit into a round hole, holds the lowly distinction of coming within a single vote of impeachment. As for Ulysses Grant, he was apolitical before being elected, and he never learned enough about the presidency to wield its

OPPOSITE: *A quaint postwar picture of the White House hides the chaos within.*

Americans commemorated felled presidents with tokens
such as this memorial card of Lincoln and Garfield.

power. He is mainly noted for using nepotism to a degree unparalleled until the Kennedy era.

The next three presidents on this list hailed from Ohio, long an important state politically and one that rapidly industrialized during this period. Grant's successor, Rutherford Hayes, deserves praise for officially ending Reconstruction, but his impact is limited because he chose to serve only one term. That was longer than James Garfield, who was killed within months of his inauguration. The favorite among the sad lot was the last: William McKinley, who still is regarded as one of the best liked presidents. Yet his laissez-faire policies toward big business led directly to the age of progressivism, when the forces of monopoly and labor abuse were severely curtailed.

This era is also remarkable for the number of presidential assassinations. In a span of 40 years, three of these presidents were gunned down in their prime. While all the killers were deranged, their sundry motives sprang from the turmoil of the times. In particular, Charles Guiteau took the corrupt patronage system of political favors to its hideous extreme. When the post he sought was not forthcoming, he regarded killing James Garfield as the next-best avenue. As for McKinley's assassin, Leon Czolgosz was an anarchist who justified killing a president because of his strong alliance with the business forces that he perceived were oppressing the masses.

Although all these men knew the violence of war, they were not prepared for the turmoil of postwar peace. The tides of Reconstruction, industrialization, and mass immigration caused social upheaval on a scale that perhaps no president could have controlled. What we do know is that the training that these men gained in battle in no way prepared them for controlling the tumultuous era that followed. ✑

JAMES BUCHANAN

THE WORST PRESIDENT

W HILE LINCOLN IS CONSIDERED the greatest of our chief executives, his predecessor is usually ranked as the worst. James Buchanan is remembered not for what he accomplished but for what he failed to accomplish at the most critical point in the young nation's history.

Buchanan grew up in Lancaster, Pennsylvania, only ten miles from slaveholding Maryland. No other important pre–Civil War Northerner lived closer to the South. This proximity early on earned him the label of a doughface—a Northerner with Southern leanings.

His first 65 years were largely uneventful, as he became a wealthy attorney in Washington. A fiancée died in 1819, and Buchanan kept his vow never to marry. One acquaintance commented that from the time Buchanan was old enough to vote, "he had been wedded to the Constitution." He shared bachelor quarters in the capital with a number of men, many of whom were influential Southerners.

Service in the two houses of Congress preceded his 1852 appointment as ambassador to Great Britain. That placed Buchanan a continent away from the increasingly heated debates over slavery. Because he was "Kansas-less" in 1856, he was considered "enemy-less." Democrats chose him to run for president. Buchanan's sympathetic attitude toward the extension of slavery won him 14 of the 15 Southern states, and longtime Northern Democrats carried him to victory over the fledgling Republican Party.

At 69, he began his term as one of our oldest chief executives. Buchanan was tall, with silky white hair. A neck injury at birth caused his head to tilt to one side, even though critics alleged that Buchanan had tried to hang himself after a broken engagement. A badly squinted eye was also distracting. The former ambassador wore an old-fashioned standing collar and a starched white shirt, looking as if he had just stepped from a Charles Dickens novel.

A pleasant fellow, he initially took daily walks along Pennsylvania Avenue, affably greeting one and all. A niece, Harriet Lane, served as hostess at the White House. Her poise and congeniality were such that the song "Listen to the Mocking Bird" was dedicated to her.

What Buchanan lacked was any ability to control the winds swirling about him. In the late 1850s one crisis after another swept across the nation: the Dred Scott decision, the Panic of 1857, John Brown's Raid, Southern steps toward secession. At one point, he shouted in despair, "My God! Are calamities never to come singly?"

He gave the impression of being timid and useless, and hence dangerous. Philosophically, he was trapped in what became known as "Buchanan's dilemma." He did not think the Southern states could legally secede from the Union, but as a lawyer and strict constitutionalist, he saw no legal way he could intervene in the dispute. He believed that if any agency of the federal government should address the matter, it should be Congress.

No one in his inner circle was helpful. John C. Breckinridge, his vice president, was a Kentuckian who would become a Confederate general. Dominating Buchanan's Cabinet were scheming Southerners. Five ultimately resigned, others threatened to step down, and one (Edwin Stanton) was actually an informant for the Republicans. Buchanan remained overlooked, unaware of details, depressed by events beyond his control. He vacillated month after month, hoping the critical decisions could be deferred until after he left office.

When three Southern commissioners came to Washington in 1861 and pressed Buchanan for assistance, the president exclaimed: "You don't give me time to consider! You don't give me time to say my prayers.

A secessionist cartoon titled "Little Bo-Peep and Her Sheep" mocks Buchanan
as a fearful lamb fleeing the South Carolina–bound flock.

I always say my prayers when required to act upon any action belonging
to Congress."

The nation was only a month before the explosion of war when Lincoln
took the presidential oath. Buchanan remarked that if Lincoln was as glad
to get into the White House as he himself was to get out of it, Lincoln
must be the happiest man alive.

"Buchanan the Blunderer," as the press labeled him, departed Washington convinced that he had done well in his tenure of office. "I acted for
some time as a breakwater between the North and the South, both surging
with all their force against me." No human wisdom, he thought, could have
prevented the process of degeneration during the 1850s. He had done his
best, and he firmly believed that posterity would do him justice.

He returned to Wheatland, his home in Lancaster. Six servants saw to
his needs, and visitors came frequently. Buchanan was a good Unionist

during the war years, never speaking out against what he considered Lincoln's repeated violations of the Constitution. In 1865 he joined the Presbyterian Church, which he had previously regarded as too abolitionist. Yet voices continued to be raised against him. Despite his voluminous mail, Congress took away his franking privileges. Buchanan's opposition to the Emancipation Proclamation brought a new rash of enemies. His endorsement of a Peace Democrat candidate, who would allow the South to reenter the Union with its prewar slave status intact, appeared to many as political suicide.

Only Richard Nixon matched Buchanan's after-the-fact effort to rehabilitate a failed presidency. The Pennsylvanian toiled long over his memoirs. Since no former associates would help him, he hired a ghostwriter. *Mr. Buchanan's Administration on the Eve of the Rebellion* was published in 1868. The book was notable for the attention paid to Northern antislavery agitation and "the malign influence of the Republican party" as major causes of the Civil War. Naturally the memoirs exonerated Buchanan of any wrongdoing, and their publication brought forth another torrent of remonstrance.

On June 1 of that year, Buchanan died of pneumonia. The day before his passing, he declared, "I have no regret for any public act of my life, and history will vindicate my memory." The problem was, no one wanted to write about him. The first biography of James Buchanan did not appear until a full 101 years after he left the presidency. ✑

ANDREW JOHNSON

ONE VOTE
FROM IMPEACHMENT

N O ONE, NOT EVEN ABRAHAM LINCOLN, has ever reached the
White House from more humble beginnings than Andrew
Johnson. Born to dirt-poor parents in North Carolina and
orphaned early in life, Johnson never attended school. He was appren-
ticed at the age of ten to a tailor. Later he taught himself to read; his wife,
Eliza, taught him to write and do simple arithmetic. He would become a
voracious reader, spending a great deal of his time in Washington perusing
tomes in the Library of Congress.

After moving to eastern Tennessee, Johnson opened his own tailor shop.
He married Eliza and fathered five children, and he was able to save money
by stern thrift. Of medium height and size, he was dark-complexioned
with black hair and eyes. Probably because of his tailoring profession,
Johnson was always neatly dressed. He was usually courteous, but he could
be crude both in thought and in diction. That he never allied himself with
any church was something that people held against him.

His political career followed the usual path: state legislature, House of
Representatives, governor, and U.S. Senate. Although he was reticent by
nature, he came alive with fire and thunder on the stump. At every level
of government, he displayed high principles, refusing help from financial
backers and political bosses. However, he was so strongly opinionated that
he would argue with anyone—including members of his Democratic Party.

THIS LITTLE BOY WOULD PERSIST IN HANDLING BOOKS ABOVE HIS CAPACITY.

AND THIS WAS THE DISASTROUS RESULT.

An American newspaper parodies Johnson during his impeachment trial.

During the secession crisis of 1860–61, he alone among all Southern senators remained in the upper chamber. He viewed the exodus of the Southern states to be "treason and nothing but treason."

That left him in an uneasy no-man's-land. Southerners considered him a traitor. Northerners regarded him with distrust. That did not stop Lincoln from appointing Johnson military governor with the rank of brigadier general in 1862, by which time Federal forces occupied a large section of Tennessee. Johnson carried out his duties in near-dictatorial fashion. He impressed slaves, suspended newspapers, confiscated horses for the army, and drafted a loyalty oath stronger than that demanded by the Union government. Tennessee became the first of the Confederate states to later qualify for readmission to the Union.

In the 1864 national election, Republicans temporarily adopted the name National Union Party for broader appeal. The leading War Democrat, Johnson was chosen as vice presidential candidate. His political

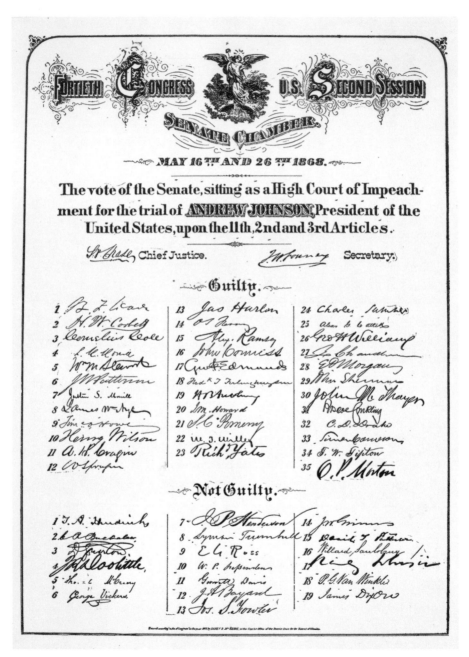

The vote for Johnson's impeachment shows a Senate divided.

downfall began shortly thereafter, at the March 1865 Inauguration ceremonies. That morning he had a hangover as well as lingering effects from a recent bout with typhoid fever. Johnson asked for a stimulant prior to taking the oath of office. He downed two glasses of whiskey, and then delivered rambling, sometimes incoherent remarks, which were described by one newspaper as "the spewings of a drunken boor." Another editor shuddered that "one frail life stands between this insolent, clownish creature and the presidency!"

A month after this national embarrassment, Johnson became president of the United States. In almost every way he was unqualified for the office. He was a staunch states' righter who championed the poor man. The very qualities that made Lincoln persuasive—especially tact and common sense   were notably lacking in Johnson. He could not compromise; hence, in this era he could not lead.

Dazed at first by the suddenness of his elevation, Johnson did little more than issue reassurances that Lincoln's lenient peace plans would be followed. That he kept Lincoln's Cabinet intact was additional evidence of that intent. However, the question of what to do with the South sharply divided the Cabinet. Seward supported Lincoln's policies, while Stanton headed the Radical faction.

Johnson's three years and 11 months in the White House consisted of open warfare with the Congress. The president advocated a conciliatory reunion of states; radicals wanted vengeance on the South. Johnson quickly concluded that Radical Republicans were bent on destroying the Constitution, and he saw it as his patriotic duty to fight to preserve it. He grew increasingly abrasive because he was certain his adversaries were wicked men out to destroy him. In an 1866 speechmaking tour, he responded to hecklers by exchanging insults with them; the dignity of the high office sank to the gutter.

His strident opposition to the Radical Republicans had an inevitable result. Never before had Congress overridden a presidential veto. Yet Johnson's term saw an oft-repeated pattern: Congress would pass a law, Johnson would veto it, and Congress would override the veto by a large margin.

Shortly after the 1867 Military Reconstruction Act—vetoed in vain—placed the South under military occupation, Johnson retaliated by firing Secretary of War Stanton for corruption. The House of Representatives retaliated by drawing up charges to impeach the president. The 45-day trial was a farce. Johnson's "high crimes and misdemeanors"—as the Constitution defines justification for impeachment—were his not agreeing with the will of Congress. The flimsiness of the 11 articles of indictment reflected how cocksure the Radicals were of their case.

In the end, Johnson escaped impeachment by a single vote. The outcome saved the authority and eminence of the presidency. Had impeachment passed, no future president would feel safe quarreling with a majority of the House of Representatives and two-thirds of the Senate. However, Johnson's victory was Pyrrhic. For the remainder of his term, he and Congress were at loggerheads. Johnson interfered with no army policies. General in Chief Grant remained in charge of executing Reconstruction laws, and he ran the army as if the president did not exist.

After both parties scorned him in 1868, Johnson returned home. He survived an 1873 cholera attack and accepted appointment in 1875 to return to the U.S. Senate. On the last day of July, however, he died from a second stroke within 48 hours. His remains were wrapped in an American flag and buried with a copy of the Constitution as his pillow.

Andrew Johnson was hardworking and honest; he was also hotheaded and contentious. As an accidental president, he failed to measure up to the demands of the office to which he could not have been elected in the first place. Historians place him beside Buchanan on the short list of presidential failures. ✌

ULYSSES SIMPSON GRANT

GOOD IN WAR, POOR IN PEACE

N O MAJOR AMERICAN FIGURE displays a more disheartening contrast in leadership between war and peace than Ulysses Simpson Grant. Anyone who knew him before the Civil War might have predicted this dichotomy, since he failed at every venture he tried outside the military. The aggression that he showed in a series of Union victories, both in the West and the East, evaporated on election to the White House, where his laxity led to an administration that was dogged by accusations of corruption. For this reason, the first of the four Union military commanders to become president has long been considered the worst of them.

Born to a leathermaking family in 1822, he was one of six children. His christened name was Hiram Ulysses, but when he arrived at West Point, a clerical error listed him as Ulysses Simpson Grant. Cadets called him "Uncle Sam" Grant, and friends thereafter knew him as "Sam."

Excellence in horsemanship outweighed his mediocrity as a cadet and enabled him to graduate from the academy. One of his close friends, James Longstreet, introduced his cousin, Julia Dent, to Grant, and the two subsequently married. Each brought a lifetime of love and stability to the other.

Alone and depressed while doing frontier duty in California, Grant turned to the bottle. In 1854, after being caught drunk in public, he involuntarily resigned from the Army. For five years he failed at every civilian task he undertook. The coming of the Civil War found Grant working in his father's leather goods shop in Galena, Illinois, where he had trouble even remembering prices. Grant so far was hardly a Horatio Alger success story.

Three months passed before he received the colonelcy of a recalcitrant regiment that no one else wanted. For the silent, unpretentious officer, a steady climb to fame ensued. Grant stood five feet eight inches tall and weighed 135 pounds. Stooped and round-shouldered, he had the expression, as one observer described, "of a man who had come way up from very far down."

Grant had more than his share of quirks. He commanded in a dozen major battles, yet the sight of blood made him queasy. Any meat he ate had to be well-done. Despite witnessing the cruelty that army horses had to endure, Grant had a strong affection for all animals. His favorite breakfast was cucumbers soaked in vinegar. Like Stonewall Jackson, Grant was tone-deaf. Lincoln once asked him what his favorite song was, and Grant replied, "I know only two songs. One is 'Yankee Doodle' and the other isn't." His daily consumption of 12 to 15 cigars later had fatal consequences.

National recognition came early in 1862 after his forces captured Fort Donelson, Tennessee. His stern demand for the garrison's capitulation earned him a new nickname, "Unconditional Surrender" Grant. Subsequent victories at Shiloh, Vicksburg, and Chattanooga made him the Union's most successful field commander. To criticism made of Grant after the terrible losses at Shiloh, Lincoln responded, "I can't spare this man. He fights."

On March 10, 1864, Lincoln named Grant general in chief of all Union armies with the resurrected rank of lieutenant general, a rank held only by the sainted Washington. Grant's subsequent ten-month campaign against Robert E. Lee's army ended the war at Appomattox. Grant then displayed a surprising humanity. Perhaps because he had known defeat in prewar years, Grant sympathized with Lee and his beaten legions. The Federal general's lenient surrender terms enabled former Confederates to go home with dignity. This was a first, vital step toward national reconciliation.

Grant appears at ease in camp during the war, when his reputation soared.

Grant was now the nation's foremost hero, trailed by crowds wherever he went. Such adulation propelled him into political realms he should have avoided. This was a man who had voted only once in his life.

That made no difference to the adoring public. In 1868, Grant probably could have received the presidential nomination from either party, and as a

*To his many supporters, Grant's campaign hat
bore the promise of better days.*

Republican he won the election by a landslide. He ran on the simple slogan "Let us have peace." What followed, asserted one historian, was "eight years in blunderland" that "are regarded as a national disgrace." However, hero-worshipping American voters elevated Grant to the presidential chair and deserved to shoulder much of the blame for what followed.

Grant entered the White House in the Gilded Age, when the country's growth ran high and wealth was amassed in stupendous fortunes. Corruption to some degree was inevitable. Under Grant it flourished. He knew nothing about politics and made no effort to find out. Family members packed the government. Old army cronies got civilian appointments with no more knowledge than the president had. The 18th chief executive became an easy tool for designing politicians as well.

Grant viewed his position as that of an administrator, not a leader. His blind loyalty to discredited cronies established a record for scandal and moral rottenness not equaled even by Warren Harding's infamous regime. Reelected by an even higher margin in 1872, Grant interpreted the victory as a mandate to continue governing in his slapdash manner. That would lead shortly to the Panic of 1873 and a depression that lasted six years. Only Hamilton Fish's admirable achievements as secretary of state stand out among the sordid record.

After his presidency, Grant spent two years being feted by the crowned heads of Europe. He returned home and barely missed being nominated for president a third time. Yet in 1884 all his money was invested in a brokerage firm that suddenly went bankrupt and he was left humiliated and penniless. Congress restored him to full general's rank with retirement pay, but the stipend was not enough to cover his mounting bills.

A friend, Mark Twain, stepped forward with an offer and large advance for Grant's memoirs. Seeking to provide for his family, the hero eagerly went to work. Midway through the task, Grant began experiencing stabbing pain in his throat. Diagnosis revealed inoperable cancer. Completing the memoirs now became a race against time. Grant spent nine months working feverishly. He dictated to a stenographer until the malignancy choked off his voice. Then he turned to writing text. Physicians prescribed morphine and cocaine to ease the pain, but the opiates also beclouded his memory.

The warrior died July 23, 1885, only seven days after completing the manuscript. Grant's two-volume war recollections were published later the same year. The work proved to be one of the most successful titles of the 19th century, notwithstanding its controversial conclusions and personal judgments.

Grant's brilliance as a general would be sterling were it not blemished by his ignorance as a president. In an exploding country awash with wealth, his solution was to leave the spigot turned on full blast. Though he was sadly lacking as commander in chief, his gifts as chief of the Union Army and contributions to national unity put him among the military's greats. ∽

RUTHERFORD BIRCHARD HAYES

PRESIDENT OF RECONCILIATION

ONE OF THE IRONIES OF AMERICAN HISTORY is that a man of impeccable honesty was the winner of the most dishonest presidential election on record. Once Rutherford Birchard Hayes was in office, however, his putting an end to Reconstruction helped heal wounds in the South, and his efforts to reform civil service removed the taint of corruption left after eight years of U. S. Grant cronyism. By the end of his one term, he proved to be the tonic that the country needed.

Hayes was born in Ohio, graduated from Harvard Law School, and was a practicing attorney in Cincinnati when the Civil War began. He was then 38 with three children. He had no military experience but did have an abiding love for the Union. "My belief in this war," he told his family, "is as deep as any faith can be."

Hayes enlisted in the 23rd Ohio, the first Buckeye regiment to organize for three years of duty. In time he came to command the unit. Long conversations with experienced officers, plus close contact with the men in the ranks, led Hayes to say that he was "one of the good colonels in the great army." He found military command responsibilities to be a pleasing contrast to the dullness of civilian careers.

Except for the 1862 Battle of South Mountain, Maryland, Hayes saw action only in western Virginia and the Shenandoah Valley. He aided in the capture of Confederate Colonel John Hunt Morgan's troopers in the 1863 Ohio raid, and gallant action the following year in the Second Valley Campaign brought Hayes a promotion to brigadier general.

He was always dedicated, energetic, gallant, and—by his own admission—lucky. When he left for war, he "fiercely wished" for a wound. He received four, the worst being a broken arm caused by flying shrapnel. Hayes considered patriotism more desirable than life. In one engagement, he was leading a charge when he saw a fearful soldier about to break for the rear. The colonel pulled out his revolver and vowed that "he would kill him on the spot" if he did not "go in and fight." The man regained control, returned to the battle, and was killed instantly. Hayes was glad to have given the soldier the death of a hero rather than that of a coward.

One of his sergeants, future president William McKinley, wrote of Hayes: "His whole nature seemed to change with battle. From the sunny, agreeable, the kind, the generous, the gentle gentleman . . . he was; when the battle was once on, intense and ferocious."

Upon his return home from the war, Hayes became equally successful in politics. First a Radical Republican congressman (1865–67), then twice a reform governor (1868–72 and 1876–77), he was a natural candidate for presidential nomination in 1876. His opponent was Samuel Tilden, the most popular Democrat since Andrew Jackson. The campaign itself, however, descended to new lows in mudslinging and dishonesty.

Democrats spotlighted the long years of Republican corruption. Republicans countered with the slogan "Not every Democrat was a rebel, but every rebel was a Democrat." Hayes promised to stress civil service reform and to end military occupation in the South. "There can be no enduring peace," he proclaimed, "if the constitutional rights of any portion of the people are permanently disregarded."

In the election, Tilden won 300,000 more popular votes than Hayes. The all-important electoral vote, on the other hand, was 184–165, and another 20 votes in four states were disputed. Weeks of heated congressional vitriol eventually led to the creation of an Electoral Commission, consisting of

A two-frame cartoon on "strong" government versus "weak" government ridicules Hayes's conciliatory gestures to the South.

eight Republicans and seven Democrats. Wholesale duplicity, intimidation, and even murder accompanied the commission's deliberations.

An informal deal materialized. If the Democrats acquiesced to Hayes's election, Republicans would agree to withdraw troops from the ex-Confederacy. That would open the door for Democrats to establish anew their dominance of the South. At 4 a.m. on March 2, 1877—two days before the expiration of Grant's term—the commission by an 8–7 vote declared Hayes to be the next president. Nationwide, Democrats never forgave Hayes for "stealing" the presidency. Republicans never forgave him for allowing the South to form a solid bloc again.

In his only major political mistake, Hayes rewarded with federal offices the four Louisiana electoral college members who had arbitrarily given their state to the Republican candidate. Thereafter, Hayes had to weather a number of unflattering nicknames: "Old Eight to Seven," "President De Facto," and "His Fraudulency" among them. Nevertheless, the highly moralistic Hayes was a more effective chief executive than his detractors claimed.

He took office quietly and resolutely, the slanders and slurs of the campaign forgotten. Hayes immediately declared Reconstruction at an end, and in his strong Cabinet he put forth the name of an ex-Confederate. The president fought for, and obtained, presidential prerogatives that Congress had usurped since the post-Lincoln years. While Hayes was unable to drive a full program through Congress, he paved the way for a badly needed civil service overhaul. One writer concluded that Hayes's "great contribution was to restore faith in the integrity of the Washington regime and to prove, despite the Grant orgy, that a Republican could be honest, courageous, and a roadblock to designing thieves."

Never has the White House been as "morally clean" as it was in the Hayes years. Hymn singing and prayers were part of every day's agenda. The high-minded Hayes and his teetotaler wife (called "Lemonade Lucy") set strict house rules: no alcohol, smoking, gambling, or dancing. After one official dinner Secretary of State William Evarts commented, "It was a brilliant affair. The water flowed like champagne."

Hayes deserved reelection in 1880, but from the start he had vowed to be a one-termer. He was grateful for making that promise. Midway through his tenure he complained that the courage and generosity he had seen in his 23rd Ohio comrades had been lost in the unstable peace after the war. He added on another occasion, "I am heartily tired of this life of bondage, responsibility, and toil." Still, he left the government more prosperous than when he entered office. That in itself was a signal achievement.

The soldier-statesman retired to private life. Following a trip to Columbus and Cleveland, Hayes boarded a train on January 12, 1892, to return to his home in Fremont. He was stricken en route with severe chest pains. He died the following day of "neuralgia of the heart." His body was eventually laid to rest in the state park established at his home. ᏚᎦ

JAMES ABRAM GARFIELD

A Term Too Short

JAMES ABRAM GARFIELD was the last of our "log cabin presidents." He was also, like Abraham Lincoln, a chief executive who was assassinated during this period in our history. Yet there the similarities end. Garfield's term in office is the second shortest on record, and his killer had no motivation beyond dreams of grandeur. While both deaths were tragic, Garfield's had the added burden of being utterly senseless.

Born on the Ohio frontier, Garfield from birth came under the strong influence of the Campbellites (Disciples of Christ). It was while he was a student at a Campbellite academy in Hiram, Ohio, that his faith accelerated. He possessed a keen intellect, a natural speaking ability, and a deeply implanted sense of right and wrong. After gaining a bachelor's degree from Williams College, he returned to the Hiram school to teach foreign languages. Garfield was only 26 when he became president of the Hiram academy.

Politics then beckoned. In 1859, the tall and handsome Garfield won election as a state senator, and his antislavery rhetoric brought him a wide reputation. With the advent of the Civil War, he organized a company of his students, and they volunteered en masse for army service. The militarily untutored Garfield became lieutenant colonel of the 42nd Ohio and by year's end commanded the regiment.

In a January 1862 skirmish at Middle Creek, Kentucky, Garfield's men scattered a ragtag Confederate force. This gave the Union control of the eastern half of Kentucky and brought Garfield a brigadier general's commission. Ill health kept him in Washington for several months, where his Radical Republican ear was ever alert. When Lincoln issued the Emancipation Proclamation, Garfield told a friend, "It is a strange phenomenon in the world's history, when a second-rate Illinois lawyer is the instrument to utter words which shall form an epoch memorable in all future ages."

Thanks to the influence of his friend, Treasury Secretary Salmon P. Chase, Garfield returned to the western theater and joined William Rosecrans's Army of the Cumberland. The two generals became close associates, despite Rosecrans's active Catholic faith and Garfield's aversion to papism. Soon Garfield became the Army's chief of staff.

Although Garfield was remarkably thin-skinned and constantly sought approval at every level, he had strong feelings of how the war should be waged. Primary among them was the need to strike boldly against the enemy. Garfield grew restless as Rosecrans made sure his army was just perfect. His impatience would have been acceptable, but Garfield went beyond the chain of command and voiced discontent in personal letters to Secretary Chase. "Thus far the General has been singularly disinclined to grasp the situation with a strong hand," Garfield stated. "I beg you to know that this delay is against my judgment."

This betrayal of trust in a superior he was duty-bound to serve was a black mark on Garfield's record, even though Rosecrans's embarrassing defeat at the September 1863 Battle of Chickamauga justified Garfield's criticisms. Two months later, Garfield resigned from the Army to accept election to Congress. He served in the House for 17 years, all the while gaining the attention and respect of his colleagues.

By 1880 the Republicans were hopelessly split into two wings. Garfield became a dark-horse candidate and won the nomination on the 34th ballot. The ensuing campaign, against Democratic nominee Winfield Hancock, was full of personal attacks and bitter recriminations. Out of the 9 million votes cast, Garfield won with a plurality of fewer than 2,000 votes—the closest popular margin of all presidential elections. (The electoral college vote was 214–155 for Garfield.) On the day after the election, Garfield had the unprecedented position of being a member of the House of Representatives, a U.S. Senate appointee, and president-elect of the United States.

The amiable Garfield found the highest office agonizing from the start. Applicants for government jobs were everywhere, Garfield always had trouble saying no to anyone, and fellow Republicans were pulling at him from opposite directions. At one point Garfield shouted, "My God! What is there about this place that a man should ever want to get in it?" To add to his misery, long-standing party scandals—some of which touched Garfield personally—began to erupt.

Garfield could have never guessed that one of the aspirants for a federal job was insane. At 9:30 a.m., July 2, 1881, after four months in office, the president walked into the Washington train station to travel to commencement ceremonies at his alma mater, Williams College. Secretary of State James G. Blaine was at his side when a shabbily dressed man walked up and shot Garfield twice from behind. The first bullet merely grazed his coat, but the second shot entered his back, fractured at least one rib, and lodged deep in his body. A physician rushed to the scene and assured the president that the wound was not serious. Garfield replied, "Thank you, Doctor, but I am a dead man."

Week after week, a dozen physicians probed with fingers and unsterilized equipment in search of the bullet. Meanwhile, because Garfield and Vice President Chester Arthur were political rivals who disliked each other, Garfield's advisers refused to allow Arthur to see the president or to assume any executive duties. Sweltering summer weather in Washington led to Garfield being taken in a specially designed railroad car to his home at Elberon on the New Jersey shore. Tracks were laid all the way to the front door.

As the search for the bullet continued, Garfield was given morphine injections (hypodermic needles had been in use for less than five years). Alexander Graham Bell, of telephone fame, had invented an electromagnetic metal detector, but no one on-site understood the contraption. It failed to pinpoint the bullet because the bedsprings interfered.

An illustration re-creates the tragic moment that ended Garfield's life, and subsequently the era of "log-cabin presidents."

Sepsis began to take its toll. Garfield became increasingly dazed and confused as the disease spread. The 79-day ordeal ended on September 19, when the president died. He was 49. A postmortem examination located the bullet, at last, behind his pancreas.

Garfield's funeral obsequies were reminiscent of those of Lincoln, but Garfield's presidency was too short for anyone to evaluate it. The second assassination of a president came not as a result of a protracted rebellion. It was the first in a pattern that would mark all the presidential murders that followed. A lone individual, overtaken by insanity, had taken it upon himself to correct what he knew was history's mistake. ◡

CHARLES JULIUS GUITEAU

MURDER "FOR THE PEOPLE"

O NE REASON IT'S DIFFICULT to prevent assassination plots is that the people who hatch them think the infamy they achieve is worth whatever price they have to pay. Charles Julius Guiteau, certainly of unsound mind, had reached that conclusion when he shot President James A. Garfield.

Guiteau, of French Huguenot extraction, grew up in an unstable family environment that shifted from Illinois to Wisconsin. In adulthood he failed at every career he pursued: insurance salesman, self-educated lawyer, newspaperman, preacher, debt collector, and political activist. His marriage to a YWCA librarian provided clear evidence of his mental instability: During the five years she endured his cruelty, he locked her in closets, beat her, and dragged her around the house by the hair while shouting, "I am your master!"

Shabbily dressed, with piercing eyes, a slanting forehead, and a feline walk, Guiteau exuded a furtive manner. In 1880 he got involved in politics. He originally favored Grant for president but switched to Garfield's side. Guiteau harassed party bosses to let him give campaign speeches, and he finally got permission to address a small group of African Americans. The closeness of Garfield's victory convinced Guiteau that his one address provided the margin of victory. He thereupon requested the ambassadorship to France.

The perpetual loser bombarded the White House and the State Department with letters and visits inquiring about his appointment. Finally Secretary of State James G. Blaine wrote him: "Never bother me again about the Paris consulship so long as you live." The White House also barred him from entrance.

One night, "like a flash," Guiteau recalled, he had an epiphany. "If the President was out of the way, everything would go better." His motive was not personal. He likened it to removing the Indians to make way for settlers and railroads. He wanted to save the Republican Party, prevent another civil war, and respond to the dictates of God. "I acted upon the inspiration of the Diety," he confessed.

The 40-year-old Guiteau became joyfully focused on his mission. As he later told a jailer, "I thought . . . what a tremendous excitement it would create, and I kept thinking about it all the week." He borrowed $15 and bought a .44-caliber pistol with an ornate handle because it would later be attractive in a museum. (The Smithsonian Institution subsequently photographed the gun, which then disappeared.) Guiteau carefully prepared an "Address to the American People," outlining the reasons for killing Garfield. The assassination "is not murder," he declared, "it is a political necessity."

On the morning of July 2, 1881, Guiteau was waiting at the train station when the presidential party entered the huge lobby. Guiteau walked up behind Garfield and shot him twice at a distance of six feet. A single policeman grabbed Guiteau while aides rushed to the fallen president.

The assassin reveled in the publicity that followed. He demanded $25 for any photograph taken. The *New York Herald* eagerly published a hastily written, disjointed autobiography. Guiteau fully expected to be released as legally insane, whereupon he planned to run for the presidency by going on the lecture circuit to speak about politics and religion. He also announced from jail that he was "looking for a wife," who had to be "an elegant Christian lady of wealth, under thirty, belonging to a first-class family."

More than 170 prospective jurors were interviewed before an impartial dozen could be selected. The trial began on November 14, two months

Utterly remorseless, Guiteau spent his last days defending the assassination as "a political necessity."

after Garfield's death, and it lasted eight weeks. The major question was Guiteau's sanity. His constant outbursts and interruptions reduced the courtroom at times to a circus. One physician after another testified that the accused was "a morbid egotist," "a moral monstrosity" who "is not only now insane, but was never anything else."

The district attorney countered: "He is no more insane than I am . . . He got tired of the monotony of dead-beating. He wanted excitement of some kind, and he got it."

Guiteau offered his own explanation: "The doctors killed Garfield. I just shot him."

The jury deliberated only one hour before bringing in a guilty verdict. Guiteau bounded to his feet. "You are all low consummate jackasses!" he shouted. When the judge sentenced Guiteau to death, cheers erupted in the courtroom. To the end, the condemned man played his role to the hilt. He planned to appear at his execution dressed only in his underwear, as a reminder of the crucifixion of Jesus. That fantasy was denied. Guiteau's request for a band to play at his hanging was similarly rejected.

On June 30, 1882, a large crowd of newspapermen and curiosity seekers jammed the prison courtyard. Guiteau smiled and waved at the assemblage as he walked to the scaffold. Standing on the gallows, his hands bound in front of him, he read first from a Bible and then a few verses of poetry he had composed that morning. The hangman placed a black hood over his face. Guiteau was mumbling, "Glory, glory, glory" when the trapdoor dropped under his feet. Wild cheers exploded from the crowd.

Of the four presidential assassins in our history, Charles Guiteau lived the longest, nine months, after his victim's death. During that time he trotted out all of his mad dreams for public display, like the publicity hounds so well known today. In an era when America was changing from a nation of farmers to factory workers, this small man was able to rise out of the faceless crowd and make his chilling mark for all the wrong reasons. ❧

WILLIAM McKINLEY

AMERICA'S SWEETHEART

I N 1896 HE SEEMED ALMOST THE IDEAL presidential candidate: a 17-year-old schoolteacher when the Civil War opened, a major in Rutherford Hayes's 23rd Ohio, a congressman with long years of honorable service, a leader in the politically potent Buckeye State, and one who "could bend like the willows in the winds of public opinion."

William McKinley was so wedded to Big Business in an age of industrialization that he was known as the "advance Agent of Prosperity" and "Napoleon of Protection." He was one of the few heads of state who maintained great rapport with his congressional colleagues. The Ohioan brought a substantial closing of the bloody gap between North and South, and he even managed to ease the distance between factions within his own Republican Party.

America was prospering when he was elected, and McKinley pursued every impetus to make the nation the industrial power of the world. Like Lincoln, he kept an ear to the ground on public opinion—despite the warning from political boss "Uncle Joe" Cannon that he might get grasshoppers as a result. Because McKinley was willing to listen, he never made a hasty decision.

He was widely known for being amiable, courteous, and impeccably dressed. Dignity and girth added inches to his short frame. McKinley never allowed himself to be seen in disarray. He was a heavy cigar smoker, but not in public for fear of being a corruptible influence on the young.

*An 1899 image of McKinley on a visit home to Canton, Ohio,
attests to his strong family values.*

Several times a day he would change his white vests when they wrinkled. So great was his self-control that he seemed not to perspire during the muggiest Washington weather.

That he was also a warm family man was common knowledge. He carefully watched over his epileptic wife, Ida. After saying "I do, so help me, God" at his 1897 inaugural, he leaned over and kissed his mother. As a person, he was probably the most beloved president thus far.

Ironically, given that McKinley was such a kind and gentle man, he is remembered primarily for taking the country into the Spanish-American War. He was no warmonger—"I have been in one war," he said in 1898, "and I do not want to see another"—but he was a keen interpreter of public wants. The people, not the president, held the ultimate authority. The masses were eager for war with Spain to establish an overseas empire.

McKinley balked and had to take sleeping powders to overcome the stress. Theodore Roosevelt, who did everything in extremes, snarled that

Sending shock waves across the nation, a September 7, 1901,
newspaper headline announces McKinley's assassination.

McKinley was "a white-livered cur with no more backbone than a choc-
olate éclair." A fight-thirsty Congress passed the necessary declaration of
war, and America's possessions soon extended across the Pacific Ocean to
Hawaii and the Philippines. Flanked by an able secretary of state, John
Hay, McKinley made the United States an active force in world leadership
for the first time. It also made McKinley a shoo-in for reelection in 1900.

McKinley developed a good technique when he had to do mass hand-
shaking. He would smile, grab the guest's right hand, squeeze it quickly.
By holding the person's elbow with his left hand, he could pull him along
and smile at the next person in line.

Such greeting was taking place on September 6, 1901, at the great Pan-American Exposition in Buffalo, New York. The president was shaking hands in a hall with a long line of people. An aide told McKinley that there wasn't time to meet them all. "Well," McKinley replied, "they'll all know I tried."

Around 4:15 a man approached with his right hand in a handkerchief. He was dressed in plain clothes and had a childish expression on his face. McKinley courteously extended his left hand to greet him. The handkerchief fell away; a .32-caliber pistol fired two shots. McKinley slumped to the floor as the gunman stood rooted to the spot. A host of bystanders pounced on the gunman and, after disarming him, began flailing at him with fists. McKinley said as loud as he could, "Don't let them hurt him."

It took a while for medical assistance to arrive. Physicians determined that one bullet had been deflected by a button, but another had cut a path through the president's stomach and lodged somewhere in the muscles of the back. A surgeon later sutured the two holes in the stomach but did not remove the bullet. The use of antiseptics lay in the future.

McKinley was alert and cheerful for the next several days. He then began to have difficulty eating. The area along the bullet's track had become infected. On the morning of September 13, his condition turned critical. That evening McKinley began murmuring his favorite hymn, "Nearer, My God, to Thee." He died of sepsis at 2 a.m. the following day. His body lay in state in the East Room of the White House prior to burial in Canton, Ohio.

One biographer concluded, "He stood at the top of American politics as a result of his own masterful skill and because he was as much the dominant political personality of his time as Franklin Roosevelt would become in the 1930s."

He was the last Civil War veteran to serve as president. With his passing also ended the domination of Civil War forces. The mushrooming industrial might that had created a country of haves and have-nots on an unprecedented scale would be halted by the reforms of McKinley's successor, Theodore Roosevelt—the nation's next great president after Lincoln. America was entering a new century, in which its concerns encompassed the entire world. ✑

LEON CZOLGOSZ

ANARCHISM IN ACTION

O F ALL THE PRESIDENTIAL ASSASSINS, Leon Czolgosz (pronounced SHO-gosh) had the clearest motive. He hated the
politics of state-supported capitalism. As America emerged
from its cocoon to take its place on the world stage, strange terms like
"communism" and "proletariat" migrated from Europe to inspire industrial workers in the United States. When viewed in this context, the
eruption of such a madman does not seem as strange.

Similarities exist between Garfield murderer Guiteau and McKinley
assassin Czolgosz: Both men were of questionable sanity; both were failures in the normal avenues of life; both became disillusioned with and
resentful of American society. Both had a burning desire for notoriety and
concluded that killing the president of the United States would unquestionably make a "somebody" out of a "nobody."

Czolgosz was the same age as the man he murdered. Born to poverty-
stricken parents in Michigan, he received little education because he had
to begin working at the age of ten. His mother died in childbirth soon
thereafter. His stepmother and his rigidly Catholic father bullied him
throughout his youth. Such abuse affected his emotional development, and
he slowly became a recluse. Though unsociable, he was never quarrelsome.
At one point he suffered a nervous breakdown.

Czolgosz despaired constantly of his lowly station in life. He developed
into a clean-shaven, bright-looking man. No record of any romantic

relationships exists. Moving from one short-term job to another, the rudderless Czolgosz almost naturally drifted into anarchism. He read radical newspapers and magazines while occasionally attending socialist meetings. Czolgosz listened intently to such radicals as Emma Goldman and Emil Schilling, who railed against America's wealthy enriching themselves at the expense of the poor. The jobless Pole came to believe that all rulers were the enemies of the people and that because the United States was the most powerful industrial nation in the world, its lower classes were forever doomed to poverty; the federal government was to blame for such inequity.

Late in July 1900, newspapers announced the assassination of King Umberto I of Italy. His killer stated that he did the deed for the sake of the common man. Czolgosz now saw his destiny. "I thought it would be a good thing for the country," he concluded, "to kill the President." Czolgosz knew what he wanted to do, just as he knew he would die if he succeeded. Yet his sacrifice might bring America to its senses in terms of social fairness.

He spent a year contemplating how and when he could act. The opportunity came in September 1901, when President McKinley would be attending the Pan-American Exhibition in Buffalo, New York. Czolgosz traveled there and purchased a short-barreled revolver, which could be easily hidden in his large hand. On the second day of the exposition, he patiently waited in line to see McKinley. As Czolgosz walked forward, the president extended his hand. The anarchist slapped it away and fired twice. "I done my duty!" he yelled before the crowd subdued him. He later confessed, "I don't believe one man should have so much service and another man should have none."

His trial began nine days after McKinley's death. Court-appointed attorneys asked for a delay: They could not make a case because Czolgosz refused to talk with them. The motion was denied, and the trial was short. A jury deliberated merely an hour before sentencing Czolgosz to death.

The shackled and heavily guarded prisoner was taken by train to Auburn Prison, New York. A large and angry mob waited at the station. Czolgosz

LEON CZOLGOSZ, WHO SHOT PRESIDENT McKINLEY.

The above pictures are snap-shots of the assassin taken just after his arrest.

Four head shots reveal the face of the misguided Czolgosz,
whose crime devastated American citizens.

was attacked and beaten before additional police officers hustled him inside the safety of the prison. The warden allowed no visitors during the ensuing month as preparations were made for execution by a method only ten years old: electrocution.

Czolgosz, resigned to his fate, made no statements and displayed no emotion. On October 29, 1901, guards awakened him from a sound sleep and led him to the electric chair next door. At 7:12 a.m., Czolgosz reportedly muttered a curse just before the first of two jolts of 1,700 volts coursed through his body. A special grave in the prison cemetery had been prepared. It was vented because, just before interment, authorities poured sulfuric acid into the coffin to hasten decomposition. Within 12 hours, nothing was left of Leon Czolgosz.

He remains the most obscure of presidential assassins, but his motives, as demented as they were, sprang from a wellspring shared by many at the time. In 1904 muckraker Ida Tarbell published *The History of the Standard Oil Company,* detailing its monopolistic practices, and two years later Upton Sinclair's *The Jungle* showed the world the horrors of Chicago's stockyards. Within a span of seven years, anarchists killed the president of France, the empress of Austria, the king of Italy, the prime minister of Spain, and the president of the United States. Amid the clamor for change, Leon Czolgosz ushered in a new era in his twisted fashion. ∾

CHAPTER 9

AMERICA RISING

In the short 35 years from Appomattox to the end of the 19th century, Americans settled half of their continent, laid out a vast railroad system, and became world leaders in the development and use of coal, oil, and metals. The industrial revolution, which began in the North in the 1830s, propelled the United States to third in manufacturing worldwide during the Civil War. The country surged into first place in the succeeding two decades. Fueling that growth were unknowns who took advantage of the tremendous spurt of wartime spending and became famous in the last half of the 19th century.

The major industrialists in the Gilded Age were entrepreneurs in areas where many temptations were offered and few restraints imposed. While they behaved with becoming vulgarity, they were men of audacity and exploitative talents—shrewd, aggressive, insatiable. One writer concluded, "They directed the proliferation of the country's wealth, they seized its opportunities, they managed its corruption, and from them the whole era took its tone and color."

Pioneering this new breed of executives was Andrew Carnegie. The undersized, ever inventive Scotsman started in railroads, and during the war he switched to telegraphs that relayed battle reports instantly. He was in England after the war when he met Henry Bessemer—and mass production of steel was born. From that time he "mounted the ladder of success so fast that it

OPPOSITE: *"The Modern Colossus of Rail Roads" encapsulates the industrial boom.*

scorched the rungs." With the gigantic piles of money he amassed, Carnegie proved to be one of the greatest philanthropists the world has known.

During the war the North's growing strength was supported by sizable investments from private individuals. Rising to the top of the heap of frantic entrepreneurs were financial giants like Jay Gould and J. P. "Jubilee" Morgan. Gould's holdings expanded from his speculation in railroad stocks during the war until his vast empire encompassed 15,000 miles of American rails. In his early days, Morgan was not above war profiteering but moved on to become legendary for his banking houses.

Some of the industrial revolution's magnates just happened to be in the right place at the right time. Selling meat to the Union Army gave Philip Armour his start in what grew into a meatpacking empire based in Chicago. The working conditions at his stockyards became so onerous that a public outcry utterly disgraced him. His labor force was hardly alone in being mistreated during this unregulated era. The growth of industrial labor inevitably brought friction with corporate leadership. Unrest led to strikes, which usually ended in bloodshed. Detective Allan Pinkerton, on whom Lincoln depended for enemy intelligence during the war, proved adept at infiltrating bands of unhappy workers and alerting corporate heads of possible activity.

The "personification of progressivism," the individual who dominated the nation's rise to economic greatness, was John D. Rockefeller. The Civil War provided a boost for America's newest mass-market fuel, oil. With those gains, Rockefeller went on to create an empire unparalleled in its size. At the turn of the new century, when the average annual wage was $400, he became America's first billionaire. For the last 40 years of his life, however, he turned his prodigious energy to charity. Indeed, his legacy today stems almost as much from his philanthropy as from his empire building.

Rockefeller's charity, while enormous, was matched by two humanitarians working alone but faithfully. Clara Barton began helping others on the battlefields of the Civil War, and that work became a lifetime crusade. An indomitable spirit who was unwilling to accept the strictures placed on women, she established the American Red Cross as a major relief agency for the needy.

Fashionable New Yorkers stroll through Madison Square in the city that was quickly becoming a commercial and manufacturing epicenter.

Reformer Frederick Douglass found that his cause did not take off so readily; society is more difficult to spur to new heights than an industry. Well known for his abolitionist views prior to the war, Douglass continued his quest for the recognition of racial equality in the postwar years. His legacy influenced successors like Booker T. Washington and W.E.B. DuBois as the nation struggled with how freed slaves would fit into the social order. This last legacy of the Civil War remains painfully unresolved to this day. ∾

ANDREW CARNEGIE

KING OF STEEL

HIS IS THE GREATEST "RAGS TO RICHES" STORY in American history. Andrew Carnegie was born into poverty in Scotland. His father operated a hand loom until he lost his job to mechanization. The family then immigrated to Pittsburgh, Pennsylvania, where young Andrew worked first as a bobbin boy in a textile factory and then as a telegrapher. In 1852, Thomas A. Scott, called "the father of American railroading," offered Carnegie a job as telegrapher and personal secretary for the western division of the Pennsylvania Railroad.

Rail lines were the first big industry in America, and Pennsylvania had the largest. Scott gave Carnegie advice, experience, and the use of his extensive library. The young Scotsman accepted all of it. When Scott advanced to president of the line, he appointed Carnegie in his place with the western division.

Carnegie's only participation in politics came during this period. His abolitionist views led him into the Republican Party. As a proponent of social equality, he wrote several editorials for Horace Greeley's *New York Tribune.*

Shortly after the Civil War began, Scott was named assistant secretary of war in charge of military transportation. He wisely brought in Carnegie to supervise telegraphic communications for Union detachments in the Washington area. Carnegie helped in repairs of the Annapolis-Washington line so Federal regiments could reach the capital. Cut in the face while splicing wire, Carnegie received praise as being one of the war's first casualties.

Scottish-born Carnegie entered the American railroad industry and shot to fame.

After collecting the best operators he could find, Carnegie helped establish the U.S. Military Telegraphic Corps. The speed that telegraph lines brought to widespread communication revolutionized the face of war. Like fellow businessman John D. Rockefeller, Carnegie then hired substitutes

*First designed in 1904, the Carnegie medal is awarded to civilians
who make exceptional sacrifices to save the lives of others.*

to avoid serving in the army. Carnegie felt no shame remaining in civilian
pursuits. He regarded himself a better patriot for improving railroads than
he would be as another soldier in the ranks.

Fame and fortune followed. While continuing work for the Pennsylvania Railroad, Carnegie invested $40,000 in the nascent Columbia Oil
Company. Two years later, the oil producer made more than $1 million in
profits. In 1862, Carnegie organized the Keystone Bridge Company, which
built the nation's first iron trestles. Wartime demands for armor, cannon,
shells, and other iron products made Pittsburgh the center of the rapidly
growing iron industry. Carnegie took advantage of the situation in 1864
by creating one iron company and buying another. His firm dominated
the production of iron for railroad use in the immediate postwar years.

In partnership with T. T. Woodruff and George Pullman, Carnegie contributed another improvement to railroads by designing an elegant sleeping car for overnight travelers.

All this was prelude to the great leap to come. The ironmaster made a fateful trip to Europe in 1882. There he met English inventor Henry Bessemer, whom Carnegie initially thought was "a crazy Frenchman." Bessemer had developed a process of forcing air through molten pig iron to produce white-hot steel. The 38-year-old Carnegie rushed home. The age of iron had passed; the blast furnace was now the way to go. "Give it thirty thousand pounds of common pig iron," he exclaimed, "and presto! The whole mass is blown into steel!"

The entrepreneur surrounded himself with capable assistants, negotiated for cheap railroad transport, and created the most efficiently operated steel plant under single management in the world. Carnegie's enterprise came to include steelmaking foundries, rolling mills, and bridge works. With headquarters in Pittsburgh, and easy access to coal, oil, and the carbon fuel coke, Carnegie turned out steel in quantities that drove away competition. In one decade, steel production leaped from 26,600 tons to 500,000 tons.

Expansion was continual and easy. The steel combine in which Carnegie held half interest was a private partnership, not a public corporation. Carnegie insisted that profits be plowed back into the business. By cost reduction, consolidation, and control of all the production stages, Carnegie reigned over the most extensive individually owned iron and steel operations ever. His annual income—at a time of minimal taxation—was $250 million by modern-day calculation.

Yet his enormous wealth was only one asset of a man known for his charm, literary knowledge, and social graces. While much of his fortune came from in-house trading and manipulations, Carnegie was a missionary for financial responsibility and social benevolence. Those who became rich, Carnegie stated, were the best fitted for wealth because competition "insures the survival of the fittest in every department." In the first of two books he wrote, *Triumphant Democracy* (1886), Carnegie thought American democracy was vastly superior in production methods than the

English monarchy. His best received volume, *The Gospel of Wealth* (1889), argued that the wealthy should use their affluence to enrich all society.

Much of his moral standing evaporated in the 1892 Homestead Strike, when laborers at one of his plants demanded higher wages. Bloody clashes followed with police and Pinkerton henchmen the company had hired. The plant reopened with immigrant employees, known as "scabs," rather than plant workers. Carnegie's reputation was permanently damaged. The Homestead dispute led to a 1901 sellout by Carnegie to financial giant J. Pierpont Morgan. The $14 billion sale was the largest personal transaction in history. Carnegie's former empire became the United States Steel Corporation.

While creating America's steel industry, Carnegie began making significant gifts to charity. He once declared in a memo to himself: "Man does not live by bread alone . . . [My] gifts have contributed to the enlightenment and joy of the mind . . . to all that tends to bring into the lives of the toilers . . . sweetness and life. I hold this the noblest possible use of wealth."

The business magnate donated more than $5 billion to worthwhile pursuits before his August 11, 1919, death from bronchial pneumonia. Another $30 million went to charities after Carnegie's passing. He was buried in Sleepy Hollow Cemetery in Tarrytown, Massachusetts.

Motivated by the demands of the Civil War, Carnegie was a key figure in the emergence of postwar America as the world's greatest source of first iron and then steel. Among his enduring legacies are also public libraries, the Carnegie Institute of Technology, the Carnegie Corporation of New York, Carnegie Hall, Carnegie Mellon University, the Carnegie Endowment for International Peace, and the Teachers Insurance and Annuity Association of America (now TIAA-CREF). ∾

JASON "JAY" GOULD

PACEMAKER FOR GREED

FOLLOWING THE WAR, a new class of super-rich industrialists made stupendous fortunes by any standards. None was more corrupt and exploitive than Jason "Jay" Gould. He parlayed his winnings on the fate of Union battles to amass an initial fortune. From that foundation he wheeled and dealed his way to America's greatest railroad speculator and developer.

Born in Roxbury, New York, he was largely self-educated, schooling himself in surveying and mathematics. His first hint of shrewdness came when he was barely 20. He began his career in a Pennsylvania tanning business, bought out his partners, and gained a modicum of prosperity.

In 1859 Gould became enamored with the burgeoning railroad field and began purchasing stock in small companies. For Gould, the Civil War was a business opportunity to be fully exploited. He paid government agents to inform him of Union victories or defeats before news became public. He could then anticipate stock market reactions and reap large profits. In one instance, he bought control of a line by purchasing stock at ten cents on the dollar. The line later flourished—and so did Gould.

Beginning in 1867, Gould became the terror of Wall Street, joining financiers Cornelius Vanderbilt and Daniel Drew to gain control of the Erie Railroad, the East Coast's major carrier. Gould was named president of the company the following year. He was not an impressive-looking executive. Undersized in body and maintaining a full beard, he was normally reserved in manner and gave only a fleeting smile. His large, dark eyes were piercing; his intense concentration gave off a demonic energy.

Gould's manipulative ways came into full view when he appointed New York political leader William "Boss" Tweed as director of the Erie line. Tweed in turn arranged legislation favorable to Gould. The two became wrathful targets for the press and cartoonist Thomas Nast. The *New York World* called him "The Little Wizard of Wall Street." The *New York Times* went further: Of "His Majesty Jay Gould," the paper suggested, "it may be time that fifty millions of Americans will allow Mr. Gould's foot to rest on their neck."

Never did Gould evince any interest in running a railroad. He enjoyed manipulating stock through what today is called insider trading. He was, on the one hand, a speculator who bought and sold stocks by guessing their future prices, and on the other hand a manipulator who caused stock prices to fluctuate for his personal gain. Using stocks from his own companies, Gould persuaded sympathetic banks to finance his activities. And always he offered bribes to men in politics, justice, and other high places.

All this became evident in 1868 when, with Daniel Drew and James "Jubilee Jim" Fisk, Gould countered an attempt by Vanderbilt to seize control of the Erie Railroad. Gould engaged in a number of outrageous schemes. Among them, he issued 100,000 shares of fraudulent Erie stock and bribed the New York legislature to legalize the action. The plan succeeded, even though Gould had to flee to New Jersey to avoid New York court action. Additional payoffs ended the Erie takeover attempt.

The following year, in what one writer termed "a plot of breathtaking audacity," Gould sought to corner the gold market. Enriched by railroad profits, emboldened by his success in buying legislators and judges, Gould hired President Grant's brother-in-law and his personal secretary as active investors. A small group then leaked word that they were buying large sums of gold with the president's endorsement. Price for the precious metal shot up to $140 per ounce.

An early photo of Gould before he sported his trademark beard

In an attempt to tamp down the market, the Treasury Department injected $4 million of its gold. That produced Black Friday, September 29, 1869, on the stock market. Gould cohort James Fisk gloated that in an hour prices plunged in "the wildest confusion and the most unearthly screaming of men to the verge of temporary insanity by the consciousness of ruin." In an hour, gold fell to $30 an ounce. Gould, anticipating an economic rout, had sold his gold at a handsome profit on the morning before the crash.

With $25 million in hand, Gould turned his attention to western railroads. He acquired leadership of the Union Pacific and added fledgling rail lines to the mother company. His position was unassailable. The government continued to give land freely for railroad development. Companies had complete control over rate settings, freight storage, transportation schedules, as well as future construction.

By 1881, Gould owned the largest railroad empire in the nation: 15,800 miles of tracks, which represented 15 percent of America's entire rail network. He ran the lines with an iron hand of efficiency. He never

*A satirical Gould watches the downtrodden people enter the "Cave of Despair"
with his metaphoric monopoly club in hand.*

hesitated to call in strikebreakers when a labor dispute erupted. He once asserted: "I can hire one-half of the working class to kill the other." Gould added the Western Union Telegraph Company to strengthen his holdings.

Yet all of his buying left his empire badly undercapitalized, and it collapsed in the Panic of 1884–85. Gould lost all his holdings except for the Missouri Pacific Lines and Western Union. Using the Missouri Pacific as an umbilical cord, he acquired the Wabash as well as Texas and Pacific Lines. This gave him a monopoly on railroads in the southwestern quadrant of the nation.

Gould's retirement from stock market dealings did not mean a retreat from business. His personal wealth was an estimated $72 million. He purchased New York City's elevated railway system almost as a hobby. In addition, the purchase of the *New York World* newspaper may have been a move to quiet one of his chief critics. His reputation as a cold and aloof capitalist never improved.

In his last year, tuberculosis began to take its toll. He seemed to have barely enough skin to cover his frame. His hair receded and made his oversize ears prominent. On December 2, 1882, Gould died in New York City. His unembalmed remains were placed in a plain casket. They rest in a huge mausoleum in Woodlawn Cemetery.

Gould's notoriety for greed and corruption contributed greatly to the negative public perception of big businessmen in the industrial revolution. That might have been predicted for a man who viewed the outcome of a battle solely in terms of the money he wagered on it. A biographer concluded, "In his expeditions he used courts and governments; his allies were many, but none his friends; at one time or another in his life he broke almost every man who worked with him; and to the last he remained what by nature he was: a lone worker." ∽

JOHN PIERPONT MORGAN

BANKING CZAR

ANAME SYNONYMOUS with American finance, John Pierpont Morgan was "the living embodiment of Wall Street and its culture." Whereas he began his career in the same scurrilous fashion as Jay Gould, he went on to become a central figure in the banking world. He became so wealthy that he was able to buy Andrew Carnegie's colossal empire. Before his death, he used his immense power to orchestrate the first steps toward what is today the U.S. Federal Reserve Bank.

Born into a wealthy Connecticut banking family, Morgan was educated at several academies and received a degree from the University of Göttingen in Germany. An 1852 attack of rheumatic fever broke his health, slowed his growth, and bothered him spasmodically throughout his life.

Morgan began his career in a London bank that his father partly owned. The cosmopolitan 21-year-old returned to America in 1858 to take up banking in his native country. The Civil War provided him with the opportunity to launch his own career. Like most wealthy Northern men of the time, Morgan paid a $300 commutation fee rather than being drafted. He quickly amassed profits from the manipulation of gold prices and other questionable dealings. His most notorious act was the purchase of 5,000 defective rifles for $3.50 apiece from an army arsenal and the resale of the weapons at $22 each to a gullible field quartermaster.

J. P. Morgan Bank in New York City, home to the world's
first billion-dollar corporation

Morgan appeared on the American financial scene just when the industrial revolution had created a huge demand for investment capital. Factories and railroads were rapidly burgeoning fields, but U.S. capital markets were seriously underfunded. To expand they needed long-term investments that reliable bankers could furnish.

In the immediate postwar years, Morgan directed several banks in the New York–Philadelphia area. Because he was always firmly in control of transactions, a new term entered banking lexicon: "Morganization," or reorganizing a business's structure and streamlining management to increase profits. His reputation for such efficiency made finding investors easy. Although remembered historically as the high priest of modern capitalism, Morgan did not believe in free markets.

His first major deal came in 1879, when he sold $25 million of New York Central Railroad stock to English investors. Morgan's brokerage fee made him wealthy for life. He eagerly accepted appointments to companies'

Fulfilling his irascible reputation, Morgan strikes a photographer with a cane in 1910.

boards of directors. When Morgan could not personally serve, he picked subordinates to man the positions.

Easily recognizable, the financier was a large man with massive shoulders, piercing eyes, and a dominating personality. One acquaintance observed that a visit from Morgan left him feeling "as if a gale had blown through the house." His brusqueness led another colleague to say, "He is an impossible man to have any talk with. The nearest approach he makes is an occasional grunt." To his few friends, he was known as "Pip." He was never without a cigar.

One physical feature plagued Morgan. As a result of an uncommon form of rosacea called rhinophyma, his nose was a huge and hideous purple bulb. Political cartoonists such as Thomas Nast made it an overriding feature of Morgan's face. The financier, who disliked publicity of any kind, reacted violently to attempts to photograph him. All his professional portraits were retouched. Yet a crude taunt persisted: "Johnny Morgan's nasal organ has a purple hue."

His preeminent characteristic was bombast. Yet Morgan was a bundle of inconsistencies. He was deliberate but impulsive, ingenuous and shrewd, domineering but flexible. Above all, Morgan enjoyed his luxuries. His Madison Avenue home was the first electrically lit private residence in New York City. One of his favorite quotations was "If you have to ask the price, you cannot afford it."

When the Panic of 1893 struck, most railroads were overexpanded and carried massive debt structures they could not maintain. The "House of Morgan" came to the rescue. His personal wealth climbed to such a pinnacle that he was accused of single-handedly controlling the flow of capital in the United States.

That was true to some degree. In 1895, as the economic panic subsided, the U.S. Treasury experienced a serious depletion of its gold reserves. Morgan visited President Grover Cleveland and offered a solution. With the cooperation of the Rothschild international dynasty, Morgan floated a 30-year loan of $65 million in government securities.

This deal wounded Cleveland politically. In the 1896 presidential election, Democratic candidate William Jennings Bryan repeatedly attacked Morgan and his banking empire. At the convention the banking houses threw their financial support to Republican candidate William McKinley, who won two terms in the White House as a friend of Big Business.

After the death of his ever watchful father, Morgan moved on to scale even higher heights. During the period 1890–1913, J. P. Morgan and Company organized or underwrote 43 major corporations. Morgan himself had become the most powerful banker in the world. After 11 years of trying, in 1901 he successfully bought out Andrew Carnegie's iron holdings and created the United States Steel Corporation. It was the first billion-dollar company in the world. Controlling two-thirds of the steel market put Morgan in the forefront of the construction of ships, rail lines, cars, wire, nails, and a host of other metal goods.

When the next depression struck, Morgan once again flexed his power. The Panic of 1907 was the second worst in American history. Major banks appeared on the verge of collapse, and no normal avenue existed to stop the downward spirals. Morgan called a meeting of leading financiers at his New York mansion. He persuaded the group to redirect funds between banks, to secure additional international lines of credit, and to buy the plummeting stock of healthy corporations to stabilize them. This private activity eventually led to the 1913 creation of the Federal Reserve System.

In 1912, Morgan was scheduled to travel on R.M.S. *Titanic*'s maiden voyage from England to the United States. He happened to be part owner of the company that built the luxury liner. Yet he canceled his reservation at the last minute because he was enjoying a leisurely trip through Europe,

The pleasant sojourn did not last for long. A series of ministrokes left Morgan increasingly weakened. He died on March 31, 1913, while vacationing in Rome. Organized to the end, Morgan left detailed instructions for both his funeral and his interment. His remains were buried in his hometown of Hartford.

America's meteoric post–Civil War growth rose in tandem with this remarkable individual. An economic analyst stated, "At a time when America had no central bank, Morgan acted as a monitor of its capital market and lender of last resort." The political right praised him as a hero of economic progress; the left decried him as an icon of capitalist greed. Later the founder of *Forbes* magazine anointed Morgan as "the financial Moses of the New World." ço

PHILIP DANFORTH ARMOUR

PRINCE OF PORK

NAPOLEON BONAPARTE DECLARED that "an army marches on its stomach." Civil War armies certainly agreed with that axiom; a lack of food was more the norm than the exception. Wartime demands for meat brought forth Philip Danforth Armour, who ensured thereafter that meat products could be sent to armies or peoples anywhere. Armour was the first of the meatpacking giants in the industrial revolution.

Raised on a New York farm by Scotch-Irish Presbyterian parents, Armour was attending a Methodist seminary at Cazenovia, New York, when he was expelled for taking a buggy ride with a girl. At the age of 14, he left New York with 30 others to seek fortunes in the California gold rush. By the time Armour reached the West Coast, the most promising land had been claimed. An uncommonly high business acumen then appeared. Young Armour began employing out-of-work miners to construct sluices that controlled the water flow in the mined rivers. He became an instantly successful businessman.

Armour decided to go to New York City to test its mercantile business, but along the way he stopped in Milwaukee and ended up buying into a wholesale grocery business. Just before the Civil War began, he and his brother established a meatpacking company in Chicago. A fortune was waiting. The one million men entering Union armies provided an unrestricted market for preserved meat.

The meat-packer quickly took advantage of changing meat prices. Around 1864 Armour expected pork prices to drop sharply as the war wore down. He bought large quantities at depressed prices and sold the meat at high profits in such metropolitan centers as New York and Boston. His most important financial coup, according to one economic historian, "occurred near the end of the Civil War when he predicted heavy Confederate losses and thus the dropping of pork prices . . . he made contracts with buyers at $40 per barrel before prices plummeted to $18 when the war ended." This arrangement netted Armour a 45 percent profit and boosted him toward the rank of millionaire.

On Chicago's South Side, he established a complex of slaughterhouses spread over 14 acres and capable of handling 7,000 hogs a day. He created a grain commission business as part of his company. Hogs—and subsequently cattle as well as sheep—were brought by rail to the Chicago stockyards and fattened by grain before slaughter. Actress Sarah Bernhardt visited the massive stockyards and found them "a horrible and magnificent spectacle."

The "horrible" epitaph applied to another side of the business as well. Operating without any federal regulations, meat-packers often caused pollution within the meat itself. Sausages might contain rat droppings, the rodents themselves, or floor sawdust, among other unsanitary detritus.

Profits soared. Armour opened meatpacking plants in Kansas City and Omaha. Armour and Company was incorporated in 1869 and became the world's largest food processing and chemical manufacturing enterprise in the world. His business transformed the food industry in two major ways: farmers sold crops to large companies that processed and packaged goods for distribution, and railroads enabled foodstuffs to be transported in high volume over long distances. To get his products to markets, Armour followed the lead of rival Gustavus Swift and established a private enterprise of railroad refrigerator cars. By 1900, more than 12,000 yellow Armour cars rode America's rails. Each bore the logo "We Feed the World."

By the 1890s the annual income of Armour's complex was $200 million. He had become one of the greatest industrialists of the so-called Gilded

Chicago meatpacking titan Armour wrangles livestock, the backbone of his empire.

*A refrigerator boxcar bearing the Armour logo distributes goods
as quickly as the assembly lines can process them.*

Age. The heavyset, clean-shaven Armour, with hair only on the side of his
head, maintained a low-key profile throughout his rise to riches.

The secrets to Armour's success were twofold. His was the first meat
company to utilize an assembly line, with each worker having a single
task to perform as carcasses moved via overhead belts and hooks—an
approach that sparked Henry Ford to manufacture automobiles using
the same procedure.

Equally important, Armour found enormous profit in the waste inherent
in slaughtering, especially from hogs. Workers harvested every product possible from carcasses: hides, hooves, horns, meat, and entrails. The Armour
Company became producers of fertilizer, glue, hairbrushes, buttons, marga-
rine, and pepsin. Armour boasted that he utilized "everything but the squeal."

He also liked to employ low-grade humor in promotions. "Ministers
would preach better," he exclaimed, "if they included more of Armour
sausages in their diet."

The road to riches soon encountered bumps. Company employees were
largely immigrants, and Chicago became a "patchwork quilt of vibrant
ethnic neighborhoods." Workers put in long hours of hard labor in a
filthy environment, for which they received meager wages. Armour was
among the first business giants to hire women in large numbers. Wives

and daughters performed menial tasks such as trimming fat from meat and tying sausages.

Strikes against the exploitive treatment were inevitable. Armour survived three major walkouts. The most prominent was the Haymarket Bombing in May 1886. Workers were striking for an eight-hour workday when several were killed by police. The next day, as law enforcement officers sought to disperse the crowd that gathered in Haymarket Square, someone hurled a bomb at the advancing police. The explosion and subsequent exchange of gunfire killed eight policemen and four civilians, while wounding 100 others. The affair is still regarded as a milestone in the development of labor unions.

Armour suffered another embarrassment during the Spanish-American War II. He did not believe that war would cause much disruption to the economy. "Better times and better prices for grain and stock," he announced reassuringly, would convert more antiwar, dissident farmers "than any missionaries we might send to talk to them." That was before Army officials claimed that Armour was shipping tainted meat ("embalmed beef") to soldiers overseas. He strongly denied the charge, and an investigation found no criminal activity involved. Yet Armour was accused in many quarters of bribing the panel. His personal reputation was permanently damaged, and his health suffered as well. He died of pneumonia on January 6, 1901, in Chicago.

Five years later, Upton Sinclair published a best-selling novel, *The Jungle*, painting a dark picture of the squalor in the meatpacking industry. The foul conditions of the Chicago plants captured the public imagination and led to the 1906 passage of the Meat Inspection Act and the Pure Food and Drug Act.

J. Ogden Armour succeeded his father as president of the corporation. During the next 20 years, Armour sales escalated to $200 billion annually. Its cans of potted ham as well as its pork and beans remain popular staples. Reminders of the founder exist on rail. Refrigeration cars, as well as the basic color of the Union Pacific Railroad, are painted in "Armour yellow." ☙

ALLAN PINKERTON

THE PRIVATE EYE

THE FORERUNNER OF TODAY'S U.S. Secret Service was an agency founded by Allan Pinkerton, who was a peculiar combination of energy and imagination. He set up the first private detective agency in Chicago, and his acquaintance with Abraham Lincoln and George McClellan brought him to Washington for the war years. During the industrial revolution, large companies sought out Pinkerton to gather intel on union organizers. His success in doing so led to outbreaks of violence that tarred his name in history books.

A Scotland native, Pinkerton immigrated to America as a young man and continued his occupation as barrelmaker. One day he chanced upon the hideout of a band of counterfeiters. The civic-minded Pinkerton rallied a group of neighbors and captured the gang. The episode, and the accompanying publicity, implanted in him a love of law enforcement. He moved to Chicago and in a short time became the city's first private detective. Pinkerton proved effective in protecting mail and railroad property, and he is considered responsible for introducing two important investigative techniques: professional surveillance and going undercover.

In 1850 he established Pinkerton's Detective Agency. Its logo, an unblinking eye, matched its motto: "We Never Sleep." That combination led to the phrase "private eye."

Pinkerton did yeoman work for the Illinois Central Railroad when George McClellan was a line executive, and the two became friends.

The agency's official logo appeared on stationery in Pinkerton's New York, Philadelphia, and Chicago offices.

During this time he also met the company's lawyer, Abraham Lincoln. Pinkerton was working for the Baltimore-Washington rail line when, in February 1861, he foiled an assassination attempt on President-elect Abraham Lincoln while en route to his Inauguration. When Lincoln arrived safely at the capital, he unlimbered his long legs and said, "Well, boys, thank God this prayer meeting is over."

A few months later, Pinkerton found himself on military assignment. The Union Army's new commander, George McClellan, remembered the detective's work for him and appointed Pinkerton as head of all military intelligence and espionage relative to the Army of the Potomac. The short, stocky, hard-eyed Pinkerton moved to Washington and assumed the pseudonym "Maj. E. J. Allen." He traveled with the army as a McClellan aide while his two dozen operatives worked from a Washington bureau.

Pinkerton's first big "catch" was one of the Confederacy's best informants, Washington socialite Rose O'Neal Greenhow. Early in 1862, while his agents continued to chip away at espionage activity in the Northern capital, McClellan ordered Pinkerton to ascertain the enemy's strength in his front. That was when the detective's usefulness for the Union cause began to spiral downward.

He had been an expert at catching bank robbers and railroad bandits. Yet as chief of military intelligence, Pinkerton was out of his element. Spying

Surrounded by intelligence operatives, Pinkerton leans against a tent pole at the Secret Service headquarters located at Antietam.

on enemy armies was beyond his field. The agents depended heavily upon accounts of Southern deserters, frightened slaves, and unfounded reports planted to mislead. Pinkerton would later boast: "My system of obtaining knowledge was so thorough and complete, my sources of information were so varied, that there could be no serious mistake in the estimate."

Pinkerton was dead wrong. At one point he warned McClellan that 150,000 Confederate soldiers were opposite Union lines. The actual figure was fewer than 60,000 enemy troops.

The miscalculations got worse. A leading factor in McClellan's defeat on the Virginia peninsula arose from false data that Pinkerton sent. McClellan's dismissal from army command in November 1862 marked the end of Pinkerton's military service. A recent authority concluded that Pinkerton and his agents were "the most unaccountably inefficient intelligence service an American army ever had."

The postwar years proved more rewarding. Pinkerton's Chicago agency expanded; new branches opened in New York and Philadelphia. Soon large corporations were hiring Pinkerton to provide information on nascent union-organizing efforts. One Pinkerton agent lived for three years among a secret society of coal miners known as "Molly Maguires." When the cult began discussing terrorist attacks, Pinkerton agents crushed the movement.

In several labor strikes, Pinkerton's harsh policy toward labor unions led to bloodshed and drew strong criticism from workers, though he repeatedly asserted that he was only helping employees avoid the grasp of union control. His greatest failure during this period was losing bank robber Jesse James after a protracted chase extending across several states.

The detective chief found time to write several books about his adventures as a "master spy." One such work, *The Expressman and the Detective* (1864), contains 14 stories brimming with conceived settings, manufactured conversations, and philosophical interludes. In the preface, Pinkerton asserts, "If there be any incidental embellishment, it is so slight that the actors in these scenes . . . would never themselves detect it; and if the incidents seem to the reader at all marvelous and improbable, I can but remind him, in the words of the old adage, that 'Truth is stranger than fiction.' "

A stroke in 1869 forced Pinkerton to relinquish management of his business to two sons. He assisted in work on a system that would centralize all criminal identification records. Today the Federal Bureau of Investigation maintains such a database.

Pinkerton died on July 1, 1884, from uncertain cause. One source points logically to a second stroke. Two other possibilities have been offered: malaria as a result of a trip through the South or gangrene acquired when Pinkerton slipped on a pavement and bit his lip deeply. He was buried in Greenland Cemetery in Chicago.

Eulogies flowed at his passing, but modern-day commentators lean heavily negative. Pinkerton's year of military duty continues to be an historical yoke around his neck. Being the punitive arm of monopolistic companies subjecting their workers to cruel conditions left a sour taste too. Still, when judged for what he did best, Pinkerton created such widespread advances in law enforcement and security that they are taken for granted today. ∾

JOHN DAVISON ROCKEFELLER

THE FIRST BILLIONAIRE

THE NATION NEVER KNEW wealth's wonder until a Cleveland oilman appeared on the scene. He became the first American worth more than a billion dollars. A devout Baptist devoted to God and money, John Davison Rockefeller did for oil what Andrew Carnegie did for steel, and his holdings increased far beyond those of the steel magnate. At the peak of Rockefeller's success, $1.50 of every $100 in circulation belonged to him. Yet he cannot be defined solely by his business practices or his wealth. Later in life, he took his stacks of money and became the premier voice of modern-day philanthropy.

The son of a patent medicine salesman and con man, Rockefeller as a youth was well behaved, studious, and determined to make his life a success. When the war started in 1861, he was doing well in a Cleveland, Ohio, grocery business. Annual profits held steady into the war years. Rockefeller had no sympathy for politicians and cranks who, he thought, had pushed the nation into war. He hired a substitute to avoid army service, but he donated generously to the Union cause. By taking advantage of inflated wartime prices, Rockefeller amassed a small fortune.

Soon he came to see the great potential of the fledgling oil industry. It supplied kerosene for lighting, lubricating machinery, and fuel for such vehicles as ships. What the business lacked, Rockefeller discerned, was a

Rockefeller's humble birthplace near Richford County, New York

major refinery close to the oil fields and with adequate rail and water connections to the rest of the country. In 1863 he picked Cleveland as the site
of his venture. With three partners—each of whom he eventually bought
out—Rockefeller launched his program of expansion and consolidation
of an economic staple.

A popular misconception is that Rockefeller owned enormous oil
deposits. What he actually developed were the refineries that processed
oil for commercial use. His undertaking was an instant success. By the
end of the Civil War, oil had become the North's sixth largest export. An
English banker observed, "It is difficult to find a parallel to such a blessing
bestowed upon a nation in the hour of her direst necessity."

By 1868 Cleveland was one of the five leading refining centers in the
nation, thanks to Rockefeller and his business practices. He borrowed money
and reinvested profits, controlled costs, and found ways to use refinery waste
for additional gain. Rockefeller's company became the largest oil refinery in
the world, and in 1870 he united all the components to form Standard Oil
of Ohio. His climb to success accelerated in spectacular fashion.

Rockefeller's mild appearance concealed the ruthless competitor underneath. Tall and thin, he sported a cropped mustache that was barely noticed
because of his small but piercing eyes. Rockefeller always wore a look of

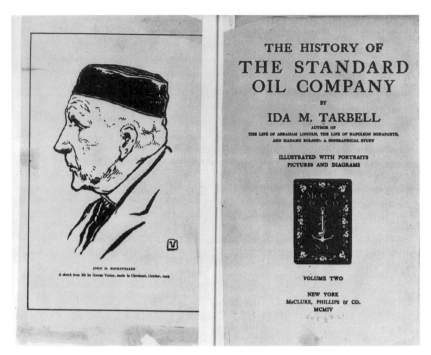

*Tarbell's 1904 exposé shed light on some of Rockefeller's
less ethical business practices.*

intense concentration. With a keen sense of religious stewardship, he
loathed alcohol, tobacco, and gambling. His thriftiness was so severe that
friends labeled him a "penny-pincher."

Always seeking business growth, Rockefeller expanded horizontally.
He purchased other refineries or undersold them to drive them out of
business. The economic wizard acquired oil supplies, built barrel factories
and storage tanks, and constructed pipelines all as "a vertical integration"
to cut costs.

Railroads soon competed fiercely for the oil traffic, and Rockefeller
formed a cartel with several lines. His volume shipments not only received
rebates of up to 50 percent but also drove smaller, competing refineries
to the wall. In one four-month period of 1872, he purchased 25 of 26
competitors in the Cleveland market. Rockefeller had no hesitation in

bribing elected officials to strengthen his monopoly. A popular statement of the day was that Standard Oil could do anything it pleased with a legislature except refine it.

"For forty years—from 1872 to 1914," a scholar of the time concluded, "the name John D. Rockefeller was the most execrated name in American life. It was associated with greed, rapacity, cruelty, hypocrisy, and corruption. Upon it was showered such odium as has stained the name of no other American."

Rockefeller did not think of himself as evil. Like Carnegie, he maintained that the growth of a large business "is merely a survival of the fittest." He thought it better "to let money be my slave than to be the slave of money." To his satisfaction, he was "an angel of mercy" who absorbed the weak in order to strengthen the industry. His was a Machiavellian strategy in purest form.

When Rockefeller began using pipelines for oil transportation, a widely publicized fight began with the organization's chief hauler, the Pennsylvania Railroad. The resultant court battle revealed much of Rockefeller's tactics: underselling, differential pricing, secret rebates, and the like. The *New York World* termed Standard Oil "the most cruel, impudent, pitiless, and grasping monopoly that ever feasted upon a country."

Undeterred by public opinion, Rockefeller in 1882 formed the Standard Oil Trust, whereby nine trustees controlled 41 companies. The New York City–based corporation became the most successful and feared company in the world. It had 20,000 oil wells, 5,000 tank cars, 4,000 miles of pipeline, and more than 100,000 employees. The trust dominated 90 percent of the world's oil refining business. However, the 1890 passage of the Sherman Antitrust Act began a slow dissolution of the monopoly.

Rockefeller then expanded his interests by entering the iron ore and transportation fields. This produced a head-on collision with Andrew Carnegie. When the smoke cleared, J. P. Morgan had purchased the ironworks of both Rockefeller and Carnegie—with all three profiting handsomely.

The oil magnate suffered a serious wound with the 1904 publication of muckraker Ida Tarbell's *History of the Standard Oil Company.* She carefully documented the company's espionage, price wars, heavy-handed marketing practices, and court evasions. Rockefeller dismissed her as "Miss Tarbarrel," but adverse public reaction forced him to loosen many of his autocratic business practices.

In 1911 the Supreme Court declared the Standard Oil Trust unconstitutional. Rockefeller reorganized it into 33 independent subsidiaries that—thanks to the advent of the automobile and a gluttonous appetite for gasoline—became such economic giants as Mobil, Esso, and Sohio. Rockefeller remarked, "I got the last laugh."

After the breakup, the man who had built America's greatest industrial enterprise retired. He spent the last 40 years of his life at his Westchester, New York, estate. But John Rockefeller proved to be the antithesis of the money-grabbing robber baron.

He turned to philanthropy in a tide of unequaled spending. Rockefeller had always donated 10 percent of his income to the Baptist Church. Now he created the University of Chicago and Spelman College, as well as three universities in Asia. He became one of the first benefactors of medical science. His Rockefeller Institute for Medical Research (now Rockefeller University) eventually employed 23 Nobel laureates. Thanks to his philanthropy, hookworm and yellow fever are now controllable diseases. As one writer concluded, "The hundreds of millions of dollars he donated to charitable causes, as well as his own Spartan life style, ultimately endeared him to a public that had once feared him."

Rockefeller died of arteriosclerosis on May 23, 1937, two months before his 98th birthday. His personal wealth was estimated at $336 billion. His influence on modern American business practices and charity is arguably greater than that of any individual in history. ∾

CLARISSA HARLOWE BARTON

ANGEL OF THE BATTLEFIELD

CLARA BARTON was rarely happy, even as one of the most honored women in American history. Unlike philanthropists of Carnegie's and Rockefeller's ilk, she put heart and soul instead of dollars into helping people in need. What started during the war as a solitary woman giving aid to fallen soldiers eventually grew into a charitable organization whose name is instantly recognizable: the American Red Cross.

Barton was born on Christmas Day 1821 and grew up alone, strong-willed, and often uncooperative. At age 15, she began teaching and later became a principal who built the student body from 6 to 600 students in a single year. That achievement ended in anger when another schoolmaster's position that she thought she would get went instead to a man. She was so mad that she abandoned the teaching profession altogether.

In 1854 the dark-haired, dark-eyed woman, who stood barely five feet tall, became one of the first female employees in the U.S. Patent Office in Washington, D.C. She worked amid persistent gender bias until the Civil War erupted across the nation.

Early in childhood, Barton acquired a love of country and things military. The war sparked the 39-year-old spinster into becoming a one-woman soldiers' aid society. With the help of a close friend, Senator Henry Wilson, the chairman of the Military Affairs Committee, Barton began to visit hospitals to distribute food and other supplies. At first she paid out of her own pocket for the goods, but soon she established a network of churches, sewing circles, local communities, and other contributors throughout New England. Barton's three-room flat at Pennsylvania Avenue and Seventh Street became a warehouse for supplies.

These behind-the-lines efforts did not satisfy her spirit. The indomitable Barton cut through red tape and the conventions of society to aid in "stanching blood and feeding fainting men" in "the open field between the bullet and the hospital." Around midnight, after a day's fighting at the 1862 Battle of Second Manassas, Barton appeared with a wagonload of supplies drawn by a four-mule team. An exhausted surgeon acknowledged her arrival by stating, "I thought that night if heaven ever sent out . . . an angel, she must be one because her assistance was so timely."

Barton wrote of her first experience on the battlefield: "All night we made up compresses and slings, and bound up and wet wounds when we could get water and fed what we could in terror lest someone's candle fall into the hay and consume us all."

Three weeks later, learning that another battle was imminent in western Maryland, Barton and four teamsters raced to the scene. She arrived in the midst of the Battle of Antietam—America's bloodiest day. Barton immediately went to work in a farmhouse converted into a field hospital. With no authority or training, she distributed food and water, assisted surgeons with amputations, dressed wounds, and comforted the dying. She was so close to the front lines that a bullet passed through her sleeve and killed the soldier she was tending. For three days she remained steadfastly at her duties, with but a single nap. An admiring surgeon pronounced her "an independent Sanitary Commission of one."

Barton displayed the same devotion to duty in December at the Battle of Fredericksburg, where she nursed alongside poet Walt Whitman. Then the Sanitary Commission curbed her activities. The woman was assuming too much responsibility and acquiring too much recognition, it claimed. Barton was transferred to tend ill soldiers in the siege of Charleston, South Carolina.

Showing tremendous valor under fire, Barton saved countless soldiers' lives.

This was the low point in her life. Barton sank into deep depression, which was finally broken in the spring of 1864 when she was recalled to Virginia to give nursing aid to General Benjamin Butler's Army of the James. There she remained until the end of the war.

Barton's postwar contributions were equally outstanding. She established a bureau to collect names of Federal soldiers missing in action. She began painstakingly recording the names of thousands of Union dead at the prison

*As president of the Red Cross, Barton addresses a class
of young nurses at their graduation.*

compound at Andersonville, Georgia. Four long years passed as she compiled the huge roster. However, credit for the listing went to a male officer.
A disappointed Barton wrote, "I make up my mind more and more that I
must be and do myself and alone . . . my affairs are as bad as they can be."

During 1866–68 she gave more than 500 lectures on her war experiences to spellbound audiences. She also championed feminism, education,
foreign aid, and civil rights. Barton never felt that she had done enough
to secure a rightful place in the world. Although she was confident of her
abilities, she was unsure whether others shared her regard.

On a trip to Switzerland, she found herself drawn to charity work
on battlegrounds. This brought her into contact with the International
Committee of the Red Cross. Barton instantly wanted the United States
to be part of the organization. She returned home with a Geneva Treaty
to that effect, only to have President Rutherford Hayes balk at a possible
"entangling alliance" with the treaty. That had been a foreign policy ever
since the days of George Washington. James Garfield proved supportive,

but he died before he could sign the pact. Finally, in 1882, President Chester Arthur endorsed the treaty, and the Senate gave quick confirmation.

In May 1881, Barton became president of the American National Red Cross. The first chapters were in upstate New York. Thanks to public and private donations, notably from John D. Rockefeller, the organization's headquarters moved to Washington. Its influence quickly spread nationwide. At first concerned with disaster relief, the Red Cross assisted the needy in the 1881 Great Fire in Michigan as well as in the 1889 Jamestown Flood. Then the Red Cross expanded to the military and offered assistance to soldiers in the Spanish-American War.

While Barton gave the impression of strong leadership, she was unable to build a reliable staff and was unenthusiastic about fund-raising. Her advancing age, plus the opposition of a bloc of social work experts, forced her into retirement in 1904. What had been "a cult of personality" became "an organizational humanitarianism."

Robbed of her work, she was never the same again. A 1908 spinal injury kept her bedridden off and on for a year. She survived one attack of pneumonia, but a second attack proved fatal. On April 12, 1912, the restless spirit emerged one last time. "Let me go, let me go," the 90-year-old Barton murmured. Death came a moment later. She was buried in a family cemetery plot in Oxford, Massachusetts.

To unknown hundreds of Civil War soldiers, Barton was "the Angel of the Battlefield." Many named their daughters for the little lady who quietly moved among the human debris of battle. For millions since, the Red Cross has been Clara Barton's memorial. Despite her melancholy, she is one of humankind's greatest benefactors.

Today the Red Cross has more than 650 chapters, 356 blood-service regions, 30,000 employees, and a half million volunteers standing by for emergency service. In addition, it remains the nation's largest supplier of blood and blood products. Its mission, just as its founder envisioned, is indispensable. ∞

FREDERICK DOUGLASS

EMBLEM OF FREEDOM

NO AMERICANS GAINED MORE from the Civil War than enslaved blacks. Tireless abolitionist pioneers endeavored to take the first, halting steps toward freedom. Standing head and shoulders (literally and figuratively) above them was a fugitive slave who rose from bondage to become one of the foremost orator-editor-activists of the abolition movement. His name was Frederick Douglass.

Douglass, initially named Frederick Augustus Washington Bailey, spent his first 21 years as a slave on Maryland's Eastern Shore. His mother was a slave, and his father probably her white master. In 1837 Douglass fled from his owner. With what he called "luck, pluck, and remarkable gifts," the fugitive slave settled in Rochester, New York, and published a newspaper, the *North Star*. (Slaves followed the celestial body north, to freedom.)

Douglass worked his way up the ranks of William Lloyd Garrison's militant antislavery organization and during 1845–47 lectured with great success in Great Britain. Upon his return home, friends purchased his freedom. In 1847 Douglass broke away from the Garrisonian movement because he thought its actions were too extreme. Likewise, in 1859 he opposed John Brown's raid. Attacking a federal installation would enrage the American public, he felt, and possibly damage the abolitionist cause.

*A former slave and a gifted orator, Douglass became
a venerated crusader for freedom.*

Douglass lectured throughout the North on behalf of emancipation and equal rights at a time when slavery was firmly entrenched in the South. His intimate knowledge of slavery and eloquent speeches drew large audiences. Through dazzling oratory and incisive writing, he was a personal indictment against slavery and racism. Awesome in appearance, Douglass was a huge man with hair slung back to his shoulders and intense blazing eyes. Walt Whitman described his voice as "splendid, loud, clear and sonorous, which would make itself heard in the largest open air assembly."

The ex-slave pulled no punches in his pleas for black freedom. As early as 1845, he said, "I do not remember to have ever met a slave who could tell his birthday." A dozen years later, as war clouds loomed on the horizon, Douglass exclaimed: "If there is no struggle, there is no progress. Those who profess to favor freedom and yet depreciate agitation, are men who want crops without plowing up the ground, they want rain without thunder and lightning, they want the ocean without the awful roar of its many waters."

By 1860, Douglass was a symbol for his cause, one who "reached the minds and hearts of white people more effectively than any other man of his race." He violently opposed any last-minute compromises with pro-secession Southerners. "If the Union can only be maintained by new concessions to the slaveholders [and] a new drain on the negro's blood," he shouted, "then let the Union perish!"

(Incredibly, Douglass never lost "a common sense of attachment" to the South. "Nothing but an intense love of personal freedom keeps us [fugitive slaves] from the South." More than once, he referred to Maryland as his "own dear native soil.")

Douglass regarded the Civil War as a moral crusade to end slavery. He relentlessly urged Lincoln to issue a pronouncement of freedom. "War for the destruction of liberty must be met with war for the destruction of slavery." Even after Lincoln announced the Emancipation Proclamation in 1862, Douglass was not satisfied. He wanted the black man to be able to demonstrate his worthiness to the Union.

He helped organize the 54th Massachusetts, the first all-black regiment in the Union armies. His eldest son was a recruit. Thereafter, Douglass became the point man in the recruitment of some 180,000 ex-slaves into the Northern armies. "Douglass's Boys" bore out his expectations and were a key factor in ultimate Union victory.

*Portraits of Douglass (center) and his intellectual contemporaries
are juxtaposed with scenes of plantation life.*

When war ended in 1865, Douglass was a fairly wealthy man. Yet the postwar years were not comfortable ones for the reformer. To the end of his life, he insisted that the Civil War had been a struggle to establish a nation that would live up to its promises. He had been instrumental in gaining freedom for his people, yet freedom and true equality were far different entities.

Douglass, it could be said, became the conscience of the nation because he repeatedly told Americans that the Civil War was not just a conflict to make the nation whole again; it was a war to end human bondage and bring equality to people of all colors. "No man can put a chain about the ankle of his fellow man without at last finding the other end fastened about his own neck," Douglass declared.

Black suffrage was his ultimate goal. "Without this," he stated, "liberty is a monkey." Yet implantation of the 14th and 15th Amendments was snail-like. President Andrew Johnson stated openly, "I know that damned Douglass. He's just like any nigger and he would sooner cut a white man's throat than not."

Soon Douglass was fighting a new war. Historical amnesia befell his race. White Northerners remembered fighting for union, white Southerners remembered defeat. Ever a critic, Douglass often appeared as a lone pilgrim crying in the wilderness. He classified himself as "one isolated in the land of his birth—debarred by his color from congenial association with whites . . . equally cast out by the ignorance of the blacks."

In the 1870s he moved to Washington after his Rochester home burned down—from suspected arson. Douglass began editing another weekly, the *New National Era*. When a young man about to begin his career asked Douglass for a word of advice, the black leader replied, "Agitate!"

He lent his reputation to the Freedmen's Bank, agreeing to serve as president. Yet the bank soon failed and brought a cloud of irresponsibility over Douglass's head. In 1884 the 63-year-old crusader married one of his clerks, Helen Pitts, who was white and 20 years younger than he. The wedding caused a national sensation. Pitts's family stopped speaking to her, and Douglass's children dismissed the marriage as an insult to their deceased mother. Douglass responded by pointing to himself as the creation of a mixed union.

Douglass held a number of minor government posts, including an 1889–1891 term as consul general to Haiti. The following year he produced a third and enlarged edition of *The Life and Times of Frederick Douglass,* an autobiography that he had first issued in 1845. The new edition, like Douglass in his final years, failed to catch attention. Millions of ex-slaves could tell similar stories of suffering. Further, freedmen seeking equality in the late 19th century found themselves facing segregation, disfranchisement, and alarming instances of lynching. The mantle of black leadership was passing to new hands such as educator Booker T. Washington and activist W.E.B. DuBois.

On the evening of February 20, 1895, Douglass received a standing ovation at a women's suffrage convention in Washington. He had just returned to his Anacostia home when he died of a massive heart attack. "The Lion of Anacostia" was buried in Mount Hope Cemetery in Rochester.

Historian David Blight has asserted that Douglass's "life and thought will always speak profoundly to the dilemma of being black in America." His dreams have not all come true, but Douglass remains the most influential leader of African Americans in the 19th century, if not for all time. His book remains required reading in many classrooms today. ℰℐ

SHOULD AULD ACQUAINTANCE <u>BE</u> FORGOT

THE LONG WAR CAME TO AN ABRUPT END once the Union president and the two great Southern armies had died. A reborn nation tottered to its feet and staggered toward what would come next. Decades passed before a lasting peace settled. The journey to a united nation was sometimes bumpy, sometimes torturous. After all, four years of violent, family-splitting, incalculably bloody war had created deep fissures. Three-quarters of a million relatives and friends had perished in battles, in prisons, and from a dozen types of lethal illnesses. Another half million soldiers stumped about on wooden legs, stood with empty sleeves, or were so physically crippled and mentally incapacitated that they were useless in rebuilding anything but memories.

Survivors of blue and gray returned to a world far different from the one they left when war began. Northerners came home to a land throbbing with forward-looking activity. The war had unleashed forces that gathered strength yearly—including business consolidations, rapid industrialization, the spread of railroads, and western expansion. These new challenges slowly began to whittle away at the older tales of suffering and glory.

OPPOSITE: *A photo titled "Freedom's Banner" shows a young former slave from New Orleans with the American flag.*

Ex-Confederates, on the other hand, returned home to desolation and emptiness. Metropolitan areas such as Atlanta, Charleston, Columbia, Mobile, New Orleans, and Richmond were stockpiles of utter destruction. Homes, farms, buildings, bridges, roads, factories, shipping ports, and rail lines were gone. Fields that once blossomed were now overgrown in weeds. Law and order was nonexistent. Hunger and want plagued a shattered population.

To compound the problems, hundreds of thousands of freed blacks wandered through the countryside in restless migration. Former slaves owned nothing because they had received only freedom.

Atop wartime defeat and devastation came Reconstruction. The 1867–1876 military occupation of the South fueled former Confederates' flames of anger. Recovery was long and bitter. By the 1870s the South had wrapped a cloak of respectability around its participation in the Civil War. The struggle for them was the "Lost Cause."

According to its tenets, the South had been forced into war to protect its constitutional rights. Confederates were Christians who had fought for a just cause. Northerners were tyrannical invaders who waged war indiscriminately and destructively against innocent civilians as well as against opposing military forces, and they won only because of an overwhelming superiority in manpower and material. The rationale helped make defeat acceptable and the future less oppressive.

Somehow, through the harsh words and political machinations, surviving soldiers of North and South put their lives back together. More than 1.5 million Union veterans were hailed as "saviors of the Union." A half million ex-Confederates became "keepers of the faith" in the South.

Brotherhoods born in battle matured into postwar fraternal orders. The largest Union organization was the Grand Army of the Republic. With chapters scattered across the nation, and a peak membership of 425,000 members, it became a powerful political and social bloc.

Southern veterans, on an understandably smaller scale, founded the United Confederate Veterans, which likewise evolved into a regionally potent weapon. Like the Grand Army of the Republic, the United Confederate Veterans lobbied hard for soldiers' pensions and other benefits.

A certificate of Union service identifies veterans and praises their sacrifice.

Members of the first mixed-race legislature of South Carolina are identified on an 1876 card.

Both associations pressured state legislatures and solicited private funds for battlefield monuments to mark critical points in the fighting, courageous leaders, and even beloved animals who were regimental mascots. The impoverished South could not keep pace in quantity, but the sincerity and intent was as devoted as that of "the other side." General Lawrence Chamberlain beautifully expressed the underlying purpose of such memorials at an 1888 monument dedication at Gettysburg:

> In great deeds, something abides. On great fields, something stays. Forms change and pass; bodies disappear, but spirits linger to consecrate ground for the vision-place of souls. And reverent men and women from afar, and generations that know us not and that we know not of, heart-drawn to see where and by whom great things were suffered and done for them, shall come to this deathless field, to ponder and dream, and lo! the shadow of a mighty presence shall wrap them in its bosom, and the power of the vision [shall] pass into their souls.

As the Civil War passed into history, former enemies found themselves linked in what *The Red Badge of Courage* author Stephen Crane called "a mysterious fraternity." They were bound by shared sympathies for the younger men they once were and for the sacrifices they made. Of all the thoughts of that war, those remembrances offered the least controversial ground upon which they could relate. Many began to realize that they had not been enemies at all but brothers in suffering.

This mutual respect was the gateway to a lasting peace in the United States. The soldiers would never forget, but they could forgive. They were all living reminders of the greatest test of American statehood. The war was bigger than individual animosity; human commonality drew them together. Johnny Rebs never apologized for what they had done, and Billy Yanks never asked them to.

On the west side of Fredericksburg, Virginia, is the site of the 1863 Battle of Salem Church. One acre is preserved amid blocks of modern commercialism. On that little clearing stands a monument to the 23rd New Jersey. The bronze plaque on the front side contains the usual tribute: "To the memory of our heroic comrades who gave their lives for their country's union on the battlefield." On the other side of that monument is an identical plaque bearing these words: "To the brave Alabama boys, our opponents on the field of battle, whose memory we honor."

The British have never erected a memorial to French gallantry at Waterloo; the Germans have never created a monument to Polish suffering at Warsaw. Yet American soldiers have always been gallant in recognizing heroism.

This postwar camaraderie manifested movingly in battlefield reunions. Ex-soldiers returned to the battlegrounds at anniversaries to stand and remember where they once fought. They came because they could not forget. Two such reunions have earned a place in Civil War history. Both were held at Gettysburg, site of the war's most famous battle.

July 1, 1913, was the 50th anniversary of the start of the engagement. Some 54,000 veterans from 48 states converged on the little town. Old men outnumbered local citizenry by eight to one. The youngest veteran was 61; the eldest, 112.

For four days, despite the hindrances of old age, veterans tramped over the fields. They sat side by side, reliving the past, sharing stories of hardship and valor. The temperature rose to 100 degrees, and a fifth of the gathered veterans had to be treated for exhaustion. But the heat and humidity did not melt the enthusiasm. Among the jokes and old yarns traded was one from an ancient Georgian soldier: "We ran those Yankees all through Georgia, only we were in front of them!"

Others reflected on what they had done a half century earlier. An Illinois private voiced the general sentiment: "I never hated the other fellow. I was overcome by a desire to get even, and I suppose the other fellow was too."

President Woodrow Wilson came up from Washington to address the reunion. He told the bearded, bent men dressed in blue and gray: "We have found one another again as brothers and comrades in arms, enemies no longer, generous friends rather . . . our battles long past."

The presidential address was anticlimactic. The emotional peak came on the afternoon of July 3. At exactly 3 p.m.—the hour of Pickett's Charge—Northern and Southern veterans stood on opposite sides of the

*Veterans from North and South bond in mutual respect
at their final Gettysburg reunion in 1938.*

stone wall that had been the battle's focal point. Silently, they shook hands; some reached over and embraced. Others stood and wept—wept at what had been, wept because they had survived when 750,000 others had not.

The *Christian Science Monitor* editorialized: "By their reciprocal gesture of friendly unity, these honored veterans are building for the future. Not only in the sense that those who follow them inherit the legacy of brotherhood which they now bequeath . . . but it calls a nation to attention that a peace unbroken is better than a peace that must be continually mended."

By the 1930s, the war's survivors were dying at a rate of 900 per year. Pennsylvania authorities decided to hold a final reunion—in 1938, on the battle's 75th anniversary. Invitations went out to 12,500 living veterans. An Alabamian responded, "I'll be there if I have to crawl!"

The Eternal Light Peace Memorial on Oak Hill honors
North and South with a continuously burning flame.

A total of 1,845 old soldiers hobbled to Gettysburg. Rhode Island was the only state not represented. The average age was 92. Sponsors of the reunion had ample supplies at hand, save one. The 27 cases of whiskey lasted only a day.

Usually the old men did little more than sit, talk, listen, and recall what they could. Emotions ran deep throughout the four days. Men in their nineties struggled to sing wartime favorites such as "The Yellow Rose of Texas" and "Eatin' Goober Peas." Almost inevitably, they would end up singing a melody meaningful for the occasion: "And here's a hand, my trusty friend / And give me a hand o'thine / We'll take a cup of kindness yet / To days of auld lang syne."

On July 3, President Franklin Roosevelt stood before an audience estimated at 400,000 people. He looked down at the front section, where old men sat wearing hats, stiff collars, and holding canes. Roosevelt said, "All of them we honor, not asking under which flag they fought then—thankful that they stand together under one flag now."

At 6:30 that evening, the president ignited the Eternal Light Peace Memorial, whose inscription reads, "Peace Eternal in a Nation United." Seventy years have passed since then, and the flame burns bright.

No event in our history up to that point had received greater media coverage than the 1938 reunion. Newspapers, radio, and the telegraph were dispatching stories almost hourly. Few events have been more enthusiastically and positively reported. Not one negative innuendo appeared; that in itself is a journalistic miracle.

Three veterans died during the reunion. Four others died on the way home. The remainder faded into history. The last veteran died sometime in the 1950s (many families claim the honor).

We say they are all gone now. They are not. The past is forever speaking to us, and it speaks with many voices. Those Civil War generations went through an indescribable hell to carve a pathway to the future. We are that future. The America we know was born in 1865. ∽

SELECTED BIBLIOGRAPHY

Ambrose. Stephen E. *Nothing Like It in the World: The Men Who Built the Transcontinental Railroad*. New York: Simon & Schuster, 2000.

Beatty, Jack. *The Age of Betrayal: The Triumph of Money in America, 1865–1900*. New York: Knopf, 2007.

Blight, David M. *Beyond the Battlefield: Race, Memory, and the American Civil War*. Amherst: University of Massachusetts Press, 2002.

Bridges, Hal. *Lee's Maverick General: Daniel Harvey Hill*. New York: McGraw Hill Book Company, 1961.

Carder, P. H. *George F. Root: Civil War Songwriter*. Jefferson, NC: McFarland, 2008.

Castel, Albert D. *Victors in Blue*. Lawrence: University Press of Kansas, 2011.

Cheever, Susan. *Louisa May Alcott*. New York: Simon & Schuster, 2010.

Cisco, Walter R. *Wade Hampton: Confederate Warrior: Conservative Statesman*. Washington, DC: Brassey's, 2004.

Cleaves, Freeman. *Meade of Gettysburg*. Norman: University of Oklahoma Press, 1991.

Davis, William C. *Jefferson Davis: The Man and His Hour*. New York: Harpercollins, 1991.

Duffy, James P. *Lincoln's Admiral: The Civil War Career of David Farragut.* New York: Wiley, 1997.

Eisenhower, John S. D. *Agent of Destiny: The Life and Times of General Winfield Scott.* New York: Free Press, 1997.

Foner, Eric. *Reconstruction: America's Unfinished Revolution, 1863–1879.* New York: HarperCollins, 1988.

Gordon, Lesley J. *General George E. Pickett in Life and Legend.* Chapel Hill: University of North Carolina Press, 1998.

Gordon-Reed, Annette. *Andrew Johnson.* New York: Times Books, 2011.

Grossman, Justin. *Echoes of a Distant Drum: Winslow Homer and the Civil War.* New York: Harry N. Abrams, 1974.

Hobart, George. *Mathew Brady.* London: Macdonald & Co., 1984.

Jones, Terry L. *American Civil War.* New York: McGraw Hill, 2010.

Jordan, David M. *Winfield Scott Hancock: A Soldier's Life.* Bloomington: Indiana University Press, 1988.

Keneally, Thomas. *American Scoundrel: The Life of the Notorious Civil War General Dan Sickles.* New York: Doubleday, 2002.

Kennett, Lee. *Sherman: A Soldier's Life.* New York: Harper, 2001.

Livesay, Harold C. *Andrew Carnegie and the Rise of Big Business.* Boston: Little, Brown and Co., 1975.

McCloskey, Robert G. *American Conservatism in the Age of Enterprise, 1865–1910.* Cambridge, MA: Harvard University Press, 1951.

McFeely, William S. *Frederick Douglass.* New York: W. W. Norton & Co., 1990.

McPherson, James M. *Battle Cry of Freedom.* New York: Oxford University Press, 1988.

Marszalek, John E. *Commander of Lincoln's Armies: A Life of General Henry W. Halleck*. Cambridge, MA: Harvard University Press, 2004.

Martin, Samuel J. *Kill-Cavalry: Sherman's Merchant of Terror—the Life of Union General Hugh Judson Kilpatrick*. Madison, NJ: Fairleigh Dickinson University Press, 1996.

Marvel, William. *Burnside*. Chapel Hill: University of North Carolina Press, 1991.

Miller, David W. *Second Only to Grant: Quartermaster General Montgomery C. Meigs*. Shippensburg, PA: White Mane Publishing, 2000.

Miller, Scott. *The President and the Assassin: McKinley, Terror, and Empire at the Dawn of the American Century*. New York: Random House, 2011.

Nevins, Allan. *The Emergence of Modern America, 1865–1878*. New York: Macmillan Co., 1933.

Niven, John. *Salmon P. Chase: A Biography*. New York: Oxford University Press, 1995.

Osborne, Charles. *Jubal: The Life and Times of General Jubal A. Early, CSA*. Chapel Hill, NC: Algonquin Books, 1992.

Paine, Albert B. *Thomas Nast: His Period and His Pictures*. New York: Macmillan, 1904.

Parks, Joseph H. *General Edmund Kirby Smith, C.S.A.* Baton Rouge: Louisiana State University Press, 1954.

Porter, Glenn. *Rise of Big Business*. Wheeling, IL: Harlan Davidson, 2006.

Pryor, Elizabeth B. *Clara Barton: Professional Angel*. Philadelphia: University of Pennsylvania Press, 1987.

Ramage, James A. *Gray Ghost: The Life of Col. John Singleton Mosby*. Lexington: University Press of Kentucky, 1999.

Ray, Frederick. *Alfred R. Waud: Civil War Artist.* New York: Viking Press, 1974.

Reynolds, David S. *Walt Whitman.* New York: Oxford University Press, 2005.

Rister, Carl C. *Border Command: General Phil Sheridan in the West.* Westport, CT: Greenwood Press, 1974.

Rutkow, Ira. *James A. Garfield.* New York: Times Books, 2006.

Scarborough, Ruth. *Belle Boyd, Siren of the South.* Macon, GA: Mercer University Press, 1983.

Sears Stephen W. *George B. McClellan: The Young Napoleon.* New York: Ticknor & Fields, 1988.

Settles, Thomas M. *John Bankhead Magruder: A Military Reappraisal.* Baton Rouge: Louisiana State University Press, 2009.

Simpson, Brooks D. *The Reconstruction Presidents.* Lawrence: University Press of Kansas, 1998.

Smith, Gene. *High Crimes and Misdemeanors: The Impeachment of Andrew Johnson.* New York: Morrow, 1977.

Smith, Jean Edward. *Grant.* New York: Simon & Schuster, 2001.

Stahr, Walter. *Seward: Lincoln's Indispensable Man.* New York: Simon & Schuster, 2012.

Taylor, John M. *Confederate Raider: Raphael Semmes of the Alabama.* Washington, DC: Brassey's, 1994.

Thomas, Benjamin P. *Stanton: The Life and Times of Lincoln's Secretary of War.* New York: Alfred A. Knopf, 1962.

Thomas, Emory M. *Robert E. Lee: A Biography.* New York: W. W. Norton & Co., 1995.

Trachtenberg, Alan. *The Incorporation of America: Culture and Society in the Gilded Age.* New York: Hill & Wang, 1982.

Trefousse, Hans L. *Thaddeus Stevens: Nineteenth Century Egalitarian.* Chapel Hill: University of North Carolina Press, 1997.

Trulock, Alice Rains. *In the Hands of Providence: Joshua L. Chamberlain and the American Civil War.* Chapel Hill: University of North Carolina Press, 1999.

Utley, Robert M. *Custer: Cavalier in Buckskin.* Norman: University of Oklahoma Press, 2001.

Varon, Elizabeth R. *Southern Lady, Yankee Spy: The True Story of Elizabeth Van Lew.* New York: Oxford University Press, 2003.

Ward, James A. *That Man Haupt: A Biography of Herman Haupt.* Baton Rouge: Louisiana State University Press, 1973.

Wert, Jeffrey D. *General James Longstreet: The Confederacy's Most Controversial Soldier.* New York: Simon & Schuster, 1993.

West, Richard S., Jr. *Lincoln's Scapegoat General: A Life of Benjamin F. Butler, 1818–1893.* Boston: Houghton, Mifflin & Co, 1965.

Williams, Frank J., ed. *The Mary Lincoln Enigma.* Carbondale: Southern Illinois University Press, 2012.

Wills, Brian Steel. *A Battle From the Start: The Life of Nathan Bedford Forrest.* New York: Harpercollins, 1992.

———. *George Henry Thomas: As True as Steel.* Lawrence: University Press of Kansas, 2012.

Wylie, Paul R. *The Irish General: The Life of Thomas Francis Meagher.* Norman: University of Oklahoma Press, 1992.

ILLUSTRATIONS
CREDITS

Note: Library of Congress means Library of Congress Prints and Photographs Division unless otherwise indicated.

12, Library of Congress, LC-DIG-PPMSCA-23855; 15, Library of Congress, LC-DIG-PPM SCA-19482; 17, The Granger Collection, NYC; 20, The Granger Collection, NYC; 24, Library of Congress, LC-DIG-PPMSCA-34562; 27, Library of Congress, LC-DIG-CWPBH-00460; 28, The Granger Collection, NYC; 32, The Granger Collection, NYC; 36, The U.S. National Archives and Records Administration; 39, The Granger Collection, NYC; 42, Library of Congress, LC-USZ62-10122; 45, Paul J. Richards/AFP/Getty Images; 46, Library of Congress, LC-DIG-PPMSCA-34938; 49, Library of Congress, LC-DIG-PPMSCA-11268; 52, Corbis; 55, The U.S. National Archives and Records Administration; 59, Library of Congress, LC-DIG-DS-01484; 62, North Carolina State University Special Collections Library; 67, Private Collection/Peter Newark Military Pictures/Bridgeman Images; 68, The Granger Collection, NYC; 72, The Granger Collection, NYC; 75, The Museum of the Confederacy, Richmond, Virginia; 79, Private Collection/Ken Welsh/Bridgeman Images; 82, The Museum of the Confederacy, Richmond, Virginia; 85, Tria Giovan/Corbis; 87, Library of Congress, LC-USZ62-25518; 88, The Granger Collection, NYC; 93, Buyenlarge/Getty Images; 97, Library of Congress, LC-DIG-PPMSCA-28365; 100, Courtesy of the Collections of the Louisiana State Museum; 103, The Museum of the Confederacy, Richmond, Virginia; 104, Private Collection/Peter Newark Military Pictures/Bridgeman Images; 110, Diagram from *Scientific American,* Vol. VI—No. 4, January 25, 1862, Courtesy of Cornell University Library, Making of America Digital Collection; 115, Library of Congress, LC-DIG-STEREO-1S02871; 119, Private Collection/Peter Newark American Pictures/Bridgeman Images; 120, Library of Congress, LC-USZ62-43958; 123, Museum of the Confederacy, Richmond, Virginia, USA/Photo © Civil War Archive/Bridgeman Images; 126, Arthur Green/George Eastman House/Getty Images; 129, Universal History Archive/UIG/Bridgeman Images; 130, Chicago History Museum, USA/Bridgeman Images; 134, Don Troiani/Corbis; 139, Corbis; 140, Buyenlarge/Getty Images; 142, PF-(usna)/Alamy; 145, Corbis; 147, Library of Congress, LC-USZ62-17254; 148, Library of Congress, LC-DIG-PPMSCA-10341; 153, Everett Collection Inc./Alamy; 154, Library of Congress, LC-DIG-PPMSCA-25378; 161, Library of Congress, LC-DIG-PPMSCA-34483; 162,

INDEX

Boldface indicates illustrations.

BUILD YOUR CIVIL WAR LIBRARY

with More Notable Books from National Geographic

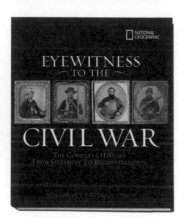

◁ This gloriously illustrated volume features a dramatic narrative packed with eyewitness accounts and hundreds of rare photographs, artifacts, and period illustrations, covering every military, political, and social aspect of the crucial period from John Brown's raid to Reconstruction.

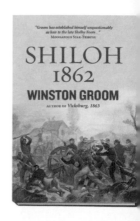

▷ "Groom has given the Battle of Shiloh the mega attention that it deserves by writing a book with the storytelling appeal of fiction but solidly backed with fact . . .This is a book that will stay with you for a very long time." —*The Washington Post*

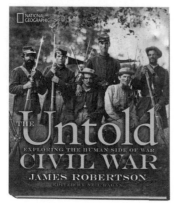

◁ "The book . . . is a beauty and should make any recipient very happy . . . a great selection of photographs." —*The Washington Post*

"Beautifully illustrated and engagingly written, this thematically arranged book reveals the human side of America's bloodiest war." –*Library Journal*

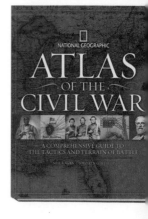

▷ In this one-of-a-kind atlas, scores of archival maps and dozens of newly created maps trace the battles, political turmoil, and great themes of America's most violent and pivotal clash of arms.

AVAILABLE WHEREVER BOOKS AND EBOOKS ARE SOLD
and at nationalgeographic.com/books

 Like us on Facebook: Nat Geo Books   Follow us on Twitter: @NatGeoBooks